Coaching and Mentoring

SAGE has been part of the global academic community since 1965, supporting high quality research and learning that transforms society and our understanding of individuals, groups and cultures. SAGE is the independent, innovative, natural home for authors, editors and societies who share our commitment and passion for the social sciences.

Find out more at: **www.sagepublications.com**

Coaching and Mentoring
A Critical Text

by Simon Western

Los Angeles | London | New Delhi
Singapore | Washington DC

Los Angeles | London | New Delhi
Singapore | Washington DC

SAGE Publications Ltd
1 Oliver's Yard
55 City Road
London EC1Y 1SP

SAGE Publications Inc.
2455 Teller Road
Thousand Oaks, California 91320

SAGE Publications India Pvt Ltd
B 1/I 1 Mohan Cooperative Industrial Area
Mathura Road
New Delhi 110 044

SAGE Publications Asia-Pacific Pte Ltd
3 Church Street
#10-04 Samsung Hub
Singapore 049483

Editor: Kirsty Smy
Editorial assistant: Ruth Stitt
Production editor: Rachel Eley
Copyeditor: Christine Bitten
Proofreader: Jonathan Hopkins
Marketing manager: Alison Borg
Cover design: Lisa Harper
Typeset by: C&M Digitals (P) Ltd,
Chennai, India
Printed and bound by CPI Group
(UK) Ltd, Croydon, CR0 4YY

Library of Congress Control Number: 2012931136

British Library Cataloguing in Publication data

A catalogue record for this book is available from
the British Library

ISBN 978-1-84860-163-5
ISBN 978-1-84860-164-2 (pbk)

'It is a pleasure to read a book about coaching that goes beyond the rather simplistic prescriptions found in most works of this genre. Far too often, contributors to the coaching literature view their clients in a rather robotic manner, ignoring the complexity and subtlety of their emotional life. In their pursuit of instant solutions, these (presumably) coaching specialists assume a Band-Aid approach to change, not paying attention to the deeper origins of executive dysfunction. Simon Western's contribution is different in that he brings back the uncomfortable complexity inherent to the human condition. By not ignoring the shadow side of human reality, his book very much enriches the coaching literature – and is highly recommended.'

Manfred F. R. Kets de Vries, Clinical Professor of Leadership and Organizational Change, The Raoul de Vitry d'Avaucourt Chaired Professor of Leadership Development

'Simon Western has a rare ability to add new dimensions to existing debates, and help us see matters from unusual angles. In this book he brings his critical perspective to bear with great acuity, focusing his attention on some key themes within the debates on coaching and mentoring. I thoroughly endorse this book.'

Professor Mark Stein, Chair in Leadership and Management, University of Leicester

'This is an unusual and path breaking book. Simon Western explores coaching in its many variations and simultaneously critiques the different discourses that comprise it. His thinking addresses what he calls the "micro practices," and macro perspectives. He inhabits that most unusual role – the scholar-practitioner – that enables him to contend with both theory and practice. As a good scholar he situates coaching historically, and as a practitioner can evaluate various methodologies, such as the cognitive-behavioral, positive-psychology and psychodynamics. I recommend this book highly to those who want to practice coaching and to those who want to understand its meaning for the wider culture.'

Larry Hirschhorn, Principal at CFAR, Professor of Human and Organization development at Fielding Graduate University, Lecturer in Organization Dynamics, University of Pennsylvania, Member, Founder and past President of the International Society for the Psychoanalytic Study of Organizations

'I see a lot of books on Coaching, and this is without doubt the most stimulating, original, thoughtful and well-founded account. When I heard that Simon Western was considering a book on this topic I wondered if even he – author of the excellent *Leadership: A Critical Text* – could bring new light to the topic. He has certainly done so – this is an authoritative, well researched, critical and appreciative account of coaching that has at its heart a profound concern for people, for social life and for the predicaments we face. It will be really helpful for anyone in coaching, for coaches and educators, for students of organization and work. In fact, the book is a substantial contribution to our understanding of contemporary practices of the self, and will be of interest to anyone intrigued with what it is to be social.'

Professor Jonathan Gosling, Professor of Leadership Studies, University of Exeter

'I recommend this book to anyone in the world of coaching who thinks that they occupy a secure niche. If you believe you have a therapeutic model that helps you to heal the wounded self of your clients, or if you use positive thinking to boost their self-esteem, then be ready for a major challenge and some rigorous thinking about your practice and the assumptions that underlie it.'

David Megginson, Emeritus Professor of HRD, Sheffield Business School, UK

Dedication

In memory of my beautiful son Fynn
Fynn, an inspiration to so many, his smile and spirit continue to light our lives. Together we shared the greatest joy and adventures. I miss him terribly. Be at peace Fynn.

In memory of my mother Enid Western
A great friend to me and others. A brilliant mentor and leader in the education sector who changed so many lives, and through her living testimony, contributed to the emancipation of women, creating a tolerant, more generous society.

I am very proud of both Fynn and Mum.

And for my father Terry Western
I thank you for your continued love.

This book has been a 'transitional object'. I located my future in this book, as it became symbolic of hope after facing the despair and grief at the shocking loss of Fynn, then my mother 12 months later. I couldn't write anything for ten months, then I found writing provided a small respite from the grief, a refuge where I became absorbed for periods. Researching, reading, using my imagination and thinking deeply then became a joy, as well as a real struggle and battle of will.

I write briefly about this experience for others who face a deep loss, grief or sadness, which can feel impenetrable, and for coaches and others helping those who face loss or despair. My experience is that the sadness doesn't pass – the loss and emptiness remain raw – but I have discovered that creativity and new life are possible as well. To survive and find emotional and spiritual health is to walk the high-wire between despair and hope, beauty and sadness, creativity and loss, to experience moments of grace whilst bearing the pain. Then alongside the grieving process, hope and love grow in the face of despair. This book is a tribute to my son and mother; they both would have demanded nothing less from me, that I write the very best book I could. I am filled with love and gratitude for their continued inspiration and presence.

Contents

About the Author

Dr Simon Western

Currently: Director of Analytic-Network Coaching Ltd, offering a researched and innovative new coaching process, which aims to transform the way coaching impacts on both individuals and organizations. www.simonwestern.com

Our task is to work in 'good faith' to build the 'good society'.

Theory and People Development: *Academia and Teaching*

Previously: Director of Coaching at Lancaster University Management School and Leading Master in Organizational Consultancy, Tavistock Clinic. Simon has a pedigree of teaching internationally and publishing on leadership and coaching (*Leadership: A Critical Text*, new edition in 2013). His thinking draws on cross-disciplinary research (psychoanalysis, organizational culture, religious studies, environmentalism) and also on his diverse and rich work experience, having worked in a factory, as a general and psychiatric nurse, a clinical manager, family therapist, organizational consultant, academic and coach working in FT100 corporate offices.

He takes a psychosocial, critical and ethical perspective, to develop innovative ideas such as Eco-Leadership, addressing ethical and business concerns in the 'network society'.

Practitioner: Strategic Coach and Consultant

Simon works internationally with C-Suite leaders across diverse organizations. His expertise is to work in depth and breadth, coaching individuals and teams through challenging times and developing strategic interventions across organizations.

Clients include: London Business School, Global OD Team HSBC Bank, CEO family business, leaders in Educational sector and CEO and clinicians in Health sector and Hospice sector.

Acknowledgements

A special thanks to everybody who contributed to this book, in many diverse ways. To those who helped work the material, including: Agata, Cathy, Pooja, Steve Fleetwood, Mary Simpson for her excellent proofing of first drafts, Maia for her artwork and contribution to my creative process. To my coaching clients, students and academic colleagues, especially Sally Watson who began this journey by inviting me to become Director of Coaching at Lancaster University.

To the friends who have stood with me: Simon Massey, Norman and Marian Warden, Eliat Aram, Laura Morales, Lynne Sedgmore, Anne-Mary McLeod, Alex Massey, Nick Jenkins, Stuart Butlin, Rosy Fairhurst, Gry, Diana, Terry and Su, Laura and Anne Simpson, Jonathan Gosling, Debbie O Sullivan, my brothers Mark and Jonathan, and the many others, who have shared this difficult journey with me. Also to Alex Wallace, Fynn's best friend who has become a friend to me also.

I am also grateful to Sage editors Kiren, Kirsty and Ruth for their patience and understanding, and am impressed by the professional and sensitive way in which they do their work.

Credits
Illustrations are original artwork by Maia Kirchkheli.
All photographs taken by author.

Introduction

Coaching – The Merger of the 'Wounded Self' and 'Celebrated Self'

Bridging the 'wounded self' and the 'celebrated self'
The organization and structure of this book
Who is this book for?
What authored the author?

This book aims to be thoughtful yet polemic, taking a critical stance, to look at coaching and mentoring from perspectives that provoke curiosity and that support practitioners and interested parties to scrutinize coaching in depth. It is a book of ideas, clearly aimed at stimulating thinking and dialogue, through situating coaching and mentoring in a broad historical and social context, and drawing on a wide range of theory from beyond coaching.

This book has four core aims:

1 To account for how coaching has emerged and what discourses and normative practices underpin and influence contemporary practice.

2 To develop a meta-theory of coaching that encourages future development based on a coherent body of knowledge with a sound theoretical base.

3 To offer clear 'frames of thinking' based on coaching discourses and theory that act as heuristic resources for coaching practitioners and educators.

4 To apply an emancipatory, ethical and critical approach to coaching, shifting practice away from a limited technocratic, functional approach and towards a more generative and progressive approach.

Box I.1   Clarification of Terms: Coaching and Mentoring

The differences/similarities of coaching and mentoring are fully explored in Chapter 2. Although their original roots are different, both mentoring and coaching in the modern context selectively draw on a range of the same narratives to describe the activity. However, it seems that coaching and mentoring are essentially similar in nature (Garvey et al., 2009: 27).

> Mentoring has a longer tradition than coaching but both activities share many of the same practices, applications and values. In the end it comes down to a choice of terminology and the meanings associated with that terminology. … Coaching has become the dominant term … For the future, maybe a new term will emerge that will satisfy all interested parties. (Garvey, 2010: 351–2)

I agree with Garvey and other scholars who make the case that the terms 'coaching' and 'mentoring' are not easily distinguishable, and it is often a matter of choice as to which is used. It is also the case that both practices draw upon very similar values and applications. Therefore, in this book, I will use the term coaching to embrace the multiple and overlapping practices of coaching and mentoring, as coaching has become the dominant term, and maybe it is becoming the dominant practice. Mentoring retains a special place in relation to unpaid approaches to 'helping' that focus on social issues, and have mutual benefits for both mentee and mentor.

Mentoring will be named separately when a distinction is necessary. 'Coachee' will refer to the recipient of coaching and the term 'client' will refer to an organization or their representative sponsoring the coaching work.

Coaching is a growing phenomenon; according to the International Coach Federation (ICF) its membership has soared from about 1,500 in 1999 to 16,000 members as of 2011.

> The coaching market is worth around $1 billion worldwide, a number that Harvard Business School expects will double in the next 2 years. (Joo, 2005: 465)

Coaching has arrived, and appears to be stabilizing itself after a period of emergence that was recently described as 'The Wild West of Coaching' (Sherman and Freas, 2004), highlighting the unregulated, diverse and hybrid nature of the practice. There is a huge investment in coaching, and the capital being invested goes beyond financial; it is social capital as well. Individuals, businesses, public and not-for-profit organizations and social enterprises are all investing in coaching and mentoring to improve either personal and/or organizational success.

Coaching is predominantly a Westernized phenomenon, and therefore this book traces its emergence through Western culture. Whilst in a globalized world it travels quickly, the dominant culture that coaching arose from is Western, individualized, democratic-capitalism. One-on-one coaching support cannot be understood without tracing its evolution from this culture. How other cultures take up coaching, shape it locally and influence it globally will be for a future book.

To help the reader situate coaching in a broader context from the outset, I will briefly offer a short narrative of how coaching has emerged from the social changes in the twentieth century and currently sits between the impact of therapeutic culture and the human potential movement. This will help situate coaching, and in Part II the book will explore in more depth a genealogy of coaching.

Bridging the 'Wounded Self' and the 'Celebrated Self'

Coaching is positioned between two contemporary social dimensions – the wounded self and the celebrated self.

The 'wounded self'

The 'wounded self' refers to a self that is damaged, fragmented or emotionally hurt and is the domain of psychotherapists and psychologists. Psychotherapists look for the 'wounded self' – this is their expertise, their business – in order to offer therapeutic intervention (the talking cure) and reparation. Therapy was created to help the 'wounded self'; as Freud's dictum says, 'Psychoanalysis turns neurosis into ordinary unhappiness' (Freud and Breuer, 1895/2004). Some argue that the therapist's gaze produces a universal 'wounded self' that has permeated society. Therapeutic culture creates a socialized way of interpreting ourselves – no longer do we believe it to be fate, God or nature that shapes us, but we believe that we are shaped by life's events, which are often interpreted as emotional traumas, or at least they evoke psychological responses and patterns which are rarely problem free: for example, '*My Mother was really caring but I was smothered and find it hard to be independent*', '*My last relationship was good; however, it made me realize how easily I lose myself – I must take more care of my own needs in future.*' The therapeutic milieu is entangled with the language of the 'wounded self' that needs healing. To be whole is to face the past, repair and reintegrate ourselves, but also to continually deal with ongoing life 'issues' of work, identity and relationships, which continually wound us and shape us. Therapeutic intervention is no longer a one-off project for those who 'break down' or need specific intervention by a Psy expert; it has colonized society and we are not *'condemned to be free'* as Sartre says, but we are condemned to *'work on ourselves'* over a life-time process of overcoming emotional issues and reparation.

The contemporary self is constantly in need of therapeutic intervention whether it is from a professional therapist or counsellor, a source of self-help or through self-reflection. We are constantly reminded of our task to work on ourselves, whether through advertising telling us to consume, to make ourselves younger, slimmer, fitter, healthier, happier and more desirable and attractive, or through the TV talk shows and multimedia, where we are constantly confronted with the injunction to self-improve. From Oprah to the problem pages of magazines, from the local yoga class to the Buddhist meditation, the message is clear – 'work on yourself'– and with it a subtext: you have a wounded self that needs repairing and improving. The world calls on us to 'tell all and tell often' (Foucault, 1978). The contemporary 'therapeutic' confessional (see Chapter 6) is a place to disclose and reflect upon our emotionally wounded selves.

Critical theorists claim that therapy culture creates a narcissistic, selfish and introspective society, focusing on 'I' instead of 'we'. Rather than liberating individuals from their concerns, they claim it entraps them in an increasingly widening array of 'ills' (Lasch, 1979).

The 'wounded self' is supported by evidence that shows a huge increase in diagnostic criteria of emotional ills, e.g. ADHD, stress, post-traumatic stress disorder, autistic syndromes, depression and treatments of anxiety and other psychic and 'emotional' ills. The pharmaceutical and therapy industries commercially profit from these increases, and governments are shown to be supporting these trends. The UK government in 2009 invested £173 million to train and employ 10,000 cognitive behavioural therapists (CBTs) to intervene in depressive and anxiety disorders (James, 2009).

Therapy has gone beyond treating the ill in four ways:

1 The definition of 'illness' has become much broader with new 'illnesses' being recognized such as posttraumatic stress disorder, attention deficit disorder, multiple personality disorder – all syndromes rather than illnesses and with them huge rises in diagnostic rates have taken place.

2 Other areas of 'ordinary' life – one's self-esteem, relationships, bringing up children, grief and loss – all became potential areas of concern and therefore areas accessible to therapeutic intervention.

3 Recognized 'illnesses' such as depression found a much wider constituency. What in the past was understood to be misery or melancholy became a treatable illness called depression. The pharmaceutical industry found a mass market for treatments such as Prozac, thereby encouraging this trend. In Britain depression accounted for 1 per cent of the population born in the First World War, 5 per cent in the Second World War and jumped to 10–15 per cent in the 1960s. Diagnosis is a very subjective matter, that is, social class, gender and ethnicity all impact on diagnostic outcomes.

4 Therapy culture entered healthy social arenas and became 'a way of thinking and being' rather than a way of 'curing psychic or emotional disorder', e.g. coaching (see Bellah et al., 1996; Furedi, 2003).

In the past decade or so, counsellors have found their way into every school and GP practice, and the social mantra is: *If you have a problem it's good to talk; if you don't talk, you have a problem.*

Until recently a 'stiff upper lip', courage and resilience in the face of struggle was socially valued, whereas today emoting and confessing our wounded selves becomes socially approved:

> A therapeutic culture has become pervasive. It is apparent in the emotional 'esteem' and 'support'; displays of emotional incontinence and claims of victimhood are guaranteed social approval. (Fitzpatrick, 2000: 64)

Heelas (1996: 146) writes that the torrent of advice from the self-help industry 'generates a climate of discontent' while Beradi (2009) claims that the 'happiness imperative' (that we should all seek to be happy) also creates this sense of failure, as the bombardment of advertising, TV and films and social demands that we should strive to be happy leaves us feeling even more wounded, as it is impossible to live up to the illusive demand and media images of happiness and success. We are constantly being asked and internalizing the questions of the subjective self: 'Am I happy?', 'Am I depressed?', 'Am I stressed?', 'Is my body perfect?', 'Is my sex life adequate?'

Coaching and the 'wounded self'

Emerging from career counselling and employee assistant programmes, early coaching in the workplace followed counselling and would focus on the 'wounded self' – the employee who was broken, stressed and underperforming. De Haan points out how the coaching trend has shifted:

> ... from remedial to developmental. The negative status and stigma that attached to managers who needed a coach for their professional development appears to have been replaced by a positive status,

arising from the fact that a manager is important enough to the organization to merit the investment in coaching. (2008: 27)

Coaching has travelled a long way and it now goes beyond the healing of a 'wounded self', offering diverse positive and action-orientated interventions. However, in spite of positive psychology, solution-focused and other goal-focused approaches to coaching, the reality of what actually happens in the coaching room still resonates in part with the 'wounded self'. The solution-focused approach, by refusing to talk about problems, uses the signifier 'solution' as a substitute for the word 'problem', thereby drawing more attention to the unspeakable word. In the English TV comedy *Fawlty Towers*, John Cleese in his restaurant receives German guests and tells his staff, 'Don't mention the war!' and of course because it's unmentionable his Freudian slips about war are in every sentence he speaks.

People come to Life-coaching to overcome something they perceive is wrong in their lives and they believe things can be better. Life coaches on TV talk shows work as 'evangelists for the talking cure' (Cobb, 2005: 254). In executive coaching, much of the work may be geared to performance and organizational aims, but coaches are very often confronted with a 'wounded' part of the executive who reveals a troubled aspect of the self that they wish to resolve. Confident and experienced coaches allow all parts to surface, including the wounded self; the difference in coaching is that the coach is not actively looking for it, nor do they regress the coachee when the wounded self is disclosed, as a therapist might. The traditional psychotherapy trademarks of dependency, regression and reparation are replaced by coaching work that encourages autonomy and proactive engagement over deep insight as a way to deal with the wounded self.

Coaches also have a different starting point from therapists, and to explain this we turn to a counter-narrative that arose during the 1960s and helps explain the rise of coaching.

The 'celebrated self'

Why drag this corpse of your memory? ... it is better to live ever in a new day. (Emerson, 1841: 137)

The 'celebrated self' reflects a more positive view of the individual that blossomed in the post-1960s milieu, where the 'turn to subjectivity' (Woodhead, 2004), the rise of a 'new individualism' and the focus on the interior life meant that individual identity became something to be celebrated. Inspired by Emerson, the transcendentalists and the Beat generation, the human potential movement of Carl Rogers, Maslow and others influenced the celebrated self to come to the fore, highlighting an innate human desire to self-actualize. This took therapy into popular culture and beyond the wounded self, and the 'therapeutic care of the soul' became placed into the hands of the Psy professions. Society became permeated with messages to celebrate the self:

> Trust your feelings, have faith in yourself, follow your bliss, do your own thing, listen to your inner child, do what feels right, be true to yourself. These messages are offered as formulas for salvation. ... Therapeutic values that are worthy of organizing one's life around, such as self-esteem, self-fulfilment, self-realisation and self-expression have come to be accepted as axiomatic, occupying the normative heights once controlled by such counter values as self-discipline, self-control and self-denial. (Cobb, 2005; 252)

Therapeutic culture can produce a wounded self as described but an alternative and in my view complementary position, rather than polar opposite, is how it supports and produces a self-reflective society, with growing emotional articulation of how we feel and how we relate to each other. Anthony Giddens says that as the modern self is more insecure and alienated, therapists are necessary and useful (Giddens, 1991):

> This is where therapeutic cultures can be helpful, according to Giddens, since they provide both solace and resources for self-formation. Solace is needed in his view, because the modern self is much more insecure. ... Therapeutic cultures, in his view, do not destroy the self, and its relationships, but make them. (Swan, 2006: 4)

Nikolas Rose also observes how therapy can help individuals' well-being:

> ... the psychotherapies of normality, which promulgate new ways of planning life and approaching predicaments, and disseminate new procedures for understanding oneself and acting upon oneself to overcome dissatisfactions, realize one's potential, to gain happiness and achieve autonomy. (Rose, 1999: 89–90)

The celebrated self offers a hopeful optimization of the self, the potential to grow and to improve our happiness and well-being. Eva Moscowitz (2001) claimed that therapy was a new religion and cited that in the 1990s Americans spent $69 billion a year managing their feelings and attending to their emotional health. To 'Celebrate the Self' was the new imperative.

In recent times, new spirituality, alternative healing and New Ageism, infused with reinterpreted Eastern and ancient traditions, have moved from the margins to become mainstream ways for individuals to seek solace, reflection and intervention in order to find their authentic selves, and to discover new ways to live. They discover how to celebrate themselves, in each moment.

New Age: spirituality and the happiness imperative

> To its (capitalism's) promise that anyone can be a millionaire, has recently been added the promise that anyone can be a celebrity. (Foley, 2010: 41)

The New Age movement is now big business in both financial and social terms. At the core of New Ageism is the 'celebrated self'. Approaches include 'new spirituality' that has emerged from a post-religious understanding of spirituality. New Ageism can be found in abundance in management texts on airport bookshelves. From the New Age perspective the inner self is a place of authenticity, a sacred space within us. There exists a myriad of techniques and interventions to help individuals discover and celebrate their true inner-selves: meditation, yoga, chanting, Eastern philosophy, Buddhist teachings, crystals, tarot cards, NLP, Reiki – the list goes on. The Life-coach, reiki master and NLP coach, informed by the New Age ethos, coach from the belief that each person has the truth within them, and the coaching task is to help them access it. Coaching, and Life-coaching in particular, have encompassed much of New Age philosophy that has become mainstream. Paul Heelas describes the New Age community as 'expressivists':

> Expressivists live their lives in terms of what they take to be a much richer and authenticated account of what it is to be human. They are intent on discovering and cultivating their 'true' nature, delving in to experience the wealth of life itself. (Heelas, 1996: 156)

Oprah Winfrey is probably the best advocate of the 'celebrated self' through her embracing, and promotion to a world audience, of Life-coaching, self-help, personal growth, the happiness movement and new spirituality, and her phenomenal success reaches millions. In 2008 Oprah Winfrey invited Eckhart Tolle, a bestselling New Age author – *The Power of Now* (1999) and *A New Earth* (2005) – to co-host a series of ten 'webinars' which were downloaded by 38 million people (Bright, 2009: 17). Tolle talks like a contemporary Buddhist but without the religious baggage – the personal narrative that sells his story claims he became enlightened like the Buddha, but whereas Buddha sat under the Bhodi Tree to become 'the awakened one', Tolle found a contemporary place to become awakened; he sat on a park bench for two years in a London park. Tolle is a New Age phenomenon; the message is about how to live in the present and how to live calmly in the face of modernity's distress – Tolle simply says 'let go'. Adam Bright writes of Tolle:

> He breathes in. He breathes out. He waits. Something comes, and he leans over the desk to write the words that will form the core of his teaching: 'you are not your mind'. (2009: 16)

> Tolle borrows from nearly every tradition (spiritual and religious) but does not belong to any of them. (This institutional nimbleness helps him win followings in unexpected communities; I'm told he's especially popular with the MBA crowd). (2009: 11)

In the workplace Stephen Covey (1990) became a best-selling author, cleverly bridging the gap between self-help, new spirituality and managerialism.

The 'celebrated self' is a phenomenon of Western culture – from post-structuralism to New Ageism – and is encouraged by Western ideologies of individualism, consumerism and choice. The post-structuralists, particularly feminists and queer theorists, don't strictly celebrate the self, but they do deconstruct the limitations of the self. They argue that binary difference like gender is as much socially constructed as biological, and they theorize and practise diverse ways in which we can choose, individually and collectively, to breach normative boundaries of sexuality and gender (Butler, 2004). In contemporary society we face the imperative to discover and then celebrate our true selves; this is our only refuge in an uncertain world.

Coaching: the merger of the 'wounded self' and 'celebrated self'

> Therapy is too good to be limited to the sick. (Furedi, 2003)

As the *celebrated self* became more prominent, and positive psychology and the happiness industry took off (Seligman, 2002), a new profession was required to administer to the 'celebrated self', one that was not restricted to the therapeutic or pharmacological treatment of the 'wounded self'. Coaching carried with it some of the therapeutic experience and techniques that enabled the coaches to work on the 'wounded self', but real success came when coaching was reinvented to focus on the 'celebrated self'. This made coaching more marketable and more accessible. Coaching meant that you could find resources to cope without having to openly acknowledge your inner demons.

The executive coach was a new innovation in the workplace. Managers and leaders wanted and needed help to survive the new demands of an increasingly stressful workplace ('wounded self') and to try to align and rediscover their passion and their authentic selves at work (their 'celebrated self'). A New Expert was required for the lost flock at work.

In the late twentieth century the workplace became more globalized, digitalized and also more alienating. Employees increasingly used their subjectivity, identities and emotions to take on multiple roles and face new complexities, but the workplace culture was no place for the rhetoric of dysfunction or failure. To achieve at work is to be successful, confident, an individual with dynamic energy and a lot of agency. The 'wounded self' was to be kept at home or at least minimized or hidden.

Coaching filled the gap – promising to enhance individual performance in both life and at work – achieving a bridge between the 'wounded' and 'celebrated' self. Popular culture (for example, Oprah Winfrey) and therapy culture produce two selves: a celebrated self to be nurtured and with a culture of entitlement, and a wounded self that constantly needs reparation. Coaching works between these two poles, and depending on how it is delivered and the demand for it, will lean towards one or the other.

It markets and brands itself by dealing with the 'celebrated-self', selling change, transformation, self-discovery, higher productivity, improved performance in work role and in life more generally. Short-term and transformational coaching clearly is a tempting offer that promises to help the individual 'celebrate the self' and, by doing so, create a cycle of success.

On the other hand, within the 'imperative for happiness' lies unspoken and hidden parts of the wounded self that appear in the coaching sessions. Whilst coaching markets itself and works well on the celebrated self, it often works at the same time with the wounded self too offering solace to the alienated, offering a post-modern confessional to the troubled soul. Coaching is a hybrid expertise that has adapted brilliantly to the complex and competing demands of contemporary society.

My experience of coaching (having worked in many other therapeutic and consultancy roles) is that it can be a hugely liberating space in which to work, where in-depth work with coachees can be achieved, alongside strategic delivery of their personal and organizational goals. For me this creates a unique space where Freud's reality principle and the social world meet 'maternal containment' and our internal lives (see the 'P–M–P' coaching process, Chapter 13). Coaching is a vital and dynamic space that enables creativity to emerge, whereas other 'helping relationships' are often saddled with more restrictive cultures (therapy, for example, is weighed down by the rhetoric of pathology, and psychology entranced by empiricism, technique and measurement; and the institutions that oversee psychotherapy are protectionist and encourage risk-averse thinking rather than being generative in their outlook).

Coaching opens up a new space to work, one that is full of potential, a 'post-modern confessional' (see Chapter 6) and a place of solace in a bewildering social environment, and at the same time an engaged space where dynamic change and new strategic thinking can occur.

Coaching, however, lacks a robust theoretical base, and here we have a crisis emerging. The tendency in coaching seems to be to mimic the institutions around it, rather than encouraging serious scholarship and theorizing about coaching itself that would lead to innovative research, education and practice. This book aims to build on existing scholarship in coaching and draw on wider social science resources to offer a refreshing critique of coaching theory and practice that delivers new insights leading to further developments. Examining the macro-social influences and the micro-practices of coaching, the book finds them inextricably linked, yet the macro-social influences are in large ignored.

There are worrying moves in 'second wave' coaching that are attempting to homogenize and control practice, taking it towards professionalization and an instrumentalized practice, where the scientific rationalism that dominates HR departments and managerial training seeps into coaching and colonizes it. Coaching then changes from an evolving and exciting new developmental practice that works between human experience and social systems (organizational change), to a practice that works on human behaviour drawing on psychology/therapy approaches. This text opens a discussion on what informs coaching practice, attempting to get coaching practitioners, academics and trainers to develop a critical reflective stance to question the norms and assumptions of coaching.

To better understand coaching and mentoring, however, we should first take a retrospective look at helping relationships, in order to give a longitudinal perspective, to observe where continuity and tradition can teach us, and to use the past as a theoretical resource to shine a new light on contemporary coaching practice. The counterpoint of the past runs unacknowledged alongside the melody of the present, and if looked at with a critical eye, it illuminates practice in fascinating ways. The fetish of the new often obscures important lessons and links from the past, and this is also true of coaching (Burrell, 1997; Case and Gosling, 2010).

This macro overview of coaching and mentoring, addressing the historical, social and organizational contexts in which coaching has emerged and thrives, is complemented by an 'in-depth' view of micro-practices analysing the broad approaches to coaching. These macro and micro perspectives are important in order to gain a clearer picture of where coaching is today and in which direction coaching and mentoring are heading. Current literature leans towards the micro-practices of coaching/mentoring, with coaching texts focusing on how to coach. The theory of coaching mimics this position, and texts quickly turn to psychotherapy theory as surrogate coaching theory (Peltier, 2001; Cox et al., 2010). Whilst acknowledging the importance and influences of psychotherapy (see Chapter 7) this book pushes for a wider theoretical base, which includes the other three discourses that inform coaching practice and also the meta-social influences that require other theoretical resources. The aim is to develop a coaching meta-theory that doesn't try to integrate all theory, but offers both a coherent theoretical framework that oversees coaching, and a standpoint from which coaching practice and theory can critique itself.

Coaching/mentoring can be an emancipatory force, a practice to help individuals achieve a fuller sense of self and become more creative and autonomous, alongside a collective endeavour to improve workplaces and society in general.

Below is an outline of the organizational structure of the book that takes you through this journey, beginning with the present state of play, to then reveal historical and social influences, before outlining the underpinning assumptions and discourses that permeate coaching practice, and then moving on to developing a meta-theory of coaching that can be used by practitioners and theorists to inform their practice and develop new research and practice. Finally it looks at coaching from an educational and development perspective and highlights key pedagogical principles.

The Organization and Structure of this Book

Part I Scoping the field with a critical lens

Part I offers a critical overview of coaching and mentoring. Chapter 1, *A Critical Theory Approach to Coaching*, describes the four critical lenses – looking awry, depth analysis, network analysis and emancipation. These frames are important to critique the literature and also to apply to coaching practice. Chapter 2, *Scoping the Field*, examines the terms, scrutinizing practice and rhetoric to reveal how diverse coaching approaches connect and where they do not. It then deconstructs and challenges some of the normative assumptions of coaching.

Part II From friendship to coaching

Part II addresses the context from which coaching and mentoring emerged. To better understand contemporary practice it is important to see it in the light of past helping relationships. The reader is taken on a journey through three historical periods – *Pre-modernity* (Chapter 3), *Modernity* (Chapter 4) and *Post-modernity* (Chapter 5). Each historical period is examined from three viewing points – friendship, the Soul Healer and the work realm – tracing how coaching has emerged as a distinct 'new' and hybrid practice, yet with continuity throughout the past. This retrospective examination sheds new light on contemporary practice.

Part III   The dominant discourses of coaching

Part III offers a description of four core discourses that underpin coaching and mentoring. The introduction sets out a table with the four discourses and clarifies *what is discourse*, and the *critical discourse analysis* used to reveal the four coaching discourses. Chapter 6, *The Soul Guide Discourse*, describes how coaching works as a 'mirror to the soul'. The coach focuses on the inner self and the human spirit, allowing the coachee to discover their desire. This also creates a contemporary confessional space where the coachee shares their fears and anxieties; the coach focuses on human experience. Chapter 7, *The Psy Expert Discourse*, reveals how coaches work as 'technicians of the psyche' drawing on established Psy professional expertise (in psychotherapy, psychology, psychiatry, psychoanalysis). The focus is to modify behaviour and cognition with psychological tools and techniques; the coach focuses on personal performance.

Chapter 8, *The Managerial Discourse*, describes how coaches are working in the discourse of managerialism. The managers' claim to expertise is their ability to deliver efficiency and productivity (MacIntyre, 1985). Coaches absorb the Managerial Discourse, and the coach focuses on supporting the executive to take up their role more effectively to improve personal and organizational output; the coach focuses on productivity. Chapter 9, *The Network Coach Discourse*, takes coaching beyond individual psychology, soul-work or performance and situates the individual in the networks of work and society. This radically repositions coaching work as the coachee is seen as an 'actor in a network of other actors' and the Network Coach's task is to help the coachee find nodal points of change, to realize the interdependencies, to form collaborations and make connections to influence networks of activity; the coach focuses on connectivity. The Network Coach is the newest discourse emerging in coaching, and has a vital role in shifting coaching from personal and operational interventions towards strategic thinking that also takes an ethical stance. Chapter 10, *Discourse Mapping*, describes how coaching works not only within the discourses but also between and across them. The coaching discourses are not discrete – they blur and coaches often draw on more than one discourse in their work. Sometimes they are complementary, at other times tensions arise. These dynamics are explored in Chapter 10.

Part IV   The future of coaching

Part IV looks to the future of coaching, arguing that there is a need to develop a coherent coaching theory and improve education. Chapter 11, *Developing Coaching Theory*, defines what theory and meta-theory is, looking beyond theory as a scientifically 'predictive' practice, and also to how metaphor and imagination can develop explanatory theory. This sets the scene for Chapter 12, *Creating a New Coaching Meta-theory*. It identifies how coaching needs to be theorized from two perspectives, firstly as micro-practice – the activity and techniques used between two people – and then as a meta-theory which draws upon the four discourses to offer a theoretical explanation of coaching practice. The second perspective is the macro-social, the collective, institutional, formal, informal and social aspects that influence coaching. The macro-social is ignored in most coaching texts, yet needs to be included if a coaching meta-theory is to fully articulate how coaching works and how it changes. The macro and the micro are not separate but are in a constant dynamic, influencing each other, and both need accounting for.

Finally Chapter 13, *Coaching Formation*, describes pedagogy and educational approaches that deliver training and development aligned to the four discourses, and urges the coaching fraternity to focus on imaginative, creative and generative education, training and development, rather than overfocus on trying to raise coaching quality through 'control mechanisms' such as accreditation and standardization. Setting out a coaching process and pedagogical guidelines for coach trainers, this chapter looks to a bright future of coaching and mentoring.

Who is this Book for?

Coaching/mentoring practitioners

For all who coach or mentor both formally and informally, this book will provide a rich source of ideas and reflection. It offers coherent and ordered ways to think about the underlying assumptions that inform a coaching practice, and offers alternative narratives. Coaches should be better prepared to strategically plan their coaching sessions, to contract more clearly, to see where their developmental needs are, and to work with more freedom in the knowledge that they are working within a broad framework of coaching that isn't limited to any singular approach or technique.

Purchasers and providers of coaching

- Individuals

- Managers and leaders

- HR professionals

- Consultants

- Business schools

- Management and leadership development, and organizational development teams

Buying and delivering coaching/mentoring is a big commitment and this book will provide an informed view of how and when coaching/mentoring can be useful, taking a more systemic and organizational development approach to understanding its impact on individuals and organizations. There can be much confusion as to what can be expected from a coach, as there is such variety and what is delivered is not always what is 'written on the tin'. Coaches themselves often lack coherence, and this book sets out clear frameworks of the discourses that underpin coaching that will aid both providers and purchasers to make sense of the diverse coaching market.

Educators, academics and trainers

The book offers a broad view of how coaching and mentoring have adapted to the contemporary world of work, and how identity, subjectivity and therapy culture are engaged in the workplace through coaching as a new and hybrid 'talking cure'. Coach educators and trainers will benefit from this book, as it reveals underlying principles and discourses they work from at intellectual and practical levels. Chapter 13 sets out eight coaching pedagogical principles, and offers some education ideas for coaches to develop unusual skill sets such as 'associative intelligence'.

Academics and post-graduate students studying management, leadership, HR and organizational studies will also find this text useful as it positions coaching in the wider field of organizational development. Social scientists, psychologists and those studying psychotherapy will also see the relations and dynamics between coaching and therapy. Many coaching texts refer to psychotherapeutic influences and in this book I claim that therapy can learn from some of the innovative and hybrid developments in the coaching field.

What Authored the Author?

All writing has a biographical element as does all coaching; we bring ourselves to the work whether this is explicit or not. Coaching is very much about the use of the self – the coach may envisage the self as an instrument, a tool, an emotional container, an intervention, a thinking partner, a sounding board, or other metaphors may come to mind. Using the self as the main currency for the work means that the coach should a) know themselves, b) be clear what their role entails, c) have an understanding of what underpins their coaching work, i.e. to know the discourses, the underpinning theories and assumptions that inform what they do (these discourses remain largely hidden unless we take a critical stance to reveal them). Explicitly naming some of the influences that impacted on me, and therefore speak through this book, will give the reader a clearer viewpoint from which to understand and critique my writing and thinking. For coaches one of the key tasks is for them to be reflective about the influences that speak through their work, as this gives them an opportunity to draw on these appropriately rather than be condemned to enact them without thought, which leads to inappropriate coaching interventions.

This book is written from three perspectives; firstly from a very broad personal experience of the workplace; secondly from a wide theoretical perspective, drawing on psychoanalysis, critical organizational theory, theology, political and philosophical theory and the social sciences (I also have led, and teach internationally on, master's programmes in leadership, consultancy and coaching, and write on these subjects); thirdly it comes from my personal experience of a lifetime spent in helping relationships.

Personal work narrative

I have been privileged in my life to have shared engagements with others in a very diverse career that has taken me into the depths of people's lives and reached across many contexts. My working life has been, and continues to be, full of 'privileged conversations'. I currently work in various manifestations – an executive coach to board level leaders and to leadership teams. My expertise is in leadership and strategic coaching and I am invited to consult on organizational dynamics offering experiential learning events, seminars and strategic interventions.

Previously I have worked in a factory, leaving school with few qualifications, then trained as a general nurse with the physically sick and dying, and then as a psychiatric nurse with 'the mad' psychotic and schizophrenic patients in a Victorian asylum. I then worked in a therapeutic community with young people as a clinical manager and group therapist, before training as a family therapist studying systems theory and leading a community clinical team in Liverpool for ten years, working with suicidal and 'disturbed' young people and their families (who were also suffering economic and social deprivation).

This journey of working 'clinically' with the body, the mind, the individual, the small group and family, immersed me in human psychology and human relationships and it confronted me head on with the existential questions we all face about life and death, sanity and madness. It was part of my 'coaching formation' and when I work with clients and coachees, I bring this experience with me. I became intrigued by the connections that link the individual psyche and emotions to the family or team, and later how individuals, teams and families are affected by institutions, power and culture. My interests moved to influencing systemic change through studying the unconscious dynamics in organizational life. Rational explanations of the workplace did not fully explain the dynamics I had witnessed in the factory, the asylum or the hospital, and how much resistance occurred to changes that would clearly help both the client groups and staff. I immersed myself in psychoanalysis, studying at the Tavistock Clinic, and later leading their MA in Organizational Consultancy drawing on psychoanalytic theory. I took this work to Lancaster University Management School to research for a PhD in leadership. At Lancaster I was privileged to learn and work with internationally renowned scholars, where my study of organizations took on a critical perspective, drawing on Foucault, post-Marxist and post-structural theory. It opened up a new theoretical world for me, and also gave me an opportunity to work internationally with managers and leaders in the corporate sector. I worked closely with Professor Jonathan Gosling in the Strategic Leaders Unit, where we established a creative partnership and launched psychoanalytic and systems-informed leadership development interventions in global companies, which drew on observation and peer coaching (see www.lead2lead.com).

Later I became Director of Coaching at Lancaster University, setting up their post-graduate coaching programme which enabled me to reflect on my coaching work and what the meaning of coaching was. It was this process that led to this book.

My current work portfolio takes me to a variety of organizations that provide me with a cross-fertilization of experience and ethnographic information, as part of the role of coach is to observe and 'associate' (in a psycho-analytic way) to the organizational cultures in which they work. I work in internationally renowned university business schools, working with their senior teams; a multi-national bank, working with their global OD team; a small high-tech firm on the west coast of Ireland; the further education and the schools sectors; the NHS, working with CEOs and also with clinicians in a fertility clinic; and in the voluntary sector, where I have worked in Sudan with the Red Cross, and recently in a hospice. Working across domains, in diverse roles, is fascinating, and is the fuel for my academic writing and theorizing, which in circular feedback loops informs my practice. As Jacques-Alain Miller explains: 'Theory was necessary in order to institute the practice, and then, retroactively, the practice modified the theory' (Miller, 2011).

I coach individuals drawing on my psychotherapeutic past; drawing on psychoanalysis and systems theory from family therapy; critical theory understanding of organizational dynamics; and my understanding and observations of leadership and organizational development. These influences will become apparent as the reader engages with this text. What will be observed is the critical ambiguity in the writing as I underwent therapy at different times in my life, yet I am highly critical of the pathologizing stance within it and how it can produce a victim-type subject. I am fully engaged in psychoanalytic theory and practice, yet sceptical regarding many contemporary psychoanalytic institutions who undermine the emancipatory and political applications, focusing only on the clinical and becoming cult-like in their approach shunning learning from other traditions, and in doing so failing to contribute to an important dialogue. This critical awareness is often counter-intuitive to coaches who are often trained and caught in coaching discourses that encourage them to accept ideological propositions without questioning them, seeing them as simply 'good' or normative. For example, these assumptions were recently sent to me by a solution-focused coach:

1 People do not need repair

2 Change is inevitable

3 Every behaviour has a positive intention behind

4 People make the best decisions they are able to make at a time

5 People have all the resources to achieve their goals

As can be seen, the positive rhetoric is underpinned by the 'naïve individualistic narcissism' that pervades much of popular Western culture (Lasch, 1979). This emerges from the human potential movement whereby people are always seen in a positive light, the happiness imperative is applied, and all answers lie within the individual. This is a very tempting and seductive ideology!

My background helps me frame questions from diverse perspectives, many of which I have firsthand experience of. My first master's was in person-centred counselling and I taught a diploma of non-directive counselling for three years, before migrating to psychoanalysis. Freud taught us that within us there is ambiguity – our unconscious minds are in tension with our conscious awareness:

> The ego is not master in its own house. (Freud, 1917)

The positivist coaching ideology that says we can achieve anything we want avoids the reality principle – that the external world may not enable an individual to achieve their desires and goals, as it depends on social and structural power and economic distribution, alongside other factors such as mental, physical and emotional health for example. Serious scholarship of coaching, and advanced coaching practitioners, need to critique practice and more importantly the ideas behind the practice in order to develop the field and a) understand how coaching works, b) explain why coaching is popular and successful, and c) develop theory, research and innovative coaching education.

We are all authored by our experiences, as individuals and collectively, through the cultures and contexts that shape us. Coaches are shaped by their personal and collective experiences in coaching and beyond, and through the coaching narratives and discourses that inform their thinking and practice. Coaches reading this book will hopefully use it both as a thought-provoking text, and also as a mirror to their experience and coaching practice, reading with a curiosity and openness that enable them to reflect on their ideas, thinking and practice, and also to let the text read them.[1]

---

[1]As the text is read, the readers emotions and thoughts will be triggered, and each reader will have a unique and personal response. Allowing the text to read the reader, means to allow these responses to be reflected upon, not only from an intellectual position, but from a personal one also; 'Why did I react strongly to that? What does it say about me or about my beliefs?'.

Part I

Scoping the Field with a Critical Lens

1   A Critical Theory Approach to Coaching

Introduction
Why coaching and why now?
Four critical frames to analyse coaching
Frames summary
Conclusion
Suggested reading

Introduction

Have you heard the good news about coaching and mentoring?

> 'Mentoring empowered me: I gained confidence and a promotion!'

> 'I can't thank my coach enough; coaching transformed my leadership style, and I have become a better husband and father.'

> 'Since I started coaching I am much more focused; my team is working more collaboratively, and we over-achieved last quarter's targets.'

The coaching gospel has been a marketer's dream and coaching success can be found everywhere – popular magazines, websites, books, journals and through narrative accounts. We hear less about the challenges and limitations, as coaching has focused very successfully on spreading the 'good news' – that it changes lives and improves work performance.

Coaching is an exciting new addition to the myriad of 'helping professions' and it offers a vibrant and energizing new social space for reflection that claims to lead to change and action. This effervescent and infectious approach has helped coaching grow to become a multimillion dollar business.

Coaching emanates from a number of sources, from psychotherapy to counselling, from positive psychology to 'new spirituality', from sports coaching to developmental theory, and finally, from management and consultancy theory and practice. Initially there was a strong resistance in the coaching field to the link with psychotherapy at a time when coaching was trying to differentiate and define itself. Although the theory and practice of coaching clearly drew on psychotherapy, it needed to be seen as separate. Coaching is now emerging into a separate practice, yet its debts to psychotherapy are deep and tenacious. What is interesting now is the shift back towards psychotherapy, particularly in reference to theory (see Chapters 11 and 12). There is currently a 'second wave' of coaching taking place, where the moves towards accreditation and professionalization demand theory and professional standards, leading the experts in the field to turn heavily to psychology and psychotherapy. Coaching approaches and theories, such as cognitive behavioural, NLP, solution-focused, non-directive approaches and psychodynamic approaches are amongst a myriad of therapeutic influences that are abundantly found, explicitly or implicitly, in the practice of coaching. Coaching/mentoring reviewed from an ethnographer's stance is clearly a formulation of Freud's 'talking cure' in the sense that *talking* is the modus operandi of the coach, and its dominant working method is the conversational and confidential dyad, replicating the therapeutic pairing.

Coaching however is not bound by the 'old', but manifests itself in an exciting new hybrid form that is both plural and diverse. But the contemporary danger is that coaching is becoming colonized by the theories and professional codes of psychology, psychotherapy and managerialism, as it attempts to become a 'legitimate' professional activity. Coaching opens up a new space, and it is this new space that can lead to important personal and workplace development. Coaching not only offers a new expert 'helping relationship' in life experiences and the workplace, it also has the potential to bring new ideas, theories and practices to associated experts in other fields of human relations. Coaching already seems to be influencing counselling as well as being influenced by it. Linda Aspey, Chair, BACP Coaching writes:

> Understanding transference, engaging in supervision and working with loss are no longer solely the domain of therapists – many non-therapist coaches are highly trained and skilled in these areas too. And many therapists are working with issues that were once the domain of coaches, using tools and models of motivation, change, leadership and performance that were once not so dominant in our therapeutic work. We are learning from each other. (Aspey, 2011)

This chapter will review coaching in its wider social, historical, economical and political context.

Why Coaching and Why Now?

The question of why coaching and mentoring have expanded so rapidly and what purpose they serve in the workplace and in our social lives is important to investigate rather than to take for granted. For a long while the contemporary belief was that coaching was simply 'a good thing', creating an unchallengeable assumption for coachers and coachees. Now coaching has come under greater scrutiny, situating itself in a wider context where academics are beginning to define it and develop it as a significant and homogeneous practice (Kilburg, 2000; West and Milan, 2001; De Haan, 2008; Garvey et al., 2009; Cox et al., 2010). However, scrutinizing coaching also brings challenges from a critical perspective, as familiar managerial, cognitive/behaviourist and psychology positions turn to 'scientific rationalism' as the tools of modernity to scrutinize practice, asking, 'Is it efficient?' This scrutiny arises from workplace demands for coaching to prove its worth, to show a return on investment (ROI). Competing coaching approaches also have an interest in 'legitimizing' the field in order to win market share and claim credibility. This has led to a big movement that attempts to prove the efficacy of coaching through evidence-based research. This latter position is very problematic and discussed in depth in Chapter 11. The danger of this approach is to reduce coaching to a functional and instrumental practice (Garvey et al., 2009).

Additionally a critical approach asks, 'What social and organizational factors have led to the massive investment and take up of one-on-one support in the workplace in the last decade?' To answer this, we have to look beyond coaching to other social phenomena, and think how work-based coaching relates to the growth in Life-coaching, confessional TV and the constant rise of the 'therapy culture' in all aspects of our lives (Furedi, 2003).

New organizations and new modes of work require new theoretical resources and new approaches to manage, lead and organize. Coaching and mentoring has to look outside its borders and that of psychotherapy and sports, on which at present it draws heavily, and use wider theoretical resources and practices. Critical management and organizational theorists offer resources that can be useful to coaching, as they help make sense of how the workplace has changed in the global and hi-tech environment, in particular how cognitive labour has replaced manual labour, and how subjectivity and identity have become an integral aspect of what work means (Rose, 1990; Parker, 1992).

The rise of coaching is clearly linked to this post-industrial, knowledge-based transformation of work and organizations. When working with cognition, emotions, subjectivity and identity, new resources of support and development are necessary – coaching fits this very aptly. However, within this modern period, a critical account of coaching must ask if the practice is merely a sticking plaster to keep 'emotionally battered' employees, suffering epidemic levels of workplace stress, in productive roles. Is coaching being used as a tool to sustain an ever problematic and dysfunctional system that requires re-thinking rather than sustaining? Or alternatively is coaching providing a vital reflective space in which individuals can be more humane, thoughtful, creative and strategic at work: a space where critical perspectives are allowed to be aired, where questioning and creativity are encouraged, in order to find innovative ways of moving forward?

Coaching is sliding towards an institutionalization and professionalization whereby individual coaches and companies will become limited in their scope under the guise of 'good practice' and safe regulations. Sherman and Freas (2004), in their paper 'The Wild West of Executive Coaching', make the point that without more work on a theory of coaching, any standards and universal regulations are little more than barriers to entry set up by institutions wanting to profit and control the business:

> … until a body of knowledge about coaching wins acceptance, we'll remain skeptical of current efforts to introduce universal standards and high barriers for entry. For now clients will best serve their needs by evaluating coaches individually. (2004: 5)

The meta-theory proposed in Chapter 12 works towards forming this body of knowledge, bringing together the disparate and competing theories and discourses into a more cohesive field of study.

Coaching: the built-in resistance to critical reflection

> The oppressed have an interest in explanatory knowledge of the structures that oppress them. But their oppressors do not need to have that explanatory knowledge and it might be better for them if they do not. The sort of knowledge they need to have is best not called knowledge, but rather information or even data, and that is about how to manipulate events and circumstances and discourses. (Bhaskar, 2010: 107)

Bhaskar's comments reflect the trend in executive coaching, managerial and HR circles for coaching research to focus on outcomes and ROI data collection. Alternative research would be useful on explanatory knowledge about the structures of the workplace and how coaching can intervene to help improve work.

The coaching fraternity is not predisposed to theory or critical thinking. Coaches on the whole prefer practice to theorizing and philosophy, preferring the simple and straightforward (for example GROW approaches and other acronyms) to the more complex and challenging. Positivistic approaches are preferred to critical and systemic thinking, and an individualistic focus is preferred to social and structural understandings. In the UK, Bristol University's Critical Research Forum dropped the word 'critical' from its title in 2010 owing to it 'putting coaches off attending'. There are strengths in this pragmatic and positivistic approach, but there are also weaknesses and gaps.

There are in-built resistances to using critical theory to examine coaching:

1 *Coaching is about being positive.* This is opposed to therapy/counselling, which is about working with dysfunction and pathology.

   Counselling managed to supplant therapy by becoming more accessible, and coaching managed to make therapeutic skills available to employees, leaving behind the baggage of dysfunction. However, this positivism linguistically and culturally inscribes the coach/mentor and the client, creating limitations about what can and cannot be said or thought in the coaching arena.

2 *Individuals as free agents.* Within this positivistic discourse many coaches work on the assumption that individuals act as completely free agents and have the innate power to change themselves. This eliminates critical reflection which situates the individual in a social context, showing how structural and systemic factors impact on the individual.

3 *Lack of coherent theory.* In spite of the many strengths of coaching and mentoring there is a lack of coherent coaching theory (Garvey et al., 2009) and the lack of a larger body of knowledge that critiques coaching from a broader perspective than focusing on its micro-practices. A key aim of this book is to be part of a galvanizing process to partake in a conversation that addresses this lack.

Laing writes:

> Most fundamentally a critical theory must be able to place all theories and practices within the scope of a total vision of the ontological structure of being human. (1967: 41)

Coaching and mentoring are ultimately a deeply human exchange, taking place in the economic, political and social core of Western society. The workplace has displaced the church as the main site of community/human exchange. It is here we spend most of our time; it is the workplace that dominates economics and politics and shapes humanity in so many ways. Developing a critical stance will help promote coaching to have a healthy impact on the workplace, and therefore on society as a whole.

Four Critical Frames to Analyse Coaching

This chapter will now outline the four critical frames used in this book. These four critical frames explain the theoretical approach used to examine the practices of coaching and mentoring in general, and they can also be used in practice. Martin Parker (2002) declares that critical management studies (CMS) have very little impact on what happens in reality:

> CMS has had little or no impact on what organisations actually do ... there are some serious and fascinating issues being discussed within CMS, but they tend to stay within the cloistered boundaries of academic work and find little echo outside those who are already converted. (2002: 115–6)

Perhaps this is because many critical academics write from a place that is dislocated from experience and are not engaged as practitioners. Laing's (1967) critique of psychiatry had a vitality, and did influence practice at micro and macro levels; he writes from personal experience of being a psychiatrist and psychoanalyst. The critical frames discussed here also emerge from practice as my work takes me into organizations as a coaching and consulting practitioner. These frames have been used in master's-level coaching and consulting training programmes, as well as practice for students and within my own coaching work. Taking a critical approach using these frames is a theoretical stance that informs practice, and the frames themselves emerge from this praxis.

The four critical frames are:

- Emancipation

- Depth Analysis

- Looking Awry

- Network Analysis

Emancipation

Ethics, liberation, autonomy and justice: coaching to help create the 'good society'

This book takes an emancipatory approach as its ethical position. This is an ideological position that I believe should also become central to coaching. If coaching is not an emancipatory project then by default it becomes an instrumental project, whereby coaching serves only to promote greater efficiency, productivity, profit, goals and performance, with little reflection on its wider impact on the social, economic or political sphere. There are many advocates of a non-emancipatory stance, where the main claim for coaching is efficiency and improving return on investment.

If we are to avoid the accumulated problems in the twentieth century that arose from modernity – social inequity, climate change and environmental destruction amongst others – growth, functionalism and improved performance must be aligned with an emancipatory vision. Focusing on improving performance is necessary in any organization, yet it cannot be the only focus. Strategy and emergence are also important; companies now work towards corporate social responsibility and sustainability agendas. A few years ago I worked in Gap Inc. (USA), and a quick search on their website demonstrates the corporate move towards a more ethical stance, not just for altruism, but also for business success. Referring to their supply chain they write:

> In an increasingly interconnected world, acting responsibly is not just a good feeling – it's good business. (Gap Inc., 2007/8)

The 2008 collapse of the finance sector is a good example of short-term targets being rewarded without reference to wider systemic forces that led to the collapse. Coaches have an opportunity to engage and influence change. There are always tensions in the work, and answers are never easy, but the worst situations arise when challenges and dilemmas go unacknowledged. Coaches can push executives on these agendas.

The emancipatory approach I take draws upon eclectic ideas from the Frankfurt School, Habermas, Alain Badiou, Slavoj Zizek and post-structuralists such as Michel Foucault and Judith Butler, who developed emancipatory agendas through their work. This book will pursue these themes in relation to coaching. For Habermas (1987), communication is a key tool of emancipation or oppression. Foucault's body of work leads the way in showing how discourses and language create a power–knowledge link (Foucault, 1980) and how our subjective selves are formed by discourses which entrap us. I draw on the emancipatory frame to explore the underpinning discourses of coaching in order to reflect on some of the tensions that are enacted in coaching. To struggle for emancipation is to reveal power relations, to look beyond our own interests and to analyse structural power in the macro system. Micro-emancipatory goals are found throughout coaching; they underpin 'Life-coaching'. Coaching empowers – personal growth, 'Aha!' moments, new insights, profound change and personal transformation are all words that are often used to evoke the micro-emancipatory claims of coaching. Whilst coaching can help an individual, this micro agenda of instrumentally improving performance or striving to deliver individual 'happiness' can ignore how coaching at a macro-level can undermine other emancipatory agendas. Furedi (2003) and Beradi (2009) claim that the 'imperative for happiness', through positive psychology and endeavours such as coaching, can create the opposite effect. They support these claims by citing the amount of depression, anxiety and unhappiness in society.

> Depression is deeply connected to the ideology of self-realisation and the happiness imperative. (Beradi, 2009: 99)

The contented coachee/employee may be unaware of their entrapment by the culture of corporate life. Casey discusses the corporate employee who is so overwhelmed by the corporate culture that they repress and lose any ability to critique their position.

> Corporatised selves become sufficiently repressed to effectively weaken and dissolve the capacity for serious criticism or dissent. (1995: 150)

Progressive corporate and political leaders are challenging the norms that place short-term profit before social and environmental concerns, realizing that radical reform and change are required. Coaches hopefully can support and lead initiatives to challenge a status quo that has left the world in a precarious place. In a world where power has shifted from national governments to corporations, coaches in business should be working with a clear agenda to support a leadership paradigm shift towards a fairer and more equitable and sustainable world. Coaching with an emancipatory agenda with senior leaders has two elements:

1   Micro-emancipation, working on personal and team challenges to help employees to both feel and work better.

2   To support employees in challenging the status quo, to realize that an ethical agenda actually can support a healthy organization, as promoted by Unilever:

> 'The business case for growing Unilever sustainably is compelling. Consumers are asking for it, retailers demand it, it fuels product innovation, it grows the company's markets around the world and, in many cases, it saves money.' Paul Polman, CEO, Unilever 2011 (see Davos, 2011) in 'Views and Comments' from a series of debates hosted by Unilever on 15 November 2010.

Coaches can and should be working consecutively on both macro and micro emancipatory concerns. Using this critical lens, a coach takes an ethical position (a non-judgmental stance does not mean a non-ethical stance). The coach becomes a 'trusted partner' not by being an echo-chamber for the coachee, but by offering thoughts, insights, holding the big picture in mind and reflecting it back, ordering ideas, and challenging norms or behaviours that are unethical or do not promote the 'common good'. The coach or coachee will not have all the answers, but by asking the questions it is surprising what emerges. Coachees find themselves thinking more strategically, and to working in a more interconnected and ethical way.

Depth analysis

Revealing hidden dynamics in individuals, organizations and the social field

Depth analysis draws upon a psychoanalytic ontology, working on the premise that much of human relations happens 'beneath the surface'. In psychoanalytic terms this is the unconscious, while in social terms the unseen dynamics might be in discourse. Psychoanalysis is characteristic of this, and is perhaps the earliest example of a critical theorist method, as explained by Johnson and Duberley (2005):

> Perhaps the prototype for critical science is psychoanalysis because it involves 'depth-hermeneutics' [Habermas, 1972: 218] in which the distorted texts of the patient's behaviour become intelligible to them through self-reflection. In this fashion emancipation occurs as the patient becomes liberated from the terror of their own unconscious as previously suppressed and latent determinants of behaviour are revealed and thereby lose their power. (2005: 120)

Psychoanalysis goes beyond the study of the unconscious; its referents are also anxiety, subjectivity and desire, and our collective emotional lives (Freud, 1930; Fanon, 1970; Lacan, 1993; Hoggett, 2000). Psychoanalysis offers not only a theory but also a methodology for studying these issues. My training and background are in psychoanalytic theory and practice; I have been a psychotherapist and recently directed a master's programme in organizational consultancy, using psychoanalytic theory to study the unconscious and emotional dynamics in organizational life. Psychoanalysis is sometimes used as a theory without reference to practice or the clinical method, and this can be problematic; Bhaskar claims that he could 'not use psychoanalysis as a potential science of emancipation without actually having experienced it' (2010: 94).

Other forms of depth analysis, such as discourse analysis and communication studies, each attempt to reveal and interpret underlying patterns and

power relations from different perspectives. Religious hermeneutic interpretation offers ancient methods of depth analysis, trying to uncover the
meaning within holy texts. Foucault teaches us that power and knowledge
are closely related and that power is exerted through normative control, 'the
way things are done around here', and to see beyond the established 'natural
order of things' means to 'unmask' what is hidden. For example, many cultural assumptions are made about heterosexuality and marriage, and whilst
these seem normal to many, to some from different cultures or from gay or
queer perspectives, they seem oppressive. Power is performed through
Westernized ideals of the hetero-normative nuclear family, and those outside
this framework are disciplined by social rules, either explicitly or implicitly
(Butler, 2004). Psychoanalysis and other in-depth analytic approaches are
employed in this text as a framework to explore the subjective and psychic
underbelly of coaching. Psychoanalysis also provides methods and theories
for coaches to draw upon, particularly the relationship between the coach
and coachee. In coaching, this relationship is less focused on than in therapy,
yet it remains vital for two reasons:

1 Without a close, trusting relationship, a coaching alliance can't be formed, which limits the
   coaching to superficial levels.

2 The information and understanding that can be gathered through interactions with a coach
   (transference, counter-transference, projections and introjections) offer a huge amount of data
   to work with.

Depth analysis works in coaching sessions to reveal what is hidden in the
coaching relationship, and what the coachee is striving to discover within
themselves (see Chapter 6).

Depth analysis also reveals what is hidden in the structures, institutions
and normative values of coaching itself. To make interpretations from a psychoanalytic perspective means to draw upon our emotions and our subjectivity as researchers, observers and coaches. It is to use the 'self' in order to
make sense of one's feelings in relation to another or to a social situation.
These psycho-social methodologies are underused and underdeveloped
outside of the clinical arena, although there is a small but growing interest
in psycho-social research. Sasha Roseneil of Birkbeck University writes of
her psycho-social research:

> the psychosocial-analysis I carried out drew on principles from clini-
> cal psychoanalysis, in its concern to explore interviewees' psychic
> reality, the non-rational, unarticulated, unconscious dimensions of

the experiences they narrated, as well as the emotions and affects that they were able to formulate expressly in discourse. (2006: 864)

Depth analysis means in general terms to look beneath the surface, to help reveal how individual and social conscious and unconscious processes operate in a given context. In addition, Foucault and Butler draw upon another form of depth analysis: the more general impact of discourse upon individuals, collectives and culture. Butler writes on gender:

In other words how do normative gender presumptions work to delimit the very field of description that we have for the human? What is the means by which we come to see this delimiting power, and what is the means to transform it? (1990: xxiii)

Butler is asking about normative discourses that entrap us through the very language we use, and how we can look beyond this to see how these discourses manifest and can be transformed. This link between depth analysis, discourse analysis and emancipation is vital.

The irrational and subjective as well as the rational and cognitive become internalized, embodied and enacted by individuals, groups, institutions and society, and depth analysis is the means to explore these psycho-social dynamics.

Applied to coaching, depth analysis means listening to the undercurrents, to what's not being said, to the emotional undertow. Depth analysis also informs us about the power dynamics and undercurrents of the social institutions that inform coaching practice, for example the workplace, coaching companies and coaching training institutions. It means to stand back and study the common assumptions made in coaching and mentoring and what purposes and whose interests they serve.

Depth analysis must also include resources and power, to offer a real contribution to understanding psycho-social dynamics. To take a hermeneutic stance and to study the discourses of coaching are vital tools that improve the practice of coaching and help to understand its dynamic relations with the social world in which it operates.

Looking awry

Bringing desire and disruption to observation and understanding

As well as depth analysis and taking a hermeneutic stance, there is another kind of investigation that is required to achieve Calhoun's (1995) critical stance of 're-examining the conceptual frameworks and look for new possibilities'.

To see something differently means to look differently. Slavoj Zizek (1992) claims that what is usually considered as the best view – a frontal view or a scientific objective view – is actually limiting, giving a linear and normative perspective. To get a fresh perspective and really see what is happening he suggests the need to look awry, taking a 'distorted' view:

> The object assumes clear and distinctive features only if we look 'at an angle', i.e. with an interested view, supported, permeated, and 'distorted' by *desire*. (Zizek, 1992: 12)

Here, Zizek argues that the observer needs to bring their *desire* and subjectivity to the viewing rather than taking an objective neutral stance. Zizek (1992) describes what it means to look awry by using the metaphor of a film director changing the camera angle to give a completely different perspective on the scene. The film director is shooting the film with *desire*; he/she wants to bring something special to the shot. Observing then becomes an active rather than passive activity, challenging modernity's obsession with the scientific gaze of the neutral observer. Communities of practices, institutions and professions create normative processes and turn our gaze in a particular direction. To look awry is to reframe and to question the norm.

When we are 'liberated' from a particular way of seeing, new options then become available. To look awry is not only an intellectual exercise but also can be a powerful change agent. As a family therapist, looking awry enables the therapist to 'reframe' problems, making a space for families to find new options to change patterns of behaviour they find destructive (Weakland et al., 1974: 147).

Likewise within coaching/mentoring, reframing opens up new perspectives whereby the coach can see different options and ways to act or intervene. To help a coachee look awry adds new dimensions and enables real shifts to be made. Sometimes change comes from depth analysis and insight; at other times insights get stuck until a pattern is disrupted; to look awry can help the coach make a 'disruptive intervention'. This is when the coach throws the coachee off guard, with a challenge, an unexpected comment, an exercise, or some interpretation that disrupts the pattern enough to allow a new thought to emerge, and a new reflection on the norm.

To reframe is one thing, but to look awry from a critical perspective means to link this to emancipatory thinking and depth analysis. This is to question the normative, to bring new resources from different traditions in order to see something new or hidden:

> Is not short-circuiting, therefore, one of the best metaphors for a critical reading? Is not one of the most effective critical procedures to cross wires that do not usually touch: to take a major text and read

it in a short-circuiting way ... such a procedure can lead to insights which completely shatter and undermine our common perceptions. ... The aim is to illuminate a standard text or ideological formation, making it readable in a totally new way. (Zizek, 2003: Foreword)

To see beyond the obvious requires us to look awry, to bring our desire to the observation and this in turns allows us to bring new resources that aid our curiosity.

Coaches are often trained to ask the wrong questions from the outset. They are so anxious to help, to be seen to be effective, that they jump to premature goal-seeking behaviours, desperate to get results. Setting goals at the outset is seen as imperative in many coaching approaches yet to set goals so early on is to close down options too early. Garvey et al. (2009) challenge the 'goal assumption', saying it has become an established norm in coaching, and as they point out, goals have a 'dark side'; they serve certain interests and they limit complexity.

Coaching in this manner is like buying a rail ticket to the wrong destination, because the journey has been planned too quickly. To look awry as a coach means to hesitate, to pause, to move your body to another place, to ask the coachee to change seating, to do some artwork, to find another way to look at the presenting challenges, to read some literature, poetry, to look for aesthetic beauty and creativity instead of problems and challenges, and finally to become associative rather than rational and linear. The results can be phenomenal, opening up new spaces that were not previously conceptualized.

Looking awry is particularly pertinent to coaching and mentoring because the dominant way of looking at coaching thus far has been straight on, and it is quickly becoming an instrumental functionalist profession, asking, 'What are your goals?', 'How can we achieve them?', 'What small steps can improve your performance?'

A master coach, however, will get the coachee to look awry. To achieve this, a safe base is required, and a coach who goes beyond the normative asks the coachee to access their desire in order to look awry. This dual process of *short-circuiting* (bringing new resources) and looking awry provides options to reveal what was previously concealed within a dominant discourse or within normative work practice. The pervasive 'natural order of things' then becomes known, and becomes open for transformation.

Network analysis

Network coaching, connectivity, interdependence, emergence

Network analysis is to take a position that accounts for the networks in which we live and work. Manuel Castells (2000) describes the 'Information Age' and the 'Network Society', addressing how technology has impacted on contemporary society.

For coaches and mentors to be effective beyond supporting micro-instrumental changes there is a deep need for more coaching education in organizational theory and social change. The world of work is changing dramatically yet many coaches are working on assumptions passed down from the past century of management thinking – particularly about how organizations function and about transformational leadership that offers an individualized charismatic formula – when what are required in today's organizations are more adaptive forms of distributed 'Eco-Leadership':

> 'Eco-leadership discourse' … this discourse is characterized by 'a growing interest in systems thinking, complexity theory, narrative approaches and also the environment as metaphors for leadership and organizing company structures' [Western, 2008a: 184].

Manual labour has been usurped by cognitive labour, with global distributed networks producing new forms of organizing and new organizational forms. The contemporary workplace is interconnected and interdependent, filled with people, technology and information communication systems (ICTs). Coaching can also be seen as an ICT when thought about from a network perspective (see Chapter 12). Churchman defines how important systemic thinking is to a critical approach. He refers to ethics, efficiency and effectiveness as the outcomes of a critical systemic approach:

> First, ethical alertness comes from thinking systemically. Second, efficiency and effectiveness come from thinking about the total relevant system. (Cited in Flood, 1999: 63)

For coaching to be effective, the impact of technology and social change has to be accounted for. Network analysis needs to become a vital part of coach training, thinking and practice. Chapter 9 discusses the Network Coach Discourse that utilizes network analysis to identify how coaches work within different discourses in relation to diverse contexts and for different outcomes. Network coaching also connects coaching practice to wider macro-social influences. Coaching supports leaders and executives to think beyond their boxes and to help them become aware of a wider context of patterns of emergent opportunities and threats. The pressures to attain short-term goals impacts on leaders and managers, and coaching sessions are an opportunity to be more reflective and more strategic. Network analysis helps managers think about their own lives, and the connections and networks in which they live and how they can influence the networks in which they work. Network mapping exercises are extremely useful in achieving this.

The Network Coach Discourse (Chapter 9) relates to coaching that applies a 'network analysis' to working with leaders, to help them take a networked perspective, emphasizing connectivity, ethics and inter-dependence. Developing Eco-Leadership is a strategy to create organizations where leadership flourishes everywhere, to help teams and organizations become more ethical and successful through full engagement of employees, and through designing connecting structures. It also means to ensure organizations have grown in their ability to adapt to external contingencies like political and environmental change. Network Coaches are focused on developing Eco-Leadership in organizations.

Coaches need to think about their work and how they are relating to these new organizational dynamics in a systematic manner. Brunning (2006) sets out the anatomy of psychodynamic-systemic coaching, claiming these are 'contemporaneously present during executive coaching':

1 The client's personality

2 The client's life story

3 The client's skills

4 The client's aspirations

5 The client's current workplace environment

6 Current organizational role

This psychodynamic-systemic coaching approach addresses systemic issues around the client: their skills, aspirations and roles, and how they apply these to the workplace. It situates the client in a micro-system, looking at their role in a team and linking their internal 'organization in the mind' with the 'organization in reality' (Newton et al., 2006).

This is a useful framework taking coaching beyond the individual psychology of NLP and CB approaches, yet there is a hesitation in the organizational role analysis approach to bring to the fore power, politics and wider social influences such as radical changes in business models, IT and technological advances, environmental concerns, or gender and diversity issues that impact on individuals and organizations alike. Network analysis goes beyond person-in-role; it shifts from an institutional view of person-in-role, to a view of person-in-networks. This work approach is influenced by Actor Network theory (Law 1993; Latour 2005) where it is claimed that networks are made up of place, nature, technology, people, texts and machines – all the things that are entangled and form constellations that we move through without reflection most of the time.

Networks are fluid, and employees these days are also in movement, between roles, project teams, workplaces, geographical places, virtual and real places. Coaching needs to work with this rich environment, and to think beyond a limited individualistic perspective or a role perspective that omits the wider network influences. Whilst some of these 'big picture' issues may initially seem irrelevant to coaches focusing on the individual, working with a person's 'network' is vital, whether you are mentoring an adolescent in trouble or coaching a chief executive of a transnational corporation. I have worked in diverse settings for many years, and my experience is that change in a person means change in a network of activity too, or it is not sustainable. Network analysis recognizes that change in an individual will mean changes in their relationships with close others, with institutions, organizations and within social networks. Change means identifying resources that support change and assessing the restraints in the network.

Leadership, like power, is not just at the top of organizations but is every-where. Getting middle managers to think about how they collaborate, about new ways to structure teams to make them more self-managing, and perhaps about new business models and new ways to save energy – creates a bottom-up transformation as well as facilitating top-down change. This is where coaching can provide real added value. Today's organizations in the post-industrial era are eco-systems and networks with fluid, moving boundaries, diverse stakeholders and a plurality of actors that are both human and non-human (Law, 1993).

Coaches will offer much more value to workplace transformation if they look beyond individual behaviours, psychology and sporting metaphors, and analyse situations from a broader network perspective.[1] Network analysis means to shift the perspective offered by individual goal and performance-focused approaches. These are welcome and useful but not enough. Coaching is now a mass enterprise and its impact and influence as a whole must be accounted for. To achieve this a meta-analysis of the coaching network is required (see Chapter 11).

Coaching providers who offer services to organizations that can improve their network capability, and build the organizational leadership capacity to become more strategic, embedding and aligning values, are very sought after.

Frames Summary

These four frames – Emancipation, depth analysis, looking awry and network analysis – *can* provide a basis for a critical approach from which to review coaching (see Table 1.1). Together they offer a place to work from an

---

[1]See Appendix: Analytic-Network Coaching, for a coaching process that addresses the individual and the network.

ethical position in a world where it is argued that corporations and the finance industry are now the dominant economic and political force in the world. Corporations, it is argued, have greater wealth and influence than nation states (Anderson and Cavanagh, 2000; Hertz, 2001; Klein, 2001). Coaches working in organizations, the public sector, not-for-profits and the private sector have an imperative to work towards developing an ethical,

Table 1.1   Summary of the critical frames applied to coaching practice

Depth analysis

Revealing hidden dynamics in individuals, organizations and the social field

Depth analysis draws upon psychoanalysis and discourse analysis, working on the premise that much of human relations and organizational dynamics happens 'beneath the surface', in our individual and collective unconscious processes, and is hidden in the texts and language we use. To understand the social relations between power, knowledge, emotions and change is to undertake depth analysis. To coach clients using a depth approach is to work in the Soul Guide Discourse (see Chapter 6), working intimately with individuals, engaging with their deepest authentic selves and unconscious processes.

Emancipation

Ethics, liberation, autonomy and justice

Coaching can work on a micro-emancipatory agenda, that is, to improve the life of the coachee, but too often this is compromised to the efficiency, productivity and goals agenda. The three questions coaches should ask are:

1   'Is this coaching working towards the "good society" and a sustainable world?'
2   'Is the coaching ethical and working towards the coachee's well-being and autonomy?'
3   'Is the coaching ethical and working towards the organization's values, well-being and sustainability?' Are any of these in conflict and need exploring with the client? Too often these questions are absent. Coaching has an opportunity (and a responsibility) to push for sustainable and socially just agendas at the three levels of individual, organization and social.

Network analysis

Network coaching, connectivity, interdependence, emergence

Network Analysis is an important lens to locate coaching in the wider social-political environment. In coaching practice it locates the coachee in their network, identifying nodal points of connectivity where they can influence change; this is very pragmatic and important work. Identifying powerful connections and groups, powerless groups, key and missing stakeholders, and resources, the coachee begins to map their organization and their social world, discovering patterns and gaps. This exercise is very powerful as it helps coachees internalize a sense of their place, and their location or dislocation, and how to make a difference. Network Analysis places coaching in the twenty-first century's organizations and life. We live in a network society, and coaches need to work in this domain. Chapter 9 discusses this in more depth.

Looking awry

Bringing desire and disruption to observation and understanding

Looking Awry is to disrupt the normative, to look differently in order to experience differently, and discover something new. It is to bring authenticity, ethics and desire to the coaching relationship, to discard the limitations of the rational for a while. To 'think outside the box' has become a tired cliché that no longer suffices. To see things differently, releasing creativity and innovation, means to bring desire and subjectivity to the looking. The coach has to create a safe container from which the coachee can reveal their desire, and step outside of their normative place, to experience something new, and from this position discover new insights and develop themselves.

progressive and emancipatory approach. This is particularly important as coaching claims to be a force for good, to help people become their authentic selves. There are also many commercial benefits to ethical practice.

These four frames together inform a critical approach to coaching, looking at depth, with an ethical frame, with a connected-network understanding, and with the potential to look awry, beyond the norms we all get trapped in unknowingly. They also inform coaching practice as well as theory. To coach is to work intimately and at depth with individuals (Depth Analysis), coaching them to enhance their autonomy, freedom and well-being (Emancipation Analysis), to help them influence their interdependent networks and to think connectively about their organizations and stakeholders (Network Analysis), and finally to see things differently, releasing creativity and innovation (Looking Awry).

Conclusion

A critical approach is therefore important for coaching, as it adds to the growing body of knowledge and theory that is developing. Critical theoretical approaches bring new resources from a broad spectrum of critical management studies, organizational theory, discourse theory, feminism, philosophy, sociology and other social sciences.

Critical theory informs the development of a meta-theory of coaching. This will help coaching be examined both as a practice and as a macro-social body, as body politic, and how coaching works in informal network influences, and adapts and informs external social influences (see Chapter 12). Taking a critical stance, however, is not just about theory but about praxis. Practice both informs theory and is informed by theory. A critical approach brings to the fore the critical frames discussed here. They offer practising coaches lenses to work through that focus on ethics, power and the psychosocial, which are as important in coaching work as in coaching theory.

Suggested Reading

Butler, J. (1990) *Gender Trouble: Feminism and the Subversion of Identity*. London: Routledge.

Foucault, M. (1980) *Power/Knowledge: Selected Interviews and Other Writings, 1972–77* (ed. Colin Gordon). London: Harvester.

Parker, M. (2002) *Against Management: Organization in the Age of Managerialism*. Cambridge: Polity Press.

Western, S. (2008) *Leadership: A Critical Text*. London: Sage. Ch. 1.

Zizek, S. (1992) *Looking Awry: An Introduction to Jacques Lacan through Popular Culture*. London: Verso.

2 Scoping the Field

Definitions and Divergence of Practice

Coaching and mentoring: differentiated or merged?
Definition of terms
Coaching and mentoring: ordering and categorizing
A typology of mentoring
A typology of coaching
Conclusion
Suggested reading

Coaching and Mentoring: Differentiated or Merged?

Coaching and mentoring are contested and confused terms that embrace multiple and diverse practices. This chapter will initially discuss the similarities and differences between coaching and mentoring and then briefly 'scope the field' to discuss the typology of the coaching and mentoring landscape, identifying the diversity that occurs under the names 'coaching and mentoring'.

The terms 'coaching' and 'mentoring' cause much confusion – some people use them interchangeably and others clearly differentiate them. There is no commonly agreed, shared view of the terms 'coaching' and 'mentoring'. Julie Hay, ex-President of EMCC (European Mentoring and Coaching Council) writes that her hopes for coaching and mentoring to become clearly differentiated over time were dashed and 'as time has passed the coaching and mentoring profession is probably even more confusing'. She describes how the EMCC made a policy decision while she was President to refer to coaching/mentoring as a single term in order to prompt people to 'spell out their definitions rather than realizing too late that they had been discussing different things' (Hay, 2007: 4). The European Mentoring and Coaching Council (EMCC) website puts it like this:

> The term 'coach/mentoring' is used to describe all types of coaching or mentoring that may be taking place, both in the work environment and outside. The EMCC recognize that there will be many types of coach/mentoring taking place and these will need to be defined when more detailed standards are produced.

In the last few years the clarity I had about the differences between coaching and mentoring has faded owing to popular usage, misunderstandings, misappropriation and simply because of the global diversity of approaches that blur all clear distinctions. Today, if you work in the field of coaching or mentoring it is important to clarify what precisely you are discussing or contracting, without assuming others are sharing your understanding of terms.

The ICF (International Coach Federation), the world's largest coaching organization, does differentiate between coaching and mentoring, whilst also acknowledging (and perhaps creating) some confusion. These quotes were from their website in 2008:

> Mentoring, which can be thought of as guiding from one's own experience or sharing of experience in a specific area of industry or career development, is sometimes confused with coaching.

They continue and reveal the confusion:

> Although some coaches provide mentoring as part of their coaching, such as in mentor coaching new coaches, coaches are not typically mentors to those they coach. (ICF, 2008)

This quote reveals the merging and overlapping between coaching and mentoring. However, there are tangible differences between them, which are discussed below.

Definition of Terms

Table 2.1 shows definitions of coaching and mentoring adapted from coaching programmes I directed at Lancaster University Management School in 2007.

Table 2.1 Coaching and mentoring: definition of terms, 2007

Coaching	Mentoring
Sports coaching	US mentoring
Life-coaching	Informal mentoring
Business coaching	Formal mentoring
Executive coaching	Internal and business mentoring
Leadership coaching	New hire mentoring
Careers coaching	Reverse mentoring
Tele-cyber coaching	Voluntary mentoring
Team/group coaching	Youth and educational mentoring
OD coaching	Peer mentoring

Note: These definitions refer to **work-based coaching and mentoring**.

Box 2.1

Mentor

A wise and trusted advisor or guide. (Collins Concise Dictionary, 5th edn)

A mentor is an experienced person who provides guidance and support in a variety of ways, by being a role model, guide or confidant(e). Caring for the mentee is an implicit part of the mentoring relationship. Mentoring is a contested term and there has been an expansive usage of the term so that it encompasses many diverse practices. However, to return to source is a helpful way to anchor the meaning of mentoring. The name came from the Greek myth where Mentor was a friend of Odysseus. He became tutor, faithful and wise advisor to his son Telemachus.

The mentor offers their experience and support to help the mentee develop. The stance of the mentor sits between listening, caring, non-judgmental support and imparting experience, knowledge and wisdom. Mentors can be more directive than some coaches as they have a clearer mandate to advise than coaches. However a mentor can't help with a problem unless they understand it first and have the confidence and trust of the mentee. This means mentors need good 'people' and relational skills (which are sometimes referred to these days as coaching skills hence some of the confusion). Many mentor relationships at work fail because the mentor has the experience and knowledge but lacks the 'people skills' to share it. Training and 'skilling' up mentors will be a vital part of an organization's success.

The primary task of the mentor is:

To offer experience to guide, advise and support the development of the mentee, resulting in improved performance.

(Continued)

(Continued)

Coach

An expert in facilitating another's personal journey, focusing on both personal and organizational success.

An organizational coach is a professional partner whose task is to improve 'role performance' thereby working towards organizational as well as individual aims. Using expert 'people skills' the coach will create a 'thinking space' and encourage reflection and dialogue, sharing insights, thoughts and posing challenges to the coachee before helping them focus on appropriate action. The organizational coach should focus on 'person in role', and an experienced coach takes systemic, organizational and strategic perspectives. However, many coaches become over-focused on the individual, bringing a Life-coaching/counselling approach to organizational coaching. Cognitive behavioural approaches for example are limited to personal change without paying a great deal of attention to power, culture or emotional dynamics in organizations which impact on individuals and their capacity to influence change. Coaching differs from counselling/psychotherapy because of the focus on person, role and an organizational perspective. Counselling/psychotherapy focuses on 'self-actualization', personal insight and individual well-being, whereas coaching focuses on 'role actualization'. Role actualization however can only occur if the individual reflects and works on themselves, and on their work.

The primary task of the organizational coach is, therefore:

'Role actualization': Coaching individuals to become fully empowered in their roles, in order to contribute to organization success.

Coaching and Mentoring: Ordering and Categorizing

Coaching and mentoring cover much ground and the typologies and divisions set out below are in some ways arbitrary; they can be arranged in many ways depending on the observer's position and interests. Ordering and categorizing is very much a modernist project, and dividing coaching and mentoring into categories such as formal and informal, traditional and non-traditional, Life-coaching and executive coaching, are useful in the sense of helping to define the terms of the relationship. However, these are not fixed boundaries and borders, and the real worlds of coaching and mentoring are actually very fluid and porous rather than static.

Coaching and mentoring: internal and external, independence and confidentiality

A coach brings their specific people and relational skills to the task of individual development, their focus being to link person, role and organization. Coaches are more often an external influence rather than an internal employee, and bring a fresh, outside perspective to the organization. The coach may have little knowledge or specific experience of the coachee's particular expertise. The external coach can offer a more independent perspective than an internal coach/manager or mentor who will inevitably be embedded in the organizational culture and politics. External coaching provides a space for confidentiality, as to have an independent sounding board has played an important part in the success of coaching. The possibility of discussing company concerns and an individual's own anxieties and challenges, without fearing judgment or causing negative 'office politics', is an important feature of coaching. This is not always sacrosanct; for example, tensions may arise when the coach is contracted/paid by the company they report to which may impact on impartiality. Also many coaches work with more than one employee in the company and can quickly become embedded in the company culture. Internal coaches are becoming more popular as a cost saving exercise and for 'capacity building', i.e. to create a 'coaching culture' in an organization. The boundaries between an internal coach, a coach-manager and a mentor once again become blurred.

Mentors, on the other hand, are more commonly internal. Internal mentors bring inside knowledge and technical expertise to their mentee, but lack some of the external independence, autonomy and confidentiality an external coach might bring. The advantage of an internal coach or mentor is to transmit organizational culture, tradition and internal tacit knowledge, and also experience and 'technical' expertise, to the mentee/coachee. There is no right way, but when choosing a mentor or coach these issues need to be fully considered.

A Typology of Mentoring

Traditionally, a mentor was not a trained professional helper, but chosen for their specific experience that could be passed onto the mentee. However, mentoring has been increasingly formalized as it has gained recognition as a powerful change agent. Previously, the key requisite to be a mentor was to have the right work experience and knowledge. It is becoming increasingly recognized, however, that people skills are vital to the process, so the mentor can communicate their knowledge and actively listen to the mentee to ensure they understand their challenges and learning process.

Whilst some mentors are naturally talented, others need more support and training. Mentoring training programmes and skills training for mentors are growing, and it is here that the overlap with coaching is closest, as many of the same skill sets are used. Mentor training is commonly focused on active listening, giving positive and relevant feedback, clarifying, summarizing and appropriate challenging methods. These same overlapping skill sets are used in both coaching and counselling training. Mentors may also have specific training focused on the specialist area they are mentoring in. If working with a minority group for example, there is often specific training on the challenges, discrimination and issues facing this particular group, and what resources are available to them. Mentoring often has a focused practical application, for example to get young people into work, or successfully through college, and so the training will include information on how to realize the practicalities of these goals.

As the push for formalization of training and evaluation continues, standards are being set (for example by the Mentoring and Befriending Foundation, a government-backed project to support mentoring in voluntary and charity groups in the UK). The emphasis on training and regulation may be positive, but it also undermines core mentoring qualities, i.e. goodwill, mutuality and voluntarism, which are replaced by modernity's measuring tools – evaluation, outcomes, rationalization, formalization and standardization.

Mentors and mentoring programmes most often have an internal function in an organization or they work across specified groups. Wanberg et al. (2003) and Megginson et al. (2006) claim that whilst definitions are diverse there is a clear concept of the term 'mentor' – 'Mentors bring eldership and/ or previous experience to a helping relationship.' Mentoring is more closely associated to 'goodwill' than coaching. It embodies the importance of giving to another, caring for another, returning favours, and making others successful out of your success. It has a volunteering ethos and a stronger sense of mutuality than coaching, as the mentor often feels that they personally gain as well as the mentee. Stead, drawing on mentoring literature, identifies two main strands to mentoring. The first is a focus on understanding how the organization operates at a cultural and political level. The second is psychosocial and includes role modelling, personal support, increasing confidence and self-awareness in the mentee's ability and professional identity (Stead, 2005). This divide between the inner self and the outer-organization is a constant theme in both mentoring and coaching. I will now outline a brief typology and themes in mentoring.

US mentoring

Mentoring in the USA deserves a special mention as it has a stronger foot-hold than in Europe. It has become an essential part of US culture, widely used in schools, colleges, workplaces, not-for-profits and faith-based organizations. In addition, mentoring rhetoric and practice has become widely used in the workplace. Mentoring fits with the US's cultural bias for self-improvement as a force for individual and social change, and it provides an excellent vehicle for both self-improvement and organizational success whether in a school or business. Charitable giving in the USA is huge:

> Without charities and non-profits, America would simply not be able to operate. Their operations are so big that during 2010, total giving was nearly $291 billion. (www.charitynavigator.org/index.cfm?bay= content.view&cpid=42)

Mentoring can be seen as another manifestation of charity, through good works rather than money.

Mentoring has become so in vogue in the US that two recent Presidents have shown support for it. In 2003, George Bush announced $450 million for mentoring initiatives in his State of the Union address, and in 2010, President Obama held a White House National Mentoring Month Ceremony (information gained from Big Brothers Big Sisters, a US mentoring organization for young people, with a 100-year history; see www.bbbsi.org). More than 4,500 not-for-profit organizations in the US provide mentoring for youth (Grossman and Rhodes, 2002).

Informal mentoring

Buell discusses two types of mentoring, formal and informal (Buell, 2004). Informal mentoring can develop organically, where an 'elder' takes an interest in developing a junior colleague. This often happens for example in academia where a Professor identifies a student or junior researcher as an informal mentee and has a longstanding relationship supporting them. Alternatively, a person may informally approach a potential mentor who agrees to take up this role.

Formal mentoring

Formal mentoring is when an organization sponsors the mentoring process. A mentee is assigned a mentor to promote employee development. Formal mentoring programmes are used 'in-company' to develop high-potential leaders. This mentoring links current leaders to less experienced leaders of the future. Other types of formal mentoring include in-school or universities training with older students supporting younger ones, and women's leadership mentoring programmes within a large organization, or across a domain such as teaching or business networks, where successful women mentor more junior women towards leadership roles. The key words associated with traditional mentoring are: caring, supporting, guiding and advising, providing wisdom, trust, experience, knowledge, development and growth.

Internal and business mentoring

Whilst mentoring is often an organizationally internal process, Rogers (2004) argues that a true mentor should not be a line manager: 'typically, a mentor is a colleague in the same or a parallel organization who is not in a line management relationship with a mentee' (Rogers, 2004: 24) – the importance being that if you are a line manager you cannot be a truly independent sounding board or confidant(e). However, this notion of independence has been blurred as today's manager is taught that coaching and mentoring skills are a vital aspect of their managerial skill set, and that their role is to both mentor/coach and line manage their reportees. HR professionals, senior managers, line managers and peers are all commonly used as internal mentors in companies. In-house mentors have advantages over external coaches as they are a cheaper resource, and they have the ability to pass on company tradition and narratives, keeping continuity and company culture alive, especially when mentoring new personnel into the company.

Business mentoring is mostly associated with developing and retaining high-potential leaders, and it overlaps with internal mentoring. Pamela Craig, Chief Financial Officer at Accenture, writing in *Business Week*, cites some company research on business mentoring:

> In recent research among 3,600 professionals from medium to large organisations in eighteen countries around the world, Accenture found that only 13% of respondents said they turn to a mentor at work for career advice. At the same time, they acknowledged the clear value of a workplace mentor: mentors helped them think differently about certain situations, helped them with their current roles, helped them see more opportunities and possibilities, and helped identify their skills and capabilities. (Craig, 2010)

These findings show a dissonance between the knowledge that mentoring is very useful, but that only 13 per cent utilize mentors. More research to explore this would be useful. One relevant reflection from experience is that many managers/leaders agree that mentoring would be really valuable but are reluctant to step into the role of mentee. Whilst this is changing, an anxiety amongst managers is to expose themselves and to accept feedback, challenge or self-critique.

When running a peer-to-peer mentoring leadership exchange in a global corporation with a colleague (see lead2lead reference), we were surprised at how very senior, bright and successful managers could achieve so highly yet be so weak at giving and receiving feedback to peers (subordinates they were used to dealing with). Giving feedback caused anxiety and they showed inexperience in their feedback skills. The most common feature was 'chronic niceness' whereby all feedback was dressed up as a positive issue and nothing contentious was discussed, meaning that often the most important learning points were left unsaid. By using mentoring and feedback training and by putting some clear structure, guidelines and expectations in their debriefing, we were able to transform this issue.

Mentoring has multiple benefits for both the mentee and mentor. For the mentor it improves people skills and 'feel-good' factors through supporting another, and also encourages in-company learning through the mentee. Benefits for the mentee include learning from the mentor in technical and specific skills, and through picking up tacit knowledge about company culture. The benefits for the organization are the building of networks across the company, knowledge exchange, building leadership capacity, and developing a company culture that values learning, knowledge sharing and creativity.

New-hire mentoring, where new employees are assigned a mentor who can pass on tacit company culture and knowledge as well as practical knowledge of their particular role, is becoming popular.

Reverse mentoring or 'mentoring up'

Reverse mentoring is a process whereby younger employees support more experienced executives in areas they are more skilled in, particularly in IT or social networking. Not only is there a skill transfer; mindsets are also changed, whereby new opportunities and strategies can emerge through the mutuality of these dynamic relationships. Miles describes how reverse mentoring began:

The concept of reverse mentoring began when Jack Welch, the CEO of General Electric, realized he and his management team had much to learn about the internet and technology applications. Welch required 600 top executives, including himself, to find younger mentors who were knowledgeable about the internet. Most of the mentors were in their 20s and 30s. ... This led to a transformation of General Electric as a technology driven organization, using the power of the internet to integrate the many components of production, suppliers, sales, marketing and customers. (Miles, 2010)

Voluntary mentoring

Voluntary mentoring programmes are widespread in educational institutions, sports programmes, faith organizations, prisoner rehabilitation support and drug support programmes. Alcoholics Anonymous is an excellent example of a successful mentoring approach. AA has utilized the power of peer 'mentor' group support and individual mentoring as change agents. Attending meetings and listening to peers, sharing personal experiences with others who have experienced similar troubles, is the first stage – the peer mentoring group. The second stage of AA is where an experienced member becomes what they call a 'sponsor' to a new member and supports them on their journey of giving up alcohol. It is a vital role as the sponsor brings their personal experience to support the mentee. Mentoring differs from coaching in this respect, as it is very much about drawing on one's own life experience – an AA sponsor/counsellor who hadn't been an alcoholic could not act in the same way, with the same authority and insider knowledge.

One of the challenges for volunteer mentoring is the attrition rate of volunteers leaving prematurely. This can damage the mentee, who can experience rejection in their lives (perhaps not the first) and then internalize further low self-esteem – 'I am not good enough to be mentored'. Attrition rates are also costly to the providers and trainers of a mentoring service (Grossman and Rhodes, 2002). With the growth of mentoring and the moves to instrumentalize and formalize the practice, a shift from 'free volunteering' to 'coerced volunteering', or volunteering which has a self-interested base, has been observed. For example, a student may undertake voluntary mentoring to impress on a CV or personal statement to get into university.

Youth and education mentoring

There are lots of examples of youth mentoring particularly in the USA. A highly successful volunteering mentoring organization based in the USA and operating internationally is Big Brothers Big Sisters, BBBS. It offers children, 6–18 years old, the chance to have an older mentor to help them navigate the challenges of growing up. BBBS is a classic mentoring programme, with the mentor bringing their life experience to a younger/junior partner. There are also anti-bullying mentoring programmes and in the UK 150 schools have recently signed up to an anti-bullying programme led by http://www.mandbf.org.uk, a government-sponsored mentoring foundation.

However, the success of youth mentoring is not clear. DuBois et al. (2002) note that the magnitude of the effects on the average youth participating in a mentoring programme was quite modest. Rhodes and Lowe (2008: 12) write in their meta-review of youth mentoring:

> As ... has been made clear, youth mentoring relationships are not consistent in their effects. Variation among mentoring relationships is influenced by program characteristics, relationship duration and structure, and mentor skills. To better serve youth, mentoring programs must be conceptualized, designed, and implemented effectively in order to produce consistent and positive outcomes ...

They go on to conclude:

> At this stage, we can safely say that mentoring is, by and large, a modestly effective intervention for youth who are already coping relatively well under somewhat difficult circumstances. In some cases it can do more harm than good; in others it can have extraordinarily influential effects. (Rhodes and Lowe, 2008: 14)

The Big Brothers Big Sisters programme is far more positive, reporting a national research study on their mentoring process.

Box 2.2   BBBS Study

Public/Private Ventures, an independent Philadelphia-based national research organization, looked at over 950 boys and girls from eight Big Brothers Big Sisters agencies across the country selected for their large size and geographic diversity. This study, conducted in 1994 and 1995, is widely considered to be foundational to the mentoring field in general and to Big Brothers Big Sisters community-based programme in particular.

Approximately half of the children were randomly chosen to be matched with a Big Brother or Big Sister. The others were assigned to a waiting list. The matched children met with their Big Brothers or Big Sisters about three times a month for an average of one year.

Researchers surveyed both the matched and unmatched children and their parents on two occasions: when they first applied for a Big Brother or Big Sister, and again 18 months later.

(Continued)

(Continued)

Researchers found that after 18 months of spending time with their Bigs, the Little Brothers and Little Sisters, compared to those children not in the programme, were:

- 46 per cent less likely to begin using illegal drugs
- 27 per cent less likely to begin using alcohol
- 52 per cent less likely to skip school
- 37 per cent less likely to skip a class
- 33 per cent less likely to hit someone

They also found that the Littles were more confident of their performance in schoolwork and getting along better with their families (BBBS, 1995–2011).

Mentoring for youth and in education seems to be growing; the research is mixed but there is an underlying belief that it is of benefit for both the mentor and mentee. In this respect it is one of the most mutual of mentoring/coaching relationships.

Peer mentoring

Peer mentoring often targets disadvantaged or marginalized groups, for example women, the disabled and ethnic minorities, where they are not achieving as well as other 'majority groups'. This deficit model aims to promote equality agendas.

Another form of peer mentoring is in education – TeacherNet, the UK government-sponsored Mentoring and Befriending site, is an example of peer mentoring working to get pupils in schools to support each other. Over recent years, peer mentoring has increased in popularity and has been introduced in a number of schools, where it is making a valuable contribution to the overall ethos of the school and pastoral support systems. The site supports many peer and voluntary mentoring projects focused to tackle 'social exclusion'. This relation between friendship and mentoring is interesting and will be explored in Chapter 3. Mentoring and Befriending claim to 'currently reach over 3,500 projects in the voluntary and community sector'. However, this figure continues to rise as mentoring and befriending becomes increasingly seen as an effective way of tackling social exclusion.

Summary of mentoring

Mentoring and coaching clearly overlap, and yet there is a theme of good-will, generosity and mutuality that runs through mentoring that is lacking in 'professional coaching' and that gives mentoring a different feel and a different capacity to engage. From a cost–benefit perspective, successful mentoring (when done voluntarily or using internal employees) can be hugely beneficial and a lot cheaper than coaching, with the additional benefit that it empowers, motivates and can improve both parties, the mentor and mentee. Whilst coaching has become the real buzz word and has grown hugely, mentoring perhaps is an 'unsung hero' in the field of development. Its potential is huge, and with careful planning and a lot of support, can be impressively effective. Innovative mentoring programmes, properly resourced and supported, should be on every HR and Organizational Development teams' agendas.

A Typology of Coaching

Coaching is an expansive and contested field with fuzzy boundaries and multiple identities. One of the strengths of coaching seems to be its capacity to receive projections from many diverse people and social groups, and then make coaching into what they desire or need. Coaching attracts attention from the business community and, at the other end of the spectrum, New Age spiritualists. To categorize it is therefore problematic and this typology is by no means complete, nor an attempt to have the final word. It is a description of some of the main influences, themes and coach offerings that are visible in the coach market today.

Two important coaching types are sports coaching and Life-coaching, and both have had a big influence on the growing field of organizational coaching.

Sports coaching: influences on organizational coaching

Football, tennis or athletics coaches are a major feature of the sports world. The team coach has a prominent role in basketball and American football and other team sports, taking both a training and motivational role for the team. The sports team coach is often in effect a team leader, and the individual sport coach is a technical expert. Individual sports coaches are employed in specialist areas such as fitness, diet and specific sporting techniques.

However, in the workplace the contemporary meaning of coaching has shifted towards a more 'non-directive' stance, and the expertise of the coach is more facilitative and relies less on specialist technical expertise. Other sporting coaches are trained in psychology, and import psychological techniques and adapt these to work on motivation and self-belief to assist performance.

Peltier (2001: 180) offers eight themes that arise from athletics coaching which can be transferred to the workplace:

1 Drive – single-mindedness

2 Teach the fundamentals

3 Use individual approaches and ingenuity

4 Play against yourself

5 Visualize

6 Video feedback

7 Learning from defeat

8 Communication, trust and integrity

Peltier (2001) summarizes by saying most coaching references to sports are 'littered with clichés' but are well meaning, simple ideas. From a metaphorical perspective, the sports coach influence offers motivation and inspiration. Through easy-to-grasp quotations and images of sporting heroes, alongside behavioural and psychological techniques, a coach claims to help the coachee focus, become motivated and improve their work performance. However, this transfer of language and skills from sports to business can be problematic. The many comparisons, analogies and metaphors between sports coaching and organizational coaching are concerning, as they conflate the idea of an organizational role holder with an individual athlete, who needs to get 'in the zone' or learn specific techniques.

The single-mindedness and drive to be a great athlete, for example, may be counterproductive when an organization needs to develop a culture of distributed leadership, knowledge exchange and collaborative working with stakeholders. These sporting metaphors are popular because they are comforting and simple, but are limited in helping an individual's work performance that in reality is part of a complex web of exchanges, transactions and emotions in a network of activity. Another aspect learned from sports coaching is focused, incremental, technical improvement and performance coaching. In organizations it might be used in voice coaching for public speaking.

This is very different from the developmental type coaching that now dominates the coaching field in its different forms (West and Milan, 2001).

Whitmore (2002) writes that Tim Gallwey made the link between sports
coaching and organizational coaching when he wrote *The Inner Game of Work*
(Gallwey, 2000), re-working his earlier text *The Inner Game of Tennis* (1974).
Gallwey's work seems to draw heavily on the ideas of the 'human potential
movement' and other therapeutic theories, for example Maslow's 'self-
actualization' and 'peak experience' (Rogers, 1961; Maslow, 1976). One of
Gallwey's core coaching theses is to free what he calls Self 1 from the inhibitions of Self 2: although Gallwey doesn't refer to the therapeutic roots of this
'discovery' it is clearly the same territory as a therapist freeing the patient from
'super-ego' injunctions (the authority figure in the mind) that inhibit individuals from performing more freely. West and Milan discuss coaching as a
continuum with skills coaching and training at one end, performance coaching
in the middle, and developmental coaching at the other end of the spectrum
(2001: 3), and on this spectrum one-to-one sports coaching focuses on skills
coaching. Turner (2010) identifies that sports coaching influences individuals
to focus on techniques and skills improvements and has a secondary benefit
of improving communication and morale.

'There is no 'I' in team': sports coaching beyond individual technique

Perhaps better analogies can come from sports that encompass individual
focus, yet go beyond the individual to demonstrate how teams and organizations have to work together. Team sports may offer analogies that are
more applicable to team performance; for example, motor racing relies on
a whole organization to provide the support necessary for the Formula
One driver to win. It is noteworthy that whenever a Formula One driver
wins they go overboard to thank the whole team, knowing that their lives
and their success are dependent on all. In the Tour de France cycling, there
is a complex relationship between individuals and teams, where riders
have to rely on their team members who sacrifice themselves for an individual, and they also have to collaborate with their opponents to succeed.
These team sports analogies and lessons may be more helpful to coaches
than spinning stories of heroic sports individuals that only serve to
massage egos and encourage heroic leadership in businesses, which is
long past its sell-by date.

Sports science and sports coaching is also now a big industry with a lot
of financial investment, and there is an interesting feedback relationship
between sports psychology and other psychological approaches. Increasingly,
sports science leads the way in some neuro-science, psycho-biological,

neuro-biological and motivation and teamwork approaches that will in turn have new applications for workplace coaching and leadership.

Life-coaching: 'Transform your life! Don't postpone your joy any longer!'

Karen Peterson, in her article for *USA Today*, writes:

> 'Life-coaching is all the Rage'
>
> Personal growth is hot. Diagnosis is not. That is one reason America has seen a boom in the number of people offering their services as 'life coaches.' These guides give clients the confidence to get unstuck – to change careers, repair relationships, or simply get their act together. They also raise some eyebrows because they work in a field that is virtually unregulated. (Peterson, 2002)

Life-coaching is a true hybrid: when web-searching Life-coaching, a multitude of approaches are found that inform the Life-coach – NLP, hypnotherapy, solutions-focused, yoga and bodywork approaches, spirituality, Buddhist mindfulness, positive psychology, happiness coaching – the list goes on. Life-coaches advertise to administer to a wide audience: to help deliver success at work, providing dating advice, giving relationship coaching, dream fulfilment, becoming more calm and peaceful, and of course being happy! At a recent coaching event I saw a book titled *How to Make a Hell of a Profit and Still Get to Heaven*, and much of Life-coaching makes this claim to help you find balance between material success and spiritual/inner happiness.

Life-coaching breaks out of the confines of therapy, but works in the therapeutic domain:

> 'We are not talking about being incompetent or weak. They are every-day, normal people who have their lives together. They realize the value of having somebody to help them think outside the box' – life coach Laura Berman Fortgang. (Peterson, 2002)

Today's self-improvement industry is huge, and Life-coaching is a part of this. Oprah Winfrey, probably the best known advocate, has built her financial and influential empire on the back of the popularity for self-improvement, which in contemporary times expresses the 'American Dream', championing the individual striving for happiness and success. West and Milan cite Thomas Leonard as one of the pioneers of Life-coaching, starting the first coach training programme with Coach University in 1982, which led to the formation of the ICF in 1992, which is now the leading professional association for personal and executive coaches (West and Milan, 2001: 17).

A London Life-coach writes a typical example of Life-coaching rhetoric that promises radical change:

> With me, you'll become someone you've always wanted to be: someone with inner spark, who feels confident, successful, and is more effective in all aspects of life. You will feel happier and more fulfilled, healthier, and in better mental and physical shape. You will communicate more effectively, creating better relationships at home, work, and with friends. In short, you will have more fun and less stress. (Zofia Life Coach)

Life-coaching is situated between the Soul Guide and Psy Discourses, as discussed in later chapters, between the coaching working on the inner self and the outward-self. The Life-coach aims to help the individual to discover their authentic self, and at the same time improve their 'performance' in life. This is achieved through managing anxiety, being more confident and becoming focused on achieving their goals. Garvey et al. (2009) links Life-coaching to person-centred counselling (which underpins many coaching approaches), and they also identify the lack of research in this area – 'there is no developed research base' – to support the huge interest.

Life-coaching is an interesting break with therapy, yet it works partly in the therapeutic domain. It extends therapy to the 'working-well', transforming the pathologist rhetoric of psychotherapy. No longer do you come with 'your issues' to work through; you come with your beautiful untapped potential, to be revealed and released through coaching.

Life-coaching comes directly from the human potential movement, and at the heart of the Life-coaching philosophy is the belief that each of us has the answers within, and the coach is there to help you contact your authentic self. Martha Beck, a famous Life-coach who appears with Oprah Winfrey, writes:

> All we try to do with our system of coaching is to move away the obstacles that are blocking people's best selves. We add nothing, just subtract what isn't working. The essential self that remains is far more sophisticated and beautiful than anything we could dream up. (Beck, 2011)

A critique of Life-coaching is its tendency to instrumentalize happiness and spirituality. When well-being, happiness and spirituality become a goal-oriented lifestyle choice, then the soul itself becomes a commodity! At a recent Life-coaching event, there were pseudo-scientific machines to measure the body's spiritual energy, and many other pseudo-scientific claims of efficiency of the spiritual/natural energy of Life-coaching approaches. This is seemingly counter-intuitive as Life-coaching often claims 'alternative status', turning to Eastern wisdom and spirituality to counter Western-rationalistic influence. In a movement that claims to offer spiritual and holistic alternatives to modernity's cold drive to progress, scientific language is used very widely and unashamedly without reflection on the tensions, confusion or conflicts this causes. More than anything Life-coaching is unashamedly a post-modern hybrid, happy to hold together counter-intuitive norms, as will be discussed in Part II.

Life-coaching is the product of a post-modern way of addressing life's existential questions. And for some it obviously works:

> Working with my Life Coach has been a profoundly transformative experience for me. ... With my Life Coach, I feel I have made more progress in a few sessions than I ever made in years of trying therapy. ... My perspective on life is forever changed, and I am truly grateful to my Life Coach for that. (Jodie, 2010)

Life-coaching is easy to critique from the viewpoint of experienced psycho-therapists, but in contemporary society there is a clear desire and need for Life-coaches, with many who find it beneficial. In spite of the myriad of techniques, experience and skill levels of Life-coaches, ranging from highly experienced coaches using sophisticated skills to those at the quackery and unskilled end of the spectrum, there is something free about it. Whilst sceptical about some of the approaches, it is better to allow freedom of practice than to try and over-regulate. At the most basic level of intervention, to have another person paying attention to you, to listen to you, to be authentically interested in you and to be upbeat about your potential might be more therapeutic than many therapeutic approaches! On the other hand, people facing difficult existential and personal challenges may find Life-coaching glosses over their real difficulties, and they may require more depth work to help them; smiling-positive Life-coaching has its limits!

Business coaching

> Business coaching makes itself distinctive by privileging business results over individual change. Business coaching addresses the client's development for the purpose of achieving business outcomes rather than achieving personal or career goals. (World Association of Business Coaches, cited in Rostron, 2009: 15)

Rostron says he differs from this statement as he believes that business coaching should also align personal drivers with company goals, otherwise stress will result (Rostron, 2009: 15). Business coaching is more directive than other coaching approaches and has a more managerial feel to it.

Recently, in a discussion with a representative from Action Coach (who claim to be the world's biggest business coaching company), he said they mainly work with SMEs (small to medium size businesses). The description of the work he described was a very functional approach that borrowed from consultancy approaches. Whilst the approach is more along the lines of consultancy, interestingly they utilize a sports coaching metaphor to sell their product:

> Business coaching helps owners of small and medium sized businesses with their sales, marketing, management, team building and so much more. Most importantly, just like a sporting coach, your Business Coach will make you focus on the game. (Action Coach, 2010)

Business coaching works across the Managerial and Psy Expert Discourses (see Chapters 7 and 8) and has a dual focus: personal performance and organizational productivity. Business coaching mimics a business consultancy stance, focusing much more clearly on organizational outputs. The business coaches separate themselves from the management consultant, however, by adding an important individual focus to how a manager takes up their role. Clegg et al. (2005), in their research study of business coaching in Australia, identified the challenges of 'defining standards of service and performance' and the need to develop 'a more coherent and well understood perception of the nature and benefits of business coaching amongst industry'.

The danger of business coaching is that it can reinforce a short-term operational approach at the expense of looking at the bigger picture. Short-term demands put pressure on managers and coaches alike to produce efficiency and outcomes (this is critiqued in the Managerial Discourse chapter). This operational approach helpfully focuses on immediate challenges and is valued by organizations, yet it can limit a more strategic approach towards change. In spite of the claims of business coaching to focus on results, there are many coaches who are skilled at creating reflective spaces and provide a thinking space and support for the overwhelmed manager. This aspect of business coaching then merges with other coaching approaches.

Business coaching is one of the fastest emerging disciplines in the field of coaching. Bringing management consultancy knowledge, and merging this with individual role support, feedback and advice, has produced a very powerful organizational developmental process and seems to be a winning approach in workplaces that become ever more challenging and complex for managers to deal with.

Executive coaching

Executive coaching is a widely used term that implies coaching in an organizational setting – public, private or not-for-profit – working with middle to senior managers who fit into the general term of being an executive (a managerial class). Executive coaching differs from business coaching through a greater focus on the individual executive rather than the company's business outcomes *per se*. It is therefore more about career advancement, performance-in-role and life–work balance. The executive coach provides a sounding board, a thinking partner to work through the immediate challenges faced by the manager. Berglas (2002), in his *Harvard Business Review* article 'The very real dangers of executive coaching', predicts a huge growth in executive coaching whilst being concerned that coaches need more psychological training (2002: 3–8). Berglas says that coaches need to distinguish between a 'problem executive' and an 'executive with a problem'. The former can be coached and the latter will require psychological help.

Kilburg subtitles his book *Executive Coaching* (2000) with the phrase 'Developing managerial wisdom in a world of chaos'. This helps explain the growth of executive coaching – the desire for sense-making and for middle and senior managers to regain some sense of control and wisdom, in the fast changing, hyper-technical, hyper-informational workplace, where many managers feel isolated, unwise when facing the speed of change, and fear that their sphere of influence is very limited.

In the contemporary work setting the mantras are speed, action and competition, rather than reflection, collaboration and friendship. Executive coaching has the potential to offer a 'potential space' where this overload might be digested. The executive coach is potentially a container for emotional and psychological overload, a sense-maker, a sounding board. The role of executive coaching potentially provides a 'privatized retreat space' in a workplace dominated by activity.

Having said this, under the banner of executive coaching, a multitude of approaches are applied, some providing very little reflection, focusing on more driven, behavioural and goal-focused approaches; in practice there is much diversity in coaching to executives. Executive coaching has been a phenomenal success – to create a thinking space, to move from the emotional-internal life of a senior manager and then to make sense of this in their work roles and relationships can be a profound help to them. In my coaching approach with executives – informed by psychoanalytic and network approaches – patterns in behaviours and big insights into their relationships to others (particularly around authority, leadership, followership and team dynamics) are uncovered, often relating to earlier experiences. This leads to insights that, to coin a coaching cliché, lead to 'light bulb' moments. When an executive understands why and when they freeze in a meeting, or when they react aggressively, they see the pattern and the insight reveals to them different possibilities of behaviour, and the emotions attached to the reaction are less overpowering when understood and found a place. This 'depth analysis' of the understanding of the patterns is then applied when undertaking relational analysis, leadership-role analysis or a coaching network analysis, i.e. how the coachee's inner-world interacts and engages with the outer-world.

A very important executive coaching skill (and one that is often over-looked) is to identify what the coaching work is. Too often assumptions are made by the coach, coachee and/or sponsor, which may be aligned or different. In business coaching the contract is perhaps clearer: performance and productivity. In executive coaching there is greater potential to work on emergent strategy (Network Coach Discourse) and also on personal values, and how to bring one's authentic self to work (Soul Guide Discourse).

Leadership coaching

> At the INSEAD Global Leadership Centre, we believe leadership coaching is more of an art of discovery than a technology of delivery. (Kets de Vries et al., 2010)

Leadership coaching has a more specific remit, but overlaps with executive and business coaching. Leadership coaching supports coachees in taking up their leadership roles to the very best of their ability. This means to work with leaders with more depth, and to provide the one place where they feel contained and safe enough to reflect openly on their insecurities, doubts and anxieties, as well as to celebrate their strengths and successes. The coaching session can be a place to let off steam, to blaspheme against the world and even to cry. Leadership can be a lonely place; being in the 'public gaze' of employees demands a certain confidence and presence. The coach can provide a space where leaders can 'free-associate' in order to make sense of their experience. Leadership coaching becomes more popular in a fast-changing world, where much younger leaders are appointed, where human talent and talent retention are vital for a high-performance organization and where information overload creates stress (Kets de Vries, 2006: 253). A leadership coach needs specific skills as they are required to work in two key domains that separate leadership coaching from other coaching approaches. Firstly, with regard to the psycho-social dynamics of leadership, leadership coaching demands a particular understanding of the psycho-dynamics applied to authority and power and influencing. A leader stimulates and receives projections and introjections that work at conscious and unconscious levels. Leaders need to learn and manage these processes and a coach can be a vital help as an external sounding board and a collaborative partner, who is able to challenge assumptions and interpret these dynamics. A skilled psychodynamic coach will utilize the counter-transference experiences, i.e. how the coachee reacts to the coach and what feelings are picked up when working with the coachee. For example, I was recently working with a global HR leader, and during a strategic discussion we were having, she appeared to dominate the discussion and I felt silenced, as if I didn't have any voice or anything intelligent to offer. I stopped the session and explained this to her. She reflected and realized that as a leader, when she is anxious about something she went into what she described as 'take-over-the-meeting' mode. The impact of this on her team was to silence them – they got to a result but her team became compliant rather than collaborating. This impacted on their morale and also limited the creativity, knowledge and experience in the room that could provide different and improved solutions.

Making the links between the self, in relation to leadership and follower-ship, influence, envy and rivalry, motivation and coercion, communication and symbolic representation, is vital coaching work. Many leaders also get sucked into operational thinking at the expense of strategic and networked thinking. A leadership coach will also hold leadership in mind that infers thinking beyond operations and moving towards strategy.

Leadership coaches should have a broad knowledge of organizational and leadership theory and practice. Leadership comes in many forms and the leadership coach should be well versed in how leadership varies from heroic approaches, to distributed, adaptive, collaborative and collective approaches (Northouse, 2004). Leadership coaches can have a vital role to play to support business and organizational transition to face contemporary chal-lenges. Unfortunately, many coaches, like a lot of managers, think in terms of individualistic, transformational and heroic approaches to leadership which offer grandiose ideas but limit organizational development. 'The Messiah Leadership' Discourse (Western, 2008a) is outdated, problematic and has been tried and found wanting. A more convincing narrative about leadership is required that understands the limits of individual charisma, and recognizes the complex nature of the global world and the need for col-lective leadership wisdom in response. Organizations are like eco-systems, fluid networks of activity, and in the contemporary post-industrial, digitized workplace, a new leadership approach is required. 'Eco-Leadership' (Western, 2008a, 2010) describes this new paradigm of leadership that is emerging in response to social, technological, political and environmental change. The challenge for leadership coaches is to act as catalysts, to educate themselves to understand the new organizational forms and dynamics, rather than repeat leadership messages relevant to twentieth century man-agement/leadership models and theories, so as to prevent perpetuation of the same problems and mistakes of the past. Organizations that encompass Eco-Leadership thinking, aligning success with ethical approaches to social justice and environmental sustainability, will be the most successful in the next decades.

Leadership coaching from an Eco-leadership perspective goes beyond the individual, and accounts for teams and a holistic, organizational and wider stakeholder approach.

> Leadership coaching implies a specific type of intervention that can be carried out strategically with individuals, teams or an entire organization. (Kets de Vries et al., 2010: xxvii)

Coaches are very well placed to influence and drive forward these positive changes, as they are able to speak to leaders confidentially, bringing new thinking to the table. Coaching leaders to 'unleash leadership' throughout their organizations is leadership coaching's task in today's organizations.

Careers coaching

Careers coaching is a spin-off from career counselling and it infers that the coach helps the employee/coachee make career decisions. Many recruitment firms employ careers coaches, as do university business schools to find employment for their MBA students (MBA rankings are linked to successful employment outcomes). Key areas for a careers coach are career change, career development and redundancy. Some utilize psychometrics to support the search, and some careers coaches are facilitative and work in a more general sense, building confidence and focusing the person's search criteria. Others are much more pro-active and expert, based in a certain field or industry, and they can offer advice and contact information. The other aspect of careers coaching is an expertise in CV and résumé writing.

Tele-coaching and cyber-coaching

Tele-coaching is to coach by telephone. One of my more intriguing and somewhat bizarre coaching experiences was debriefing five senior executives from a global company on their 360-degree feedback reports. They worked in five different countries – the USA, South Korea, Germany, Australia and India. I was employed by a colleague who trusted my ability, yet I had never met the coachees or worked in the company. Adapting quickly to culture and language, as well as relating to their time zones, was a challenge. Whilst sceptical about the potential success of this project what was surprising was how quickly we created a warm working relationship, and that in spite of my newness to them, they all seemed to get some help from the hour's coaching session.

Undertaking a pilot research on the effectiveness of tele-coaching, Western and Findlater (2008) found, after interviewing coaches who worked face to face and by telephone, that there was a slight preference for face-to-face coaching, although one coach in particular felt individuals sometimes disclosed more easily on the phone.

Jackee Holder, a Life coach, writes:

> 'But do not be fooled into thinking that many of the benefits gained from face to face Life-coaching are lost in the Telephone coaching relationship. During some recent Telephone coaching research I carried out at Lancaster University (2006) most Telephone coaching clients reported that:
>
> 1 The anonymity of telephone coaching allowed them to give themselves permission to be emotional because they were not face to face with their coach.
>
> 2 Telephone coaching is focused and direct and that's what they loved about it'. (Western and Findlater, 2008)

Cyber-coaching/mentoring, which refers to coaching over the internet and includes video/Skype coaching, is becoming increasingly popular through reducing cost and travel time, and opening up accessibility. As technology becomes increasingly user friendly and more commonplace, it is becoming more accessible and accepted in work-based coaching. Whilst coaching a team of six in an executive workshop we debriefed a stakeholder mapping exercise, with one member in Hong Kong whilst I was in London with the five others. I debriefed his work, then he interacted with the group all very naturally by video link; we worked seamlessly, virtually and in real time.

There are research studies being undertaken on how young people (young men and boys in particular) may be able to use forums like cyber-mentoring more productively to discuss bullying or other difficult issues which they find difficult to disclose face to face. Another advantage with cyber-coaching is the potential for multimedia interactions: PowerPoint presentations and chat rooms can be used interactively with talking. There can also be ongoing email discussions, or the coach can set up chat rooms for a group of coachees to self-manage working with others, which promotes interaction and learning from each other, and saves on costs.

Cyber-coaching is a very interesting and growing phenomenon. Improving technologies and a new Facebook/Skype generation entering the workplace are going to mean it increasingly becomes used and accepted as legitimate. The question of what it means to have a disembodied coaching experience requires a lot more research. Questions arise about missing body language (or virtual body language if using video), whether the work can be as deep and meaningful, and what proximity means to a relationship – all are areas for research where practitioners need to share experiences and learn from each other. Coaching is well positioned to take advantage of these new innovations of technology as it is more flexible and willing to adapt than other one-to-one approaches, namely therapy and counselling.

Team/group coaching

Team coaching overlaps with other activities such as team consultation and team facilitation. Like other aspects of coaching, team coaching devours some of the territory from others and at the same time can bring something new, and this will depend on who is delivering the coaching.

Kets de Vries and the INSEAD Global Leadership Centre specialize in coaching teams and groups. They take a clinical and psychodynamic approach and believe coaches need to understand the psychology of groups and have a systemic understanding to coach teams:

> Deciphering the interaction and interpersonal relationships between members of a group and the ways in which groups form, function and dissolve, is of central concern. (Kets de Vries et al., 2010: xxiii)

Coaching teams and groups requires a specific skill-set from the coach; and in order to understand the unconscious and the power dynamics that occur in teams/groups, psychodynamic concepts are important. Group Relations training, such as the Leicester Conference pioneered by the Tavistock Institute in 1957, continues to run today and provides coaches with invaluable experience of these group processes. Hackman and Wageman (2005) researched team coaching and concluded that 'team effectiveness only occurs when four conditions are present. Two of these conditions have to do with organizational circumstances and two with coaches' actions':

1 The group performance processes that are key to performance effectiveness (i.e. effort, strategy, and knowledge and skill) are relatively unconstrained by task or organizational requirements.

2 The team is well designed and the organizational context within which it operates supports rather than impedes team work.

3   Coaching behaviours focus on salient task performance processes rather than on members' interpersonal relationships or on processes that are not under the team's control.

4   Coaching interventions are made at times when the team is ready for them and able to deal with them – that is, at the beginning for effort-related (motivational) interventions, near the midpoint for strategy-related (consultative) interventions, and at the end of a task cycle for (educational) interventions that address knowledge and skill.

Their approach is the polar opposite to Kets de Vries and a psychodynamic approach, suggesting that the coaching focus should be on function rather than dynamics. Their requirements for coaching success seem to rule out teams who 'aren't ready', and many coaches would argue that a coach works with the team in the room, and a good coach will help them find their way, from whatever starting point. The diversity of coaching approaches is reflected in team coaching too.

Finally, coaching teams is best done (where possible and affordable) in pairs. When group dynamics are flying around the room, it really helps to work with a coaching partner, so that one coach can lead and the other reflect; and two insights can be invaluable when a lot is going on in a group. Allowing the team to observe the coaches in dialogue, discussing the dynamics of the group live, in front of them, also is a very important learning experience.

Organizational developmental (OD) coaching

I briefly wish to mention OD coaching as it has huge potential yet is very under-developed. Coaching with organizational development in mind often gets stuck between individual coaching and theoretical discussions about organizational culture, or how to coach individuals as a form of 'behavioural modification' to align their behaviours with company values for example. I would advocate that senior teams, OD and HR functions, should have a mantra: 'no personal development without organizational development'. Applied to coaching and mentoring, this would push organizations to think beyond individual behaviour change. In my delivery of coaching to organizations, we have had 100 managers receiving one-on-one coaching debriefs, and have designed 'discourse analysis' of the key themes emerging from these coaching sessions which are put together to form 'thick descriptions' and a 'cultural audit' of the company, without giving away confidentiality. My current interest and focus is to design coaching interventions within organizations that specifically deliver personal development and organizational development together. This involves designing coaching interventions for individuals, teams and organizations that enable movement between individuals and the organization. This work includes leadership exchanges and large-scale experiential leadership events, both of which utilize coaching and peer mentoring to deepen individual insight and broaden the coachees' organizational perspectives. This also creates new connections and new networks, and transfers knowledge, skills, experience and understandings across company boundaries.

Taking an OD coaching perspective also means that when working with individuals, the coach is alerted always to the organization in the coaching room (internalized by the coachee). The OD perspective is to use this data and also to coach the employee towards a connected, networked understanding of their work that brings OD into the coaching equation.

Conclusion

To summarize, having scoped the field of coaching and mentoring as outlined in Table 2.1, this is not a complete review. The world of coaching and mentoring has so many varieties that this outline just touches the surface. Reviewers wondered if these typologies should be categorized, into tables of similarities and differences, yet coaching and mentoring are hybrid activities and therefore I feel it is better to describe them through their genealogy and their underpinning discourses; these come later in the book.

Coaching as an expansive term

There has been an expansive use of the term 'coaching' such as 'coaching culture', 'leaders as coach', 'coaching skills' and 'team-coaching'. Under scrutiny these terms reflect how coaching has become a generic signifier for terms such as 'soft skills' and 'people skills'. A coaching culture means an organizational culture which values, and has embedded within it, people skills such as listening and giving feedback and support, and which promotes a learning organization. The same is true with coaching skills, which in general terms means good people and communication skills.

'Team coaching' is used and often replaces what was called team facilitation, team consultation and team building. This expansive use of the term 'coaching' demonstrates the power and influence the coaching discourse has in the workplace and beyond. Coaching in particular signifies good practice in dealing with employees; it reflects good people skills, communication skills and empathetic management styles. Coaching however remains an enigma, and whilst universally used, it has multiple meanings and practices.

Beyond differentiation: mentoring and coaching in common usage

Valerie Stead (2005) writes of mentoring:

> Mentoring can be seen as a holistic and fluid concept that attends to professional, corporate and personal development [Clutterbuck 2001; Kram 1983; Parsloe & Wray 2000]. (Stead, 2005: 178)

This description is apt and yet also describes coaching, and this is the challenge in separating the terms. Mentoring and coaching both offer different and diverse interventions and yet the approaches overlap and utilize very similar skills. The terms are now used so loosely that differentiation in common usage is not possible. Garvey et al. (2009) asked the question: 'Are mentoring and coaching distinctive and separate activities or are they essentially similar in nature?' Their answer:

> In conclusion, there can be no 'one best way' in coaching and mentoring and therefore no one best definition. ... The above evidence suggests that although their original roots are different, both mentoring and coaching in the modern context selectively draw on a range of the same narratives to describe the activity. However, it seems that coaching and mentoring are essentially similar in nature. (Garvey et al., 2009: 27)

Throughout this book, as stated previously, I will follow Garvey, Stokes and Megginson's lead, and will use the name 'coach' to cover both activities, simply for the reason that it is better to merge them than constantly separate them.

What is important is to clarify what is the appropriate intervention for any specific context: in-house, external providers, peer mentoring/coaching, expert technical performance coaching, coaching for culture change, executive coaching, leadership coaching, reverse mentoring and so on. The possibilities are endless; what it is called matters less than understanding what actually is being provided and why. The field of coaching and mentoring is still young and continues to develop.

Coaching in particular has a fluidity about it that is both exciting and can also be a little confusing and disconcerting. Encouraging diversity of approaches rather than attempting to standardize a conformist unified practice will produce continued innovation, growth and success in the field. Improving quality in coaching and mentoring will come about through excellent training, continued professional development and through developing critical thinking and robust theory (see Chapter 13). Coaching and mentoring provide developmental and learning processes to influence and shape some of the central issues facing the contemporary workplace and society. Diversity is welcomed; overlapping terminology can be clarified in local and specific contexts. What is important is quality of coaching and mentoring practice rather than attempting to limit practice through a drive towards conformity or standardization.

Suggested Reading

Cox, E., Bachkirova, T. and Clutterbuck, D. (eds) (2010) *The Complete Handbook of Coaching*. London: Sage.

de Haan, E. (2008) *Relational Coaching*. Sussex: Wiley and Sons.

Garvey, B., Stokes, P. and Megginson, D. (2009) *Coaching and Mentoring: Theory and Practice*. London: Sage.

Kets de Vries, M., Guillen, L., Korotov, K. and Florent-Treacy, E. (eds) (2010) *The Coaching Kaleidoscope: Insights from the Inside*. Hampshire: Palgrave Macmillan.

Megginson, D., Clutterbuck, D., Garvey, B., Stokes, P. and Garrett-Harris, R. (2006) *Mentoring in Action*, 2nd edn. London: Kogan Page.

Rostron, S. (2009) *Business Coaching International: Transforming Individuals and Organizations*. London: Karnac.

Part II

From Friendship to Coaching: A Brief Genealogy of Coaching

Introduction

A genealogy of coaching traces its line of descent, its evolution and its kinship relations to other helping relationships.

The original sources of coaching are informal helping relationships that evolved into social, sanctioned relationships, and the starting point must be friendship. Paying attention to how friendship and other social relations have evolved through different historical periods and social institutions such as the church gives a perspective on the contemporary practice of coaching and mentoring. Coaching is often thought about in an ahistorical and de-contextualized way; it is spoken about as being new. It is removed from the wider social changes, the context that surrounds it and the impact on its development and practice. Irvine Yalom, renowned author and psychotherapist, makes a similar point in regards to psychology:

> Histories of psychology often begin with the advent of the scientific method and the pioneering experimental psychologists like Wundt and Pavlov. I have always considered this a short-sighted historical view: the discipline of psychology began long before, in the works of great psychological thinkers who wrote about the innermost human motivations: Sophocles, Aeschylus, Euripides, Lucretius, Shakespeare and especially for me the great psychological novelists, Dostoevsky, Tolstoy, and later Mann, Sartre, and Camus. Freud identified himself as a scientist, yet not a single one of his great insights was born from science; invariably they arose from his deep intuition, his artistic imagination, and his deep knowledge of literature and philosophy. (Yalom and Yalom, 1998: 269)

One of the key questions which remains unasked in the coaching literature is how traditional friendship relations and historical helping relationships have become transformed, formalized, instrumentalized and socially sanctioned into today's manifestation called 'coaching'. Part II explores the deeper roots of coaching and mentoring, tracing the journey through pre-modernity, modernity and post-modernity.

G.K. Chesterton in his book *Orthodoxy* critiqued modernity, observing that whilst people think they are ahead of the times, bringing something new, they are often undertaking repetition in new clothes:

> I did try to found a heresy of my own; and when I had put the last touches to it, I discovered that it was orthodoxy ... I did try to be minutes ahead of the truth. And found I was eighteen hundred years behind it. (Chesterton, 2004: 4)

Coaching falls into this paradoxical position, claiming newness but without taking enough heed from the past.

The following genealogy is a narrative account of coaching rather than a definitive account (which would take a separate book), and as with all narrative accounts, a plurality of readings is possible. Coaching has emerged from a Westernized culture and is dominated today by the US culture. This genealogy therefore focuses mainly on Westernized influences such as Christianity and its influences on individualism, pastoral care and the modern self (Gray, 2007).

The aim of this section of the book is to bring into view some of the strengths, experience and thinking that coaches/mentors have left behind and forgotten in the rush to be new. Looking back retrospectively is paradoxically about illuminating the present and pointing the way to the future.

This chapter will take three frames and three historical periods to look at the sources of coaching and mentoring. The three frames are:

Friendship

Soul Healer

Work Realm

Friendship is overlooked in the therapeutic and coaching fields as they attempt to differentiate themselves from it. However, even today with all the professionalized helping relationships on offer (with the expectation of family), friendship is the first place we turn to for psychological and emotional sense-making and support. Friendship and socially sanctioned helping relations are symbiotic in their relations, i.e. friendship today is informed by the language of 'therapy culture' and therefore is very different from 100 years ago but at the same time there is continuity.

Soul Healer refers to the helping relations where the role is sanctioned by society and the helping is related to healing the 'soul/psyche' in its many forms. The form of helping and the imagination of the soul/psyche are both fluid depending on social context and historical period.

Work realm, the final frame, looks at conceptions and changes in the workplace and, in particular, developmental ideas regarding employees. Changes in work change the way we interpret helping employees, and a brief historical overview reveals how coaching may already be behind the times, responding to the twentieth century workplace rather than the twenty-first century workplace.

The three periods are:

Pre-modern

Modern

Post-modern

Table II.1   A genealogy of coaching

	Pre-Modern	Modern	Post-Modern
Friendship	Kinship, tribal bonds, more communal than pairing friendships. Ancient utilitarian friendship.	Modern individualized reflective-self means friendships become more intimate and more paired. Self-disclosure and emotional sharing mimics therapeutic culture.	Friendship becomes iconic: Facebook friends, TV 'Friends'. Friendship increases but develops with weaker ties, being more disposable and transient. Returns to a more utilitarian friendship.
How Coaching is influenced	*Utilitarian friendship sets early model for coaching.*	*Pairing intimate friendships offers helping coaching model. Caring and advice giving.*	*Coaches become a form of utilitarian/disposable friend.*

	Pre-Modern	Modern	Post-Modern
Soul Healer	Oracle, shaman, Desert Fathers, priest's and religious Confessional.	Talking cure (Freud). Modern psychotherapy.	Post-institutional religion, new age spirituality, hybrid therapy approaches, lead to new soul healers, e.g Life-coaching. Post-modern confessional emerges.
How Coaching is influenced	***Soul Guide** **Coaching discourse** emerges through ancient expert helpers.*	*The talking cure underpins the pairing professional relationship that leads to contemporary coaching.*	*Coaching reflects the Post-modern hybrid, bricolage of approaches, that are epitomized by the four discourses.*

	Pre-Modern	Modern	Post-Modern
Work	Learning at work is via guilds and apprentices, i.e. on the job 'contextual learning'.	Managerial culture focuses on efficiency. The Human relations movement, and therapeutic culture enters workplace.	Atomization and fragmentation. Increasing use of self, emotions and identity at work. Globalization and digital labour.
How Coaching is influenced	*Coaching and mentoring mimic pre-modern context learning: bringing the 'learning' close to the individual's work experience.*	*Therapeutic culture at work paves way for coaching and **Psy Expert and Managerial** coaching discourses emerge.*	*Atomization and use of self at work increase the need for personalized development to help employees. **Network coaching discourse emerges**, reflecting globalization and network society.*

3   Pre-modernity

Helping Relationships

Figure 3.1   **Artefact from the British Museum (photograph taken by author, 2011)**

Pre-modern friendship
Pre-modern Soul Healer
Pre-modern work realm
Conclusion
Suggested reading

The pre-modern period (Western culture) describes the period before the enlightenment in the seventeenth century, a period before the criteria for truth became based on the scientific method, and before the printing press, when oral traditions passed on knowledge. In the pre-modern period religious life was central to social life; the institutions of the church and monastery played a key role in the life development of culture. These influenced the modern sensibility and how individuality and selfhood became defined. This had a particular influence on helping relationships, expert helpers, and what Rose calls 'governing the soul' (Rose, 1990).

This chapter explores the pre-modern helping relationships that pre-empt contemporary coaching; it is divided into three sections: pre-modern friendship, pre-modern Soul Healer and pre-modern work realm.

Pre-modern Friendship

> The desire for Friendship comes quickly, friendship does not (Aristotle)

Aristotle's writing on friendship still sets the philosophical agenda to this day. In Book VIII of Nicomachean Ethics he identified three groupings of friendships (Vernon, 2007: 2):

Friendships of Utility

Friendships of utility are about friendships based on the assumption that friends are useful to each other. Aristotle said that if you take away the utility the friendship fades. Perhaps this resonates with today's professional friendships, contemporary workplace networking and with coaching.

Friendships of Pleasure

These friendships are based on the pleasure of sharing an activity; today this might be tennis, the theatre, football, cooking or any number of alternate pastimes. Like utility, the friendship only thrives whilst the activity is active.

Friendships of the Good

This is friendship at its most pure – people who love each other for who they are, for their innate characteristics. Friendship is based on mutual respect, and Aristotle claims that whilst these friendships are few, they tend to last a lifetime.

It is clear that during the pre-modern era friendship was highly valued, and the subject of how different ancient friendships were in relation to modern friendships is a contested one. Konstan (1997) argues that the ancients did have intimate friends, whereas other scholars point to a friendship that was less intimate and more utilitarian. Meilaender (1999) claims that ancients did not see friendship as a way by which one unique self builds a bridge to another, because the idea of self-identity was less personal, reflective and less unique:

> Modern scholars have often argued that ancient friendship – certainly in the Homeric period but also later – was more an economic or political relationship than a personal one. It was marked more by 'obligatory reciprocity' than by 'sentiment.' ... Thus, for example, where modern discussions of friendship might emphasize the importance of 'self-disclosure as the basis for intimacy and trust between friends', ancient thinkers simply did not value self-disclosure. They praised qualities such as candor and frankness as essential for friendship. (Meilaender, 1999)

Friendship and personal identity began to change during the transition from the ancient Greek period to the Christian domination of the West. The early Christian Desert Fathers treasured their friends as guides and helpers on the path to virtue. However, as the communal monastic tradition developed (as opposed to hermit monks), friendship became an issue of suspicion. In the community of a monastery there developed a fear of friendship and intimacy, as it was thought to cause divisive relationships or favouritism that could undermine the community. Fear of encouraging homosexuality was also probably a contributing factor (Roby, 1977: 17). A more brotherly, fraternal love was encouraged in these Christian communities that still resonates in the Christian church today. In the monastic tradition personal self-disclosure was encouraged, not as an intimate sharing between friends, but as a way of surveillance and governance to create group cohesion (this links with the peer surveillance experienced in organizations in the twenty-first century; see Chapter 5).

> Self-disclosure, indeed, may work to advance the cohesion of small
> societies precisely by *inhibiting* private relations among individuals.
> (Konstan, 1997, cited in Meilaender, 1999)

This brief sojourn into antiquity and friendship shows links between the
work of a coach and the friendship of old. A coach shares some of the
domain of the friend, particularly the utilitarian ancient friend. A core difference is that a friend is an informal relation and the coach is usually a formal
relationship. St Ambrose, writing in the fourth century of the friendship
between monks, shows a clear understanding of what are now described as
'coaching/mentoring skills':

> Preserve then my sons, that friendship you have begun with your
> brothers, for nothing in the world is more beautiful than that. It
> is indeed a comfort in this life to have one to whom you can open
> your ear, with whom you can share secrets and to whom you can
> entrust the secrets of your heart. It is a comfort to have a trusty
> person by your side who will rejoice with you in prosperity,
> sympathise in troubles, encourage in persecution. (Four Incorporeal
> Creatures, 2011)

Close analysis of this text shows that St Ambrose realized the value of a
number of factors: listening, offering support, disclosing to another, having
a trusted guide, encouraging the other when down, and celebrating success – all
very modern understandings of coaching skills.

We can also see how friendship in the ancient world provided both a
utilitarian and subjective function – the former linked to living and work,
and the latter linked to the caring of another. These values relate strongly to
what modern day coaching has become – a caring/supportive activity and
a utilitarian one to enhance work and life performance.

As the monastic tradition counselled against intimacy for fear of fractur-
ing the community, I wonder if coaching also reflects the dangers of intimacy in 'the community' of the workplace. Intimacy is both sought after
and at the same time is dangerous in the workplace. To show one's weakness
to another can leave one exposed; it could lead to the loss of promotion or
even the loss of a job. It can also lead to claims of nepotism and favouritism.
The work environment can therefore be a dangerous place for intimate
friendship. Coaching might therefore be considered in Aristotle's terms as
a 'utilitarian friend' ... a friend who is in both a confidential, often intimate,
yet transactional relationship.

Perhaps one of the reasons for coaching's popularity is that it offers the
space where intimate self-disclosure can take place (see Chapter 6).

Disclosing the intimate self to a professional rather than a friend/colleague can also be safer; the former is paid to listen, to be confidential and be caring or at least non-judgmental and supportive in their response, while the latter may reject you, become judgmental and hurt you, or spread gossip. However, the friend can also provide greater intimacy, mutuality and love, what Aristotle calls the 'friendship of the good', as opposed to the professional friend who provides only utilitarian friendship. Mentor from Greek mythology also provides us with a bridge between friendship, tutoring and personal guidance, as is well documented in coaching and mentoring texts.

The Greek Myth: origins of the modern use of the term 'mentor'

Mentor appeared in Homer's *Odyssey*. Mentor taught Odysseus' son, Telemachus. Before going off to fight the Trojan Wars, Odysseus asked Mentor to look after his household, especially grooming his son in readiness for the day when he would become king. Odysseus spent ten years or more trying to get home after the wars, during which time Telemachus grew up in Mentor's care. Telemachus set off to search for his father and was accompanied by Athena, Goddess of War, who took Mentor's form. When father and son were eventually reunited, they returned home and were able to throw out the pretenders to Odysseus' realm. From then, the term 'mentor' came to have its current meaning: experienced and trusted advisor, friend and counsellor (TVU, 2002).

Spiritual friendship

A classic text entitled *Spiritual Friendship*, written by Aelred of Rievaulx in the twelfth century, is a 'must read' for anyone interested in religious/spiritual friendship. Aelred bucked the trend in monasteries, advocating 'pure' friendships as a way of getting closer to God, and believing that:

> he who dwells in friendship dwells in God, and God in him ... The fountain and source of friendship is love, there can be love without friendship but friendship without love is impossible. (1977: 16)

Aelred counselled to develop friendship as a way of developing virtue, goodness and a deeper relationship and closeness to God. I am not sure he would approve of our modern coaches/advisors!

If coaching is an offshoot from the utilitarian friend, rather than a *spiritual friend* or a *friendship of goodness* (Aristotle), then what impact does utility have on the activity of coaching? When utility is at the heart of a relationship, there lies a question about morality, values and ethics. Does the utilitarian friendship of a coach that involves finance and transaction distort the work of a coach? Undoubtedly! There is always a tension in coaching between collusion to keep the coachee/client happy, not to be too challenging and to show loyalty and support that can distort the true friendship described by Oscar Wilde who famously quips, '*A true friend stabs you in the front*'.

Coaches have a variety of different relations with clients, and can be seen as friends in some cases, particularly those coaches skilled at working authentically with their emotions and working in the realm of 'Soul Guide', which takes a special kind of trust. I have experienced the tensions and strengths that can occur between deep work over a period of time between coaching and friendship. When a coach is getting paid for work, there is a clear demarcation, therefore there is a transactional element to the relationship. Yet the coaching work can be very intimate, and at the same time link the deeply personal to the strategic. A chief executive wrote about her experiences of our coaching sessions in an article we co-authored for the *Journal of Management and Spirituality*:

> The main impact of the coaching sessions was an enabling, flowering, liberation and further integration of my professional and spiritual life. It also provided a safe and sacred space for me to push the boundaries of creating new organisational designs and processes for CEL. (Western and Sedgmore, 2008)

This coaching relationship has now ended and we have developed a mutual friendship. Yet whilst in coach and coachee roles, we kept a clear boundary that enabled the work to continue in depth and in focus, whilst developing the basis for a deep friendship. In Aristotle's terms we moved from Utilitarian to Goodness friendship, yet we would both also speak of Aelred's *spiritual friendship* that underpinned and transcended the coaching relationship too. For those coaches working from within a spiritual or deeply human context, the work of Aelred perhaps encourages us to be less 'professionally modern' in our coaching work, which can swallow us in realms of technocracy and rationality. Tuning into the fraternal friendship of monastic communities, which enabled friendship within a role and context, might give us new ground to work from. The role of a coach might work as a Soul Guide (Chapter 6) by holding onto a clear, differentiated role, different from an informal and intimate friend, yet offering *spiritual friendship* or what we might call more generically *coaching friendship* – a deep and real friendship, yet set within the bounds of a formal coaching role and relationship.

Pre-modern Soul Healer

In Ancient Greece, the word 'psyche' encompassed the essence of an individual and their physical being, their life spirit and soul, their heart, their personhood, as well as their spirit after death. (Morwood and Taylor, 2002)

The ancients used oracles, shaman and spiritual guides in many forms, all of which are the predecessors to the professional 'helping' roles of today, i.e. the priest, the therapist or the coach. One of the core differences in the pre-modern forms are the communal, ritualistic and clearly spiritual/divine aspects of the interventions that were key to the work of ancient Soul Healers. Often masks and fetish objects were used in these ceremonial events to evoke the power of the Gods (Campbell, 1959).

Collective and public religious rituals preceded the dyadic helping relationships so prevalent in modernity; even the Christian confessional was initially a public rather than private act. In pre-modernity the public and communal were the privileged site of soul/psyche healing and ritual, whereas in modernity the individual and interior self became much more important. Foucault traces therapeutic culture and 'therapeutic governance' back to the early pre-modern Christian ideas of 'pastoral power'.

Pastoral power

Foucault traces what he calls 'pastoral power' using the metaphor of the flock and the shepherd from the Bible, seeing how this became internalized into individuals and society as a way to 'govern our souls' (Rose, 1990). From the ancient Greek culture, Foucault claims that Christianity appropriated the Hellenistic instruments of self-examination and guidance of conscience (widespread among the Pythagoreans, Stoics and Epicureans on their path to self-mastery) but altered them considerably through the metaphor of the shepherd and pastoral care. He writes that the Christian appropriation of pastoral care meant that 'primitive Christianity shaped the idea of pastoral influence continuously exerting itself on individuals' (Foucault, 1990: 71).

John's Gospel gives an example of how Christianity used the pastoral metaphor:

I am the Good Shepherd; I know My sheep, and My sheep know Me – just as the Father knows Me and I know the Father – and I lay down My Life for the sheep. (John 10: 14–15)

Figure 3.2   Sculpture of Jesus the Shepherd, Theological Seminary, Krakow, Poland (photograph taken by author, 2012)

Christianity changed the Jewish emphasis from the 'flock' or 'the chosen people' to give much greater emphasis on the individual soul. God was interested in every single one of us, as in the parable of the lost sheep:

> 12 What do you think? If a man owns a hundred sheep, and one of them wanders away, will he not leave the ninety-nine on the hills and go to look for the one that wandered off?
>
> 13 And if he finds it, truly I tell you, he is happier about that one sheep than about the ninety-nine that did not wander off.

14 In the same way your Father in heaven is not willing that any of these little ones should perish. (Matthew 18: 12–14)

The shepherd and his lost sheep became a metaphor for the church and how it would develop pastoral power. Individuals became more important and the 'modern self' began to form as an individual, self-reflecting self, which did not exist in the pre-modern mind. This modern self began to be formed by the early Soul Healers, the spiritual guides such as the Desert Fathers who, acting in 'imitation of Christ', became the shepherd, offering spiritual wisdom, counselling and confession to save the individual's soul.

Later, in the middle ages, an individual monk became accountable for his self in the eyes of God, and the monk was encouraged in his formation to become a more reflective self. St Romauld (950–1025) formed a new charism, 'the Calmaldolese' from the Benedictine order, and his brief rule below reflects the move towards the individualized reflective self.

St Romauld's brief rule

Sit in your cell as in paradise. Put the whole world behind you and forget it. Watch your thoughts like a good fisherman watching for fish. The path you must follow is in the Psalms – never leave it. (Matus, 1996: 73)

To 'watch your thoughts like a good fisherman watching for fish' is indeed a worthy phrase for any contemporary coach encouraging self-reflection in their coachee. Rather than collectively follow the monastic rules to save the soul, we can see the move towards individual self-reflection, to empty oneself, to become contemplative and reflective, and to learn about oneself by studying one's thoughts and deeds. This is the precursor to a very modern way of thinking about ourselves in the world.

The idea of self-examination, of a sense of being watched by an immanent force in the middle ages, became fused to the modern ideas of being watched by our conscience or our super-ego. Rose (2011) indicates the importance of the Christian confessional:

From the 12th Century onwards, a new practice of Christian administration of 'the cure of souls' made advances across Europe: 'After 1215, when annual confession became the obligation of all Christians, these treatises became the guides to Christian souls everywhere'. (Nelson, 1965: 64).

This pastoral power became a greater force through the Christian confessional; here your soul was examined by a priest, but more importantly by the self. The monastery was the forerunner where individuals formed themselves, examining their thoughts and deeds. McLeod links the spiritual director with psychotherapy:

> The final facet of 'primitive' equivalents to psychotherapy was the participation of a powerful spiritual guide or *spiritual director*, who would facilitate and engineer the whole process. (McLeod, 1997: 8)

The confessional produced the subject with the condemning super-ego, aware of 'bad thoughts and deeds', sins of the flesh and of the mind. Pastoral power works on the individual to help them self-control their impulses and determine how they should behave in the world.

Directors of souls

The early example of dyadic soul-helping relations were, as has been mentioned, the Desert Fathers, who 'treasured their friends as guides and helpers on their paths to virtue' (Aelred of Rievaulx, 1977: 16). They also offered spiritual support to the many who came for guidance. The Desert Fathers were not spiritual directors as we know them, nor were they like Zen masters. There was no system or method, they had a great economy of words, and their relationship to those coming to them was that of Abba or Amma (Father or Mother) to their son/daughter in Christ. This relationship might offer insights into coaching particularly when working in the discourse of Soul Guide. Coaches are not therapists or spiritual directors, but they listen – a good coach has an economy of words. Nancy Kline, keynote speaker at the BACP Coaching conference, clearly coaches in this tradition.

> Nancy Kline, creator of The Thinking Environment, will suggest that coaching in our uniquely changing world is not a technique or a toolbox. It is a *way of being* that liberates the mind of the client, an art that is at one with the transformative nature of silence. (BACP, 2011)

Spiritual directors in monasteries also provided a prototype coaching/mentoring role. They worked in groups and with individuals on their 'personal development and spiritual formation'. Their task was to act as formal spiritual guides to ensure that young monks went through a process to develop the prayerful humility that helped them to become 'formed as monks'.

The development of the interior life and the using of a guide/coach can be traced back to these pre-modern monastic orders. The *Devotio Moderna* movement of the late medieval period (fourteenth/fifteenth century) focused on:

> inner devotion, the individual's efforts, the interior life, the spiritual dimension of manual labour, the imitation of Christ, freedom in the Holy Spirit, conversion … (Belisle, 2002)

As we can see this is very different from the community, ritualistic ceremonial focus of the shamanic healer. The individual focus, the interior life, the spirituality of work, and the freedom in the Holy Spirit (which has now become the free individual spirit) all have echoes in our conceptions of modern self-hood and contemporary coaching.

Asceticism: the practice of bodily exercise

> The word *asceticism* comes from the Greek *askesis* which means practice, bodily exercise, and more especially, athletic training. The early Christians adopted it to signify the practice of the spiritual things, or spiritual exercises performed for the purpose of acquiring the habits of virtue. (New Advent, 2009)

We see here the link between the Greek practice of askesis, the interior work of purifying, and what moderns would term 'self-improvement'. The Cynic ascetics were a bridge between the pre-modern and the modern. They renounced worldly goods, wealth and power, paving the way for the Desert Fathers and Franciscan Friars in the Christian tradition. This monastic asceticism was then taken into the mainstream church and later into mainstream society.

Instead of being left outside the church, the monastic ideal was brought inside.

> … Asceticism itself was changed in this process … not only must a believer's external and public life be lived in obedience to higher power, but even the private and intimate stirrings of the body and its desire must be constantly controlled. (Woodhead, 2004: 56)

Ignatius of Loyola (1491–1556), founder of the Jesuits, designed spiritual exercises which became the central component of the Jesuit monastic training. He believed that the *examin*, the self-examination of the soul, was the most important part of these exercises. His turning of spiritual asceticism into a formal methodology was a move from the pre-modern to the modern, hence the popularity of spiritual exercises today, which are used by lay people worldwide and continue to be used for Jesuit training. This reflection on the interior life and the practices to develop a virtuous self consisted of both spiritual/psychological and bodily/physical work. The Eastern traditions of yoga and meditation – body, mind and spirit exercises – best exemplify this, and as we know have travelled a long way from their ancient Eastern roots to become mainstream practices in modern life today.

Life coaches in particular will suggest yoga or other meditation, breathing and associated techniques to help individuals 'work on themselves'. When leading the post-graduate coaching programme at Lancaster University Management School we began the day with a yoga teacher leading a session. Participation was voluntary, but the group was told that 'doing yoga for oneself meant doing it for all' as it brought a certain ambience and resonance to the day's teaching. The point was to bring the body into play, which the ancient Greeks, ascetic early monks and Eastern traditions believe is so important for any well-being. Sadly, in many of our contemporary cures for professionals, including coaching, the role of the body is often forgotten.

Coaching, and self-development in general, borrows heavily from Ignatius' exercises and 'method', the pre-modern Soul Healer, particularly through the Christian tradition which pre-empted the developments in the modern era. Here we can see the beginning of the Soul Guide Discourse emerge, a discourse that begins in pre-modernity and remains just as powerful in post-modernity, and informs coaching practice today.

Pre-modern Work Realm

The work domain in pre-industrial, pre-modern societies differed radically from our conceptions of work today. Much of it was rural/agricultural or craft-based, as opposed to modern-day industrial working conditions. Knowledge exchange occurred in less formal, more flexible networked approaches, and took place in public spaces such as trade routes and the market place. Communities of practice formed naturally around crafts and trades, often with informal rather than formal training.

Pre-modern work involved apprenticeships, on-the-job learning, in contrast to the modernist era where much management training is classroom-based, such as the MBA. Apprenticeships were an in-house training form whereby a master craftsman took on an apprentice who learnt the trade mainly through observation and practice, usually over a seven-year period. Apprentices often paid for the privilege of learning a master trade (Wallis, 2007: 2).

Guilds were the formal institutional bodies that regulated apprenticeships, though as Wallis (2007) points out, the guilds often favoured the master rather than the apprentice. Mentoring was an informal skill; a master craftsman would mentor his apprentices – this was the art of learning a trade.

Modern life and the industrial revolution marked the end of the traditional guild and diminished the apprenticeship model, as work became less of a craft and more of an industrial process where the division of labour meant tasks were simpler and more functional.

Peer coaching: contemporary applications of learning from practice

In relation to coaching the important lesson from the apprenticeship model and the pre-modern focus on apprenticeship, is the focus on observation and on-the-job practice, as opposed to contemporary off-site training courses and learning knowledge rather than tacit skills. In coaching the focus is very often on the individual coachee and self-improvement, yet good leadership is often the result of an informal apprenticeship and coaching, whereby a leader learns their 'craft' from observing and learning from practice. In collaboration with Professor Jonathon Gosling we researched how leaders learnt from each other through observing another leader at work, and being observed by a peer and receiving feedback. From this we developed a method to develop a peer coaching and observation process (Western and Gosling, 2002).

Pairing for leadership

We trained leaders in coaching skills, feedback and reflection, and observation skills (informed by ethnographic and psychoanalytic child observation techniques). We then carefully matched leaders into pairs so they could learn from observing another leader practise their craft of leadership and management. Each leader observed the other, and gave each other feedback and tips. Finally, we offered a professional coaching debrief to embed the learning.

This powerful intervention is an example of drawing upon the lessons of apprenticeship and the value of observing the craft and nuances of work, which changes the emphasis from learning through gaining knowledge to learning through experience, practice and observation. Coaches can design peer coaching and mentoring exchanges between managers to encourage this process, or they can coach individual leaders to become an ethnographic observer in their own workplace.

Coaches too can learn from the apprentice model of learning on the job, through pairing up and observing each other work. This obviously needs to be agreed with the coachee, but it can be a helpful learning process for all involved.

Coaching and mentoring can learn a lot from the potential ideas of learning through observation – tacit approaches. As a coach I often ask if I can spend a day observing the workplace, as it informs my practice hugely. I also encourage coachees to take this approach themselves or with their team, to learn from observation and practice, as the apprentices of old did.

Conclusion

The pre-modern era has a lot to teach us. Burrell argues for a 'retro-organization', that organizational theory needs rejuvenating by looking back to a pre-modern period:

> In recognizing the centrality of the enlightenment to the modern world, [Burrell] argues that it is in need of rejuvenation through the medium of dawn-picked extracts of the pre-modern period in European thought and seeks in the pre-scientific era ideas and themes of relevance for today. (Burrell, 1997: 5–6)

This also applies to coaching as the pre-modern has both informed the development of coaching and has much to teach coaching and mentoring.

Coaching in some ways is an interesting return to the past: it continues an oral tradition that is linked to contemplation and reflection. This juxtaposes against modernity and post-modernity, which value action and doing, and the written and visual presentation of texts over the oral tradition of the past.

The apprenticeship ideas of learning from another, from context, and learning from experience and practice, rather than from knowledge and books, are also formative to coaching. Coaches pass on knowledge through their behaviours and presenting selves, as well as the content of their dialogue. They also encourage their coachees to learn from experience, to reflect on their practice, and to practise what they reflect on between coaching sessions. Coaching is very grounded in contextualized learning.

Coaching mimics learning from the early wisdom traditions, through experts of the soul. The Desert Fathers and later the monasteries provided embryonic coaching and mentoring models, which pointed towards today's individualism and the pairing relationships we now call coaching. The pre-modern can also teach us much we have forgotten or lost through the journey of modernity. A return to desert wisdom may offer something important to counter the coaching rush to modernity's rationalism, goal seeking and functionalism, which is currently dominating the field.

Suggested Reading

Aelred of Rievaulx (1977) *Spiritual Friendship* (trans. Mary Laker). Kalamazoo, MI: Cistercian Publications.
Burrell, G. (1997) *Pandemonium: Towards A Retro-Organization Theory*. London: Sage.
Foucault, M. (1972) *The Discourse on Language*. New York: Pantheon Books.

4 Modernity

Experts, Tools and Technology

Figure 4.1   **Fragment from the Wapping Hydraulic Power Station (built 1890) – now the Wapping Project (photograph taken by author, 2011)**

> Modern friendship
> Modern Soul Healer
> Modern work realm
> Conclusion
> Suggested reading

This chapter will look at the influences on coaching from the modern perspective through the three lenses of:

- Modern friendship

- Modern Soul Healer

- Modern work realm

Modernity both is a historical period and, as John Gray explains, also informs who we are and how we think: we are formed as modern subjects (now entering a post-modern or late-modern period). Below are a few definitions of modernity:

> Scientific knowledge would engender a universal morality in which the aim of society was as much production as possible. Through the use of technology, humanity would extend its power of the earth's resources and overcome the worst forms of natural scarcity. Poverty and war could be abolished. Through the power given to it by science humanity would be able to create a new world. (Gray, 2003: 2–3)

> Modernity refers to the post-medieval period marked by industrialism, capitalism, secularization, the nation-state, and its constituent forms of surveillance. (Barker, 2005: 444)

Anthony Giddens describes modernity as:

> ... a shorthand term for modern society, or industrial civilization. Portrayed in more detail, it is associated with (1) a certain set of attitudes towards the world, the idea of the world as open to transformation, by human intervention; (2) a complex of economic institutions, especially industrial production and a market economy; (3) a certain range of political institutions, including the nation-state and mass democracy. Largely as a result of these characteristics, modernity is vastly more dynamic than any previous type of social order. It is a

society – more technically, a complex of institutions – which, unlike any preceding culture, lives in the future, rather than the past. (Giddens and Pierson, 1998: 94)

Modernity produced huge social gains, through science and rationalism, such as health care, urbanization, democratic institutions, nation states and mass production of essential goods, making them accessible. However it also brought world wars fought with weapons of mass destruction, huge environmental damage, and its impact on the individual and collective psyche brought both more choice and individual freedom but at the expense of community and alienation.

Modern Friendship

Friendship became increasingly valued in the modern world. As communality and collectivism shrank, individualism and dyadic relationships grew in stature. The nuclear family replaced the extended family, while traditional sites of support in institutions such as the church went into demise as the process of individuation and secularization increased. In this scenario of the nuclear family, the pairing couple of husband and wife assumed a new intimacy, as did friendships, and they stepped into the ever-widening communal void. Friendship became highly valued, people you could share your closest thoughts and feelings with. Friendship also became an important source of finding meaning in life, to have a reflective space with an intimate other. Seeking 'soul mates' in love and in friendship meant more dyadic and more personal, subjective engagements. The modern subject sought to find themselves in 'special' others. To constitute the self, to be worthy and whole, was to have close friends who would not only support you but also help construct the identity you desired. Modern friends would help make you.

This opened the way for other 'intimate' dyadic relationships through the burgeoning number of helping professionals, for example, doctors, nurses, counsellors and coaches. Likewise friendship relations were affected by social changes, and 'the triumph of the therapeutic' (Rieff, 1966) meant that friendship mirrored this social milieu. Your friends become your personal 'pop' psychologists and mutual confessional partners. Friends disclose their 'secret selves' to each other and share therapeutic interpretations and explanations of their emotional, psychological and physical states. The role of contemporary friendship overlaps with the role of coaching, both providing a conversational space, a sense-making space and a 'psychologizing' process of discovering the self in an 'intimate relationship' with another.

Perhaps this is another explanation of why coaching has been such a success. Modern men and women like and need close intimacy and friendship. They also like coaches because they mimic much of what constitutes modern friendship but with an expert/professional edge, and coaching usually leaves the coachee in control. Coaches offer a conversational and confessional space, enabling us to self-disclose, which opens up the safe, psychological, reassuring and sense-making space we 'moderns' seek. Coaches, however, are deemed the people experts, and there is the financial and transactional element to the exchange. It can be argued that an expert in a paid role gives the coach more power that is not always openly acknowledged or understood. A transactional relationship, it is argued, also frees the coachee from moral obligation. The coachee is more free to confess, to use the paid conversational time more openly, as it's professional and confidential and involves less risk than confessing to a friend. The coachee is in control: they can stop it when they wish, no follow-up telephone calls to deal with. Pure friendship is a site of moral reciprocal obligation – this makes it more risky and also more deep and authentic.

Coaching and modern friendship are not the same, but they clearly overlap and inform each other.

Modern Soul Healer

In modernity a shift took place from the religious to the secular and from the public-communal to the private-dyadic. The Soul Healers in the pre-modern period drew their credibility and legitimacy from the divine, whereas the modern Soul Healer has drawn on the new 'religion' of science (Gray, 2003). McLeod notes that as religion gradually diminished, somebody was required to continue the work of 'cure of souls' (McLeod, 1997: 10).

One of the outcomes of modernity is the division of labour and the rise of specialists and experts, resulting in managerial experts and psychological experts. In modernity the Psy Expert was born and flourished.

Sigmund Freud and the talking cure

Nikolas Rose (2011) traces the link between psychoanalysis and its predecessors:

> From this perspective, I think we can trace a line between psychotherapeutic practices of the self and these ancient spiritual exercises. For example, Benjamin Nelson argued that Freud was also central to the invention of a whole novel scheme for the direction of souls. (Nelson, 1965)

Freud started a new paradigm of Soul Healing at the turn of the twentieth century called psychoanalysis. Freud has an immense influence in the West, not only on the development of psychotherapy technique and theory, but also on our social and cultural lives. Psychoanalysis paved the way for the proliferation of Psy experts who affect us directly and indirectly; therapy culture has truly triumphed (Rieff, 1966) whereby therapy now colonizes the modern mind. Freud's ambition was a very modernist one: to find a rational explanation for the irrational and emotional aspects of our lives. In an explanation of Freud's model, Bettleheim (1982: 12) in his book *Freud and Man's Soul* argues that Freud brought together the word 'psyche', meaning soul in Greek, with 'analysis', suggesting scientific rigour. Psychoanalysis therefore was analysis of the soul in its widest sense. Bettleheim claims the current interpretation of 'psyche' as purely psychological is misleading, as the early Viennese understanding of the word was also related to the understanding of the soul. Freud, with his colleague Joseph Breuer (2004), discovered a cathartic method, developed from hypnosis. They discovered that the physical symptoms of hysteria reduced or disappeared when a patient was encouraged to 'free talk' about their anxieties, and they jointly published *Studies in Hysteria* in 1895.

Freud went on to develop a dynamic theory of the psyche – the Ego, Super Ego and Id – analysing the unconscious to discover its drive and defence mechanisms, such as repression and projection. Freud's research method was through psychoanalysis of his patients and through his own self-analysis. Freud theorized his findings and wrote prolifically. Psychoanalysis became both a theory and a practice, as Freud also developed a clinical method that lies at the heart of psychotherapeutic practice today, and remains as the basic form for coaching. The method consists of the dyadic pair, confidentiality, and where the analysand/patient is asked to free associate (speak about whatever is on their minds without censoring this) while the analyst interprets the spoken material. The psychoanalyst also interprets the relationship between the patient and analyst, through what is known as transference and counter-transference.

Whilst Freud's work is contested and challenged, it should be remembered that he was a product of his time, that is, Vienna at the turn of the century; and whilst alive he continually developed his theories rather than hold them rigid and fixed. Post-Freudian psychoanalysis has many diverse schools, such as the Lacanian, Jungian and Kleinian approaches, which differ quite fundamentally in their theory. Interestingly the diverse schools can have a 'cult-like' following, and have constantly fallen out with each other, from the very early splits between Freud and Jung.

From psychoanalysis, a burgeoning amount of psychotherapy and psychology developed, much of which can be seen in various guises within coaching today. Behaviourism radically departed from psychoanalysis in the 1950s. Primary initiators of this change were Skinner and Eysenck, who focused on behavioural conditioning, which developed into cognitive behavioural therapy (Beck, 1976) – very popular today. Psychological interventions were developed, which linked cognition and behaviour. The rationalism of modernity featured highly, and rational-emotive therapy (RET) is based on the assumption that human beings can rationally change their perceptions through ABC interventions:

- A is the activating event

- B is the belief

- C is the consequence (emotional and behavioural)

RET and other cognitive approaches suggest that we assume that A (the event) causes C (the consequence) to the individual, whereas in actuality it is B (our belief) that causes C (the consequence). If our belief causes the emotional and behavioural consequences, then the therapist/psychologist can work with the client to change their perceptions, their belief (their cognition) so that the consequence (their behaviour) also changes. The CBT therapist (or coach) disputes and helps the client to 'change their irrational beliefs'. This modern rational approach to behaviour and thought change is becoming increasingly popular, particularly as it fits well with evidenced-based research. However, it is also heavily critiqued, with claims that it reduces complex human issues to bite-size behaviours, missing the systemic and deeper issues. Each therapy has its advocates and its detractors. In an interview with *Le Point* the eminent Lacanian psychoanalyst Jacques-Alain Miller discusses cognitive behavourial therapy:

> *Le Point*: And how would you define cognitive behavior therapies?
>
> JAM: You see, they are trainers of humans, like there are bear, horse or seal trainers. Having triumphed in animal training, they embark upon the same thing with human beings. Only, just hold on a minute! In humans, the cause and effect relationship of 'stimulus-response' is always upset by what we call as we may; the unconscious, desire or jouissance ... (Miller, 2005)

Other modern psychotherapy developments emerged from the human potential movement, a diverse group of psychologists and alternative thinkers:

> ... including Fritz Perls, Timothy Leary, Abraham Maslow, and Carl Rogers who constituted a kind of brain trust for the Esalen Institute in Big Sur, California. Esalen was a great cross-roads, beginning in 1962 when it opened, for these already established scientists of human consciousness who were joined by people like Carlos Casteneda, Alan Watts, Ken Kesey, Jack Kerouac, Maharishi Mahesh Yogi, and Aldous Huxley, all of whom took an interest in re-awakening the life

of feeling ... Esalen is remembered for generating what came to be called the human potential movement. (Cobb, 2005: 256)

The human potential movement has had a huge influence on therapy and the self-help movement, and it acted as the formative bridge between therapy and coaching (see Introduction). Carl Rogers developed person-centred and non-directive counselling (Rogers, 1951) and has had a huge impact on coaching, offering both ideology and method. The underlying belief promoted by the human potential movement is that humans have the tendency to self-actualize and therefore the counselling method is to focus on creating the conditions for self-actualization to occur. Person-centred counselling shuns the 'elitist' and distant role of the psychoanalyst, claiming the therapist needs to be authentic, empathetic and congruent (the core conditions). It also challenges the diagnostic and technique-ridden approaches of cognitive behavioural therapies. Rogers' (1951) work has resonance with many coaching approaches that lean towards the humanistic philosophy that claims the answers to our challenges lie within us. Rogers' work tried to democratize and humanize the influence that 'cold modernity' had on therapy, privileging the machine metaphor of scientific efficiency, elite expertise and technique-driven approaches. His influence underpins many coaches' practice and theory (whether they are aware of this or not). Rogers' work, alongside other human potential theorists, spread to many other fields, particularly in education and management (Maslow's ideas about self-actualization are commonly used in management for example). This was therapeutic practice breaking into mainstream fields, paving the way for coaching to follow.

Beyond therapy to governance

Psychotherapy goes beyond being a professional discipline, or a technique to change people. Rose (1990) argues that therapy is deeply embedded in our culture and impacts on how we think, how we behave and how we make sense of ourselves in the world. Drawing on Foucault, he claims with others that 'therapeutic governance' offers both a way of understanding and being in the modern world, whilst at the same time the logic of the therapeutic governs our thinking.

Modern Work Realm

In the workplace, modernity brought industrialization, the factory, mass production and later the office, and with it the division of labour and the creation of new modern work subjects – what we now call 'Human Resources'. The first work subjects created by modernity were the industrial workers who brought their bodies to the factory as labour. Following this came 'organization man' (Whyte, 1956), a subject who rose from the factory floor to the office the white collar worker who entered the burgeoning middle class, a consuming, suburban class. Whyte wrote of organization man that 'for them society has been good, very, very, good' (1956: 395), yet he points to the lack of autonomy and the conformist culture that ensnares them at the office and at home.

> Most see themselves as objects, more acted upon than acting – and their future, therefore determined as much by the system as by themselves. (Whyte, 1956: 395)

Individuality and consumerism became dominant features of modern life, and capitalism became a dominant feature of modernity (Giddens, 1991). Paradoxically the espoused and real freedoms of choice and individuality also brought with them the side effects of atomization, alienation and a demise of community (Putman, 2000). It also brought a sense of conformity; not the conformity one sees in religious fundamentalism, dictatorships or state communist societies, but the conformity brought about by a culture of peer surveillance, whereby the work colleagues in open-plan offices, the organization with new social technologies and ultimately the self, act as an observing super-ego, keeping our behaviours in line with normative expectations as to how we should behave and think (Barley and Kunda, 1992). Modernity brought about the division of labour, specialisms and experts. Coaching was influenced by the emergence of new managerial experts and also, as discussed in the Soul Healer, the rise of the Psy expert. In Chapter 8, I fully discuss the Managerial Discourse and how coaching operates within it, but (for now) two impacts from the modern manifestation of the manager for coaching are:

1   The manager as expert was a new social class founded in modernity, with the inherent idea that managers were experts in efficiency and control, drawing on scientific rationalism (Taylor, 1947; MacIntyre, 1985). For coaching this provided a social group to work with, and in spite of the claims that managers operate in the realm of science and control – evidently this is problematic and many managers feel both a lack of control, and that science and rationalism won't save them!

2   Management ideology and culture infiltrated coaching itself, and the Managerial Discourse within coaching focuses on rationality and instrumentalism to increase production and efficiency (Chapter 8).

In modernity, two world wars, secularism, capitalism, bureaucracy, urbanization and new institutions also had an impact on the psyche and the human spirit (Bauman, 1989).

This loss of community, sense of alienation and existential angst, and the conformity demanded by organizations, leaves the individual confused and dislocated. The social response has been to fill this void with Psy professionals, and in late modernity, coaches emerged as another Psy expert. The Psy professionals used modern language and modern techniques to become ever more scientific and rational, to fit and gain credibility in the modern age.

Coaching emerges as a new modern Psy Expert in the workplace

The Psy discourse and therapy culture expanded into all realms of life, and the workplace provided a void to be filled. Therapy and counselling didn't fit easily; they were still regarded as for the ill, emotionally troubled or weak. Therapeutic culture was embedded in organizations and management training in particular, but the Psy experts themselves were marginalized in patriarchal work cultures. Occupational psychology found a place through psychometric testing and evaluation, and they became involved in HR and Organizational Development work. Employee assistant programmes utilized confidential counsellors, and careers counsellors pre-empted careers coaching. However, this was not enough to satiate the alienated employees, lonely leaders at the top and managers struggling with increasingly complex work that demanded their cognition and their emotional engagement.

Put simply the workplace demanded a greater input from the Psy experts. Coaching emerged as a new expertise to fill the demand. Coaching focuses on positive aspects of human nature, inspiring hope and change rather than pathology-focused or medical models. This was a new reframing and also a rebranding of Psy expertise and therapeutic culture for the workplace, and its success has been phenomenal.

Conclusion

The strength of modernism and its concept of science led to the way in which it made visible a particular perspective on structure and order, as the basis of the age of enlightenment. ... But modernism achieved this at a price, which became evident over the ensuing two centuries. Like all strengths, in excess or when made exclusive, they increasingly became weaknesses. (Griffin, 2002: 178)

Modernity produced a new reflective subject, a vessel of human potential and an autonomous individual – yet also a more alienated and estranged individual, leading to more intimate dyadic friendships to compensate for the loss of community. Science and rationalism dominated modernity, which also produced many specialists and experts, one of them being the 'technician of the psyche'. Therapists became prolific and colonized the wider social world. Therapeutic governance produces the effect of an inner voice that tells us that we are entitled to much, that we are individually unique and deserving, that our emotional needs are important, that the world is a place of risk (and abuse) and that we need special places to process ourselves, support ourselves, find ourselves, mend ourselves and celebrate ourselves. The modern self is a needy, demanding and therapeutic self.

In terms of influencing coaching and mentoring, it was Freud who brought the Psy discourse into being. The basic formula for coaching is a continuation of this process of the 'talking cure', i.e. the client talks and the expert coach listens, offers sense-making and insights, and perhaps 'expert' interventions depending on their approach. As pointed out, modernity encourages specialists and experts: for example in the field of sports, coaches became ever more important, developing coaching expertise in physical technique and in psychological motivation. These modern expert interventions pave the way for contemporary workplace coaching – a new Psy expert, who bridged the gap between therapy and positive well-being, between the 'wounded and the celebrated self', and between modernity's scientific-rational drive for efficiency and production (Managerial Discourse, Chapter 8) and our struggle for identity and meaning in an alienated world (Soul Guide Discourse, Chapter 6).

Coaching arrived at the end of the twentieth century, a product of late modernity, and of post-industrialism.

The workplace had changed for most people in the West, from a place of manual labour to a place of cognitive and emotional labour, where soft management skills came to the fore, and where subjectivity and the emotions were ever more important. Coaching arrived in late modernity as the new Psy expert for the workplace. Coaching also imported modernity's discourse of Managerialism into its foundations. Today we see increasing influence from the Managerial Coaching Discourse and the Psy Coaching Discourse; both focusing on efficiency and technique, and both underpinned by modernity's scientific-rational gaze.

Suggested Reading

Giddens, A. (1991) *Modernity and Self Identity: Self and Society in the Late Modern Age.* Cambridge: Polity Press.

Gray, J. (2003) *Al Qaeda and What it Means to be Modern.* London: Faber and Faber.

Rieff, P. (1966) *The Triumph of the Therapeutic: Uses of Faith after Freud.* London: Chatto and Windus.

Rose, N. (1990) *Governing the Soul: The Shaping of the Private Self.* London: Routledge.

5 Post-modernity

Coaching Hybridity

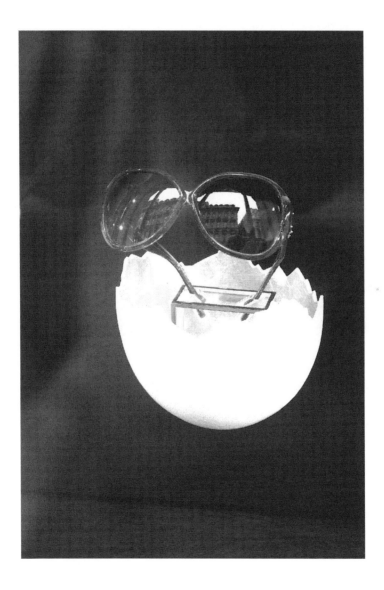

Figure 5.1   Ostrich egg and sunglasses: window display from Louis
Vuitton (photograph taken by author, London, 2011)

Post-modern organization
Post-modern friendship
Post-modern Soul Healers
Post-modern work realm
Conclusion
Suggested reading

I'd like to think (and

the sooner the better!)

of a cybernetic meadow,

where mammals and computers

live together in mutually

programming harmony

like pure water

touching clear sky.

(From 'All Watched Over by Machines of Loving Grace',
by Richard Brautigan)

Brautigan's poem of 1967 captures a vision of a post-modern future where computers and nature come together in a perfect harmony. Today machines, technology, nature, humans, discourses and texts, and systems and processes combine in hybrid networks that are complex, fast changing and fluid.

Box 5.1   Post-modernism

Post-modernism began in the mid to late twentieth century (Lyotard, 1984; Baudrillard, 1988), although the term is contested and some claim this is a period of high or late modernity (Giddens, 1991) or liquid modernity (Bauman, 1989). The post-modern self is viewed as fragmented rather than in unity, as always becoming rather than formed. The post-modern condition is a world filled with hyper communications and cyborg relations, whereby machines and humans interact inseparably (Callon and Law, 1995). Our bodies have machines and materials inserted in them, for example, pacemakers, cochlea implants, breast implants, with micro-chips now also being used. Our bodies also have technical extensions in the form of prosthetics, from limb attachments and hearing aids, to the prosthetic extensions of our laptops and cell phones that are exponentially extending our bodily selves, to reach across the virtual world to others. As Haraway writes:

> By the late twentieth century, our time, a mythic time, we are all chimeras, theorized and fabricated hybrids of machine and organism; in short, we are cyborgs. (1991: 151)

Post-modernity is a place of plural worlds that interact simultaneously, where reality and the virtual co-exist indiscriminately, and according to Baudrillard we live in a hyper-reality that is exemplified by Disneyland:

> The Disneyland imaginary is neither true nor false: it is a deterrence machine set up in order to rejuvenate in reverse the fiction of the real. Whence the debility, the infantile degeneration of this imagery? It's meant to be an infantile world, in order to make us believe that the adults are elsewhere, in the 'real' world, and to conceal the fact that real childishness is everywhere, particularly among those adults who go there to act the child in order to foster illusion of their real childishness. (Baudrillard, 1988)

For the purposes of this chapter I will describe post-modernity as the current period, which is characterized by post-ideology, where we have become sceptical about grand narratives, where there are no universally agreed beliefs, which and where everything is therefore contingent (Lyotard, 1984).

This chapter briefly describes organizations in the post-modern era, before working through the three lenses:

- Post-modern friendship

- Post-modern Soul Healer

- Post-modern work realm

Post-modern Organization

If the modern world mirrors the industrial age, working on mechanistic metaphors where parts interact to make a whole, the universe is conceptualized in Newtonian scientific terms, working like a machine; the social world operates with clear structures, and nation states and organizations are deemed to have clear boundaries. In the post-modern world, boundaries are blurred or non-existent except where we choose to draw them. The world is deconstructed and organizations are better thought of as complex systems and networks rather than buildings, with ordered, clear structures (Castells, 2000; Wheatley, 2006), and trans-nationalism undermines nation states that, like organizations, are in constant flux regarding their boundaries and identities.

Lyotard claims post-modernism presents us with the unpresentable, as expressed by abstract conceptualism in art. Lyotard ends his book *The Post-Modern Condition* with a post-modern plea to activate differences, which has a lot of relevance for coaching:

> ... to wage a war on totality; let us be witnesses to the unpresentable, let us activate the differences and save the honour of the name. (Lyotard, 1984)

In this post-modern condition, the self and identity are always in a process of 'becoming'. Judith Butler argues that gender is an unstable notion; it is not just a 'natural fact' but also a 'cultural performance' that is affected by social discourses and power relations (Butler, 1990: xxxi). Similarly, the post-modern self is a nomadic self, always in transition, both in a global sense and in an internal sense, forever migrating across networks, and often dislocated:

> A self does not amount to much, but no self is an island; each exists in a fabric of relations that is now more complex and mobile than ever before ... a person is always located at nodal points of specific communication circuits. (Lyotard, 1984: 15)

Coaching and mentoring take place within this place of post-modernity, and yet the majority of coaching practitioners, training schools and text books remain in the realm of modernity.

Post-modern Friendship

In the post-modern condition, friendship becomes vital in a fragmenting world. Sasha Roseneil (2006) claims that friendship is becoming ever more important. She argues that friendship should be taken seriously by social scientists when planning welfare and care, claiming that new and expanding friendships are a counterpoint to the rhetoric about the demise of community:

> (Friendship) provides an important counterpoint to the pessimistic tone which characterizes the work of sociologists such as Zygmunt Bauman (2001, 2003) and Robert Putnam (2000), whose ideas have been taken up in a widespread public discourse about a supposed crisis in personal relationships and community. Such ideas feed into, and implicitly express, a patriarchal, conservative hankering after a lost golden age of stable families and seemingly more secure structures of care. (Roseneil, 2006: 415)

The post-modern condition demands new friendships and new social relations, which helps explain the rise of coaching. Friends become ever more important as they enable us to attach to another, to have intimacy whilst also maintaining the nomadic autonomy demanded in the post-modern world. Roseneil offers some research to support the value of friendship in the contemporary world.

> Against this backdrop, the findings of the 'Care, Friendship and Non-Conventional Partnership' project add weight to the idea that friendship is an increasingly socially significant relationship ... They placed a high value on the way in which friends offer care and support, love and affection without infringing personal boundaries, and without the deep emotional risks of sexual/love relationships. Catriona Mackenzie and Natalie Stoljar's (2000) phrase 'autonomous relationality' captures well this moral ontology (Butler, 1999), which values both attachments to others and self-determination. (Roseneil, 2006)

Friendship has become iconic in contemporary society: the TV programme *Friends* became a massive global TV hit. The show's finale episode, *The Last One,* had 52.2 million viewers in the US alone. Facebook and other social networking sites rely on the concept of virtual friends as core to their success. Facebook had 135.1 million monthly US visitors in October 2010 (Quantcast, 2010). According to *Social Media Today* (2010), in April 2010 an estimated 41.6 per cent of the US population had a Facebook account.

Some people question whether these friendships are genuine or not:

> Dr Will Reader, of Sheffield Hallam University, found that the typical social networking user now lists at least 150 friends on their home page. His research, based on interviews with around 200 users, found that only a handful are genuine friends. The rest are the online equivalent of friendly faces on a train or high street. (Derbyshire, 2007)

However, it is not so much a question of whether friends are genuine or not, but how friendship evolves and changes under new social and technological conditions, and has gained an iconic status in the post-modern world. Friendship comes in many forms, deep and shallow, long lasting and fleeting, real and virtual, close and distant. Post-modern friendship, as a cultural phenomenon, helps us to understand how coaching works so well in today's society. *Coaching, like post-modern friendship, offers intimacy and a close 'other' whilst allowing us to retain our autonomy and distance.*

The coach mimics this 'autonomous relationality' of friendship, allowing intimacy within autonomous conditions. The coach is an expert to whom we can confess our interior lives and experiences, share anxieties and fears, our dreams and successes, but also not see for weeks, and abandon when we so choose.

Post-modern Soul Healers

In the post-modern era, New Age 'therapists', natural healers, spiritualists, counsellors and coaches (particularly Life-coaches) dominate the field of Soul Healing, replacing the pre-modern shaman and priesthood and challenging the modern secular priest, i.e. the psychoanalyst and traditional therapist. They draw upon a heady and diverse mixture of ancient wisdoms, appropriated Eastern spirituality and bodywork (Bell and Taylor, 2003).

Naturalism is a core theme, a return to 'Edenic purity', to find our true selves (before the Fall) and to become whole again. In line with a hybrid post-modern approach, New Age Soul Healers and Life-coaches are also happy to appropriate science and pseudo-science in their marketing and discourse, without fear or awareness of contradictions in their approaches.

At one level New Age Soul Healers preach a counter-cultural message to the capitalist sensibility, claiming an alternative non-materialist heritage emerging from the 1960s hippy movement, yet this is challenged by Carrette and King (2005) and others who claim that whilst there are alternative elements to New Ageism, it is also a product of hyper-capitalism and consumer society:

> Heelas pays much attention to the 'prosperity wing' of the New Age whose trainers, writers and consultants have assumed the role of clergy in enabling people, especially business people, to experience spirituality. (Carrette and King, 2005: 1246)

Carrette and King (2005), in their book *Selling Spirituality*, propose that new spirituality is merged with psychological and narcissistic tendencies, and that whilst claiming to open the self up, they actually close the self down, reinforcing the atomization of the self, where every answer can be found within, rather than found in interdependent social relations with others. Other critiques are that the soul healing/life-coaching business mirrors capitalist consumerism: 'choose your spirituality off the supermarket shelf', 'create your own personalized narcissistic religion'. There is no working through of frustrations, just an 'entitlement culture' to material wealth and to be happy. At a recent 'Life-coaching' gathering I saw a book entitled *How to Make One Hell of a Profit and Still Get to Heaven*, demonstrating this viewpoint.

The new secular evangelism: the happiness project and positive psychology

The New Age movement is a huge force in Life-coaching and it seeps heavily into workplace coaching, alongside positive psychology. There is a growing new movement in search of happiness and well-being that merges scientific psychological approaches with the New Age spirituality and its interpretations of how we become happy. Positive psychology, claims scientific status and shifts psychology away from psychology, focusing on the 'wounded self' and focusing on how to support individuals to be happier, to increase their well-being and to 'celebrate the self' (Seligman and Csikszentmihalyi, 2000).

Seligman, the guru of the Happiness Movement, has moved on and now critiques the term 'happiness' in order to promote the idea of 'flourishing'. This work seems largely a reinterpretation of the existential ideas of finding meaning through engagement.

> Flourishing includes happiness (or Positive emotion), along with Engagement, Relationships, Meaning, and Accomplishment (summarised as the acronym PERMA), which Seligman (2011) claims are the building blocks of a fulfilling life. (Sachdev, 2011: 7)

Coaching for happiness is big business, especially in the USA and increasingly in the UK and Europe (Holden, 1998). Even the British Prime Minister David Cameron has joined the happiness fan club, hoping to measure well-being and happiness:

> Mr Cameron said in a speech at the Treasury ... Measuring the nation's 'wellbeing' as well as its wealth will make it easier for the Government to help British people attain 'the good life'. (*The Independent*, 2010)

The workplace is also a site where there is a rising interest in well-being, to counter the cost of stress and ill-health and loss of engagement from employees (Taris and Schreurs, 2009). The post-modern individual consumes treatments, coaching, healing, self-help magazines and Oprah Winfrey wisdom. The aim is to improve the self, to find the true self, to become self-realized, to be self-fulfilled and ultimately to be happy individuals. Another critique of the 'happiness industry' of Soul Healers is that whilst they authentically claim happiness as a goal, they spread discontent in order to sell their wares, even though this is done without conscious knowledge of it.

> ... the interest in self-improvement is fed by a general understanding that most people are not happy with their lives. Heelas (1996) writes that the torrent of advice from the self-help industry 'generates a climate of discontent' (p. 146). (Cullen, 2009: 1246)

Whilst there are an array of critiques of this New Age movement, there are positive dimensions to the concept. It has the potential to reach beyond the dominant consumerist ideology and, like post-modern friendship, provide new forms of engagement, of community, of collective identity and of shared experience that are important in this post-modern unsettling world.

> Many 'spiritual-but-not religious' people find new communities and collective identities from diverse practices such as those associated with the New Monastic movement, the Emergent church, yoga, meditation, dance and healing groups. These activities also provide meaningful relationships to the divine, which increasing numbers of people are failing to find in institutional religious settings. (Western, 2010: 355)

There is not a right or wrong account of these new Soul Healers. There are many flaws, many reasons to critique it, but also recognition that there are many possibilities too. Hybrid forms of psychology and spirituality, new initiatives to form communities and identities, are linked to sustainability and the green movement, where compassion and caring, nature and beauty are privileged; these provide important anchors in fluid and fast-changing environments.

Post-modern Work Realm

> Work has become a zone that is as much psychological as economic. We are no longer merely productive or unproductive bodies or even normal or maladjusted workers. We are 'people at work' and we bring to work all our fears, emotions and desires, our sexuality and our

pathology. The activity of labour [is] transformed into a matter of self-actualization, in which the cash return is less important than the identity conferred upon the employee. (Rose, 2004: 105)

The shift to a post-industrial, post-modern workplace has had profound impacts on employees. Globalization and digitization mean that the factory, office, hospital, school, small business and the corporation are going through a process of profound change. Cognitive labour in a digitized workplace has amplified the relationship between work, organizations and personal identity. As David Collinson, discussing his journal paper 'Identities and insecurities: selves at work' (2003), says:

Organisations not only create products and services, they also produce people by regulating and shaping their identities in numerous ways. In contemporary workplaces where performance monitoring seems to be increasing, employee insecurities about identity are also growing. (Collinson, 2003)

The emergent organizational culture became a surveillance culture, whereby managerial and peer surveillance took place in the new architectures of open-plan offices. Contact by mobile phones and emails meant that employees could be contacted day and night, and whilst on annual leave. Information sent by emails is traceable and monitorable by the company. The demarcation between work and home diminished, and employees' identities became ever more closely associated with their company and their work. Organizations push for employees to bring their whole selves to work, and employment engagement surveys have become consistently more important. HR departments argue this is about appreciating diversity, yet it could also be a totalizing manoeuvre, whereby employees give to the company not only their physical time, and their cognitive and emotional labour; they are also required to give to the company their souls.

The business schools and consultants encouraged CEOs to be transformational and to lead with vision and values, taking on the roles of transformational leaders (Bass, 1990) with the explicit aim to create strong and aligned organizational cultures. This Messiah Leadership (Western, 2008a) meant that employees were expected to bring their souls and identities to the workplace, and to follow leaders who were paid fantastic sums to act as saviours for the company. Barley and Kunda point to three tenets of this new leadership:

1   The company as community; the company being the main site for many employees to experience community would mean that ultimately the company would become fully-fledged communitas – bringing pride and a feeling of belonging.

2 Strong cultures could be consciously designed and manipulated.

3 To value conformity and emotional commitment would foster financial gain.

> Management was advised to exorcise unwanted thoughts and
> feelings from the workforce to replace them with beliefs and
> emotions that benefited the organisation. To make the point propo-
> nents employed an imagery of cults, clans and religious conver-
> sions [see Ouchi and Price 1978, Deal and Kennedy 1982]. Authors
> exhorted managers to become 'highpriests' of their organisation's
> values to appoint mythic heroes and fabricate sagas. (Barley and
> Kunda, 1992: 383)

Collins and Porras, in their book *Built to Last*, claim that 'understanding that cult-like tightness around an ideology actually enables a company to turn people loose to experimental change, adapt and – above all – act' (2000: 123).

In a paradoxical situation, the post-modern fragmentation and the loss of grand narratives led companies to seek new ways of 'containing' the anxieties of individuals and new ways (beyond coercion and pay) to get them to commit to work. Companies attempted a counter-cultural move to 'produce' not only their goods for sale but also to produce employees who had strong collective identities. In post-modernity the company brand became the most valued asset (beyond material assets), as post-modern consumerism relies on sign exchange (Baudrillard, 1988) more than material exchange; this can mean vast profit if the sign/brand is populist, yet it also means that the company has a huge vulnerability, as the sign/brand can lose its potency with great speed (if consumers rebel on social media against unethical practice for example). For companies to be successful they need employees both to be committed and to 'believe' in the brand as well as the customers. Employees are consid-ered not only as workers but as brand ambassadors, carrying the message and the sign within them, to spread the word. The best example of this is probably Apple Computers, where Steve Jobs represented a charismatic leader (Messiah) who created huge brand devotion within his employee and customer base.

This post-modern workplace produces a disconnection – the expectation that workers are engaged and passionate, bringing their whole selves to work, contrasts with another experience, that many employees feel dislo-cated and worn down. Global corporations, corporate hotels, international airports and global shopping malls merge into a bland, minimalist oneness, dulling our spirits.

The film *The Truman Show* offers us a parody of our world, reflecting back to us our post-modern existence, where reality and hyper-reality blur. The architecture of global business has a totalizing sameness: the same shops in the malls, each corporate open-plan office the same, each reception area the same, and each receptionist smiling and greeting, a product of emotional labour (Hochschild, 1983). Catherine Casey describes cognitive workers as 'designer employees' who, after being 'culturalized' by the company, become a 'capitulated-self' which has undergone a 'wearied surrender' (Casey, 1995: 191).

> Overt displays of employee resistance and opposition are virtually eliminated. Corporatised selves become sufficiently repressed to effectively weaken and dissolve the capacity for serious criticism or dissent. (Casey, 1995: 150)

The flip side of these critiques of the post-modern work environment is the huge potential for creativity, for new start-ups, for new design and for new products. New business models provide alternative ways to think about business. There are exciting social entrepreneurships finding new ways to help communities and participate in them. Post-modern organizations break down the barriers between consumer and producer, opening up potential for new global and local connections that offer an array of potential. Some argue that corporates are far more accountable than they have previously been, as activists and consumers are now able to quickly utilize modern communication networks to expose poor treatment of workers and other malpractice. Companies are being far more attentive to issues such as corporate responsibility and sustainability. Nike was exposed in late 1996 by activists, which brought this response:

> On May 12, 1998, Nike CEO Philip Knight stood before the National Press Club ... Knight was brave: He described his company's product as 'synonymous with slave wages, forced overtime and arbitrary abuse', and announced a series of reforms. (Canizeras, 2001)

This inside report from a Google employee writing on a blog suggests some employees find contemporary workplaces creative, dynamic and caring:

> What it is like working at Google?
>
> Interesting, fun, surprising, insightful, inspiring, impactful, and more such words. Here are ten insights from / cool things about / reasons for / delightful surprises from almost a year of working at Google:
>
> 10   The amazingly fantastic food and impressive digs.
>
> 9   'Micro Efficiencies'.
>
> 8   A company that truly cares.
>
> 7   Brain expansion opportunities.

6   The sheer amount of brilliant Google employees.

5   Empowerment (The big small company).

4   The scale of your impact.

3   Doing Good: Green & .org.

2   It's a happening place. The energy, the vibe, the passion.

1   The brand.

(Kaushik, 2008)

Others critique this, saying the employee's identity is so associated to the brand that they are colluded into working long hours, without the capacity to escape the totalizing gaze of the company that fixes them, not as the generic 'Organization Man' of modernity (described by Whyte, 1956), but around a specific brand persona, and the employee becomes 'Appleman', 'Applewoman' or a 'Googler'. Google creates a brand identity for its buildings and employees. Its Californian complex is nicknamed Googleplex, and its employees are called 'Googlers'. On its website under 'Culture' it says of Googlers that they have:

1   Bicycles or scooters for efficient travel between meetings; dogs, lava lamps, massage chairs, large inflatable balls.

2   Googlers sharing cubes, yurts and huddle rooms – and very few solo offices.

3   Laptops everywhere – standard issue for mobile coding, email on the go and note-taking.

4   Foosball, pool tables, volleyball courts, assorted video games, pianos, ping-pong tables, and gyms that offer yoga and dance classes.

5   Grassroots employee groups for all interests, like meditation, film, wine tasting, and salsa dancing.

6   Healthy lunches and dinners for all staff at a variety of cafés.

7   Break rooms packed with a variety of snacks and drinks to keep Googlers going.

(See www.google.com/intl/en/about/corporate/company/culture.html.)

As can be seen, the aim is to create a 'cool' identity that employees engage with and at the same time encourage creativity and brand loyalty.

Multiple stories emerge claiming that the post-modern workplace such as Google can be totalizing and encourage conformity (the above list encourages a certain type of employee and excludes others) or alternatively it can be considered dynamic and liberating, reflecting the bricolage within organizations.

Deleuze and Guattari (2004: 7–8) describe this bricolage as 'the characteristic mode of production of the schizophrenic producer', whereby the employees are split subjects – they feel whole, aligned and engaged as part of the brand community, yet at the same time feel lost, empty inside and dislocated.

Coaching and mentoring in the post-modern workplace

The post-modern workplace seems a perfect fit with coaching, from the perspective that new mobile workforces and employees with less individual security need new forms of support. Jobs are more fluid, project-based, portfolio-based and transitional, demands tailored and responses individual. Coaching that gives one-on-one support offers precisely this. The hybrid nature of coaching means it draws on diverse streams of knowledge and skills, which reflect a multitude of needs in the workplace. Coaching has adapted quickly in some areas, using Skype or 'tele-coaching' to maximize the potential for virtual, global reach.

As I wrote in the opening chapter, there is a resistance within coaching to take a critical stance, and this resistance shows up in how easily coaches mimic the corporate cultures they enter. Unfortunately many coaches are colonized by the corporate rhetoric of transformational leadership and employee engagement, without questioning how this reproduces conformist employees, or how transformational leadership reproduces heroic, 'great man' leadership approaches (Messiah Leadership) at the expense of distributed leadership, networked approaches to organizations and stakeholders with autonomous and creative employees (Eco-Leadership). Coaches working to reproduce the Messiah Leadership, following company transformational leadership competency models, are working in the wrong period. The post-modern workplace calls for a rethink in leadership and in coaching – approaches to support a new paradigm of leadership.

This is the challenge for coaches; to see that they have an opportunity and a responsibility to bring a fresh, challenging, ethical and external perspective. This means that the coaches themselves are not simply sounding boards or non-directive facilitators, but that they challenge the norm, and take a lead, asking ethical, existential and networking questions that open up new dialogues, and connect their coachees to the networks they need to influence.

Conclusion

Post-modern coaching is a continuously adapting field, which poses many questions regarding contemporary workplaces: How does coaching fit into an organization's quest, explicit or implicit, for employee commitment and conformity?

a   Are coaches part of the hegemonic system, brought in to support the company achieve its aims of colonizing individuals so they bring their souls to work, to perform with ever greater commitment and productivity?

b   Or do coaches find themselves subverting the company aims and helping the individual resist this colonization process? Can coaches stand outside of this hegemony and support individuals to find their authentic selves, find ways to emancipate themselves?

c   Or are coaches working on the edge, supporting economic and organizational success, whilst at the same time helping individuals hold onto their authenticity, helping them to become resilient and use all of their talents?

Coaching in its diversity is probably doing all of these and more. One of the challenges for coaching is: Can coaches learn from the most adaptive and progressive companies/organizations (and I would add social movements), and transfer best practice, ideas, business models and networked approaches to support stakeholder engagement, and ethical stances for socially and environmentally responsible workplaces?

The post-modern subject, it seems, desires closeness and distance, with both real and virtual relations, and as friendships adapt to this, so do the Psy experts. Coaching has emerged as one of these adaptations and utilizes the technology of this post-modern era to coach (Skype coaching and cyber-mentoring, for example).

The huge take up of coaching reflects the dislocation experienced, and the hybrid nature of coaching practice, drawing upon multiple sources, reflects the fragmented, hybrid bricolage of the post-modern world.

Coaching is part of this hybridity. Building itself on the remnants of modernity, it resists easy definition and categorization, as it embraces multiple and plural approaches. The call for professionalizing and institutionalizing coaching into a homogeneous body of knowledge carries with it great dangers, as this is a modernist project being carried out in an emergent post-modern world. Any move towards professionalization or unity of coaching practice has to be tempered by the knowledge that coaching is at its strongest when it can be fluid, adaptive, entrepreneurial and reads the contemporary social times. The Network Coaching Discourse emerges to answer these contemporary challenges, to meet the demands of the networked society. Coaching will need to embrace and develop this discourse rather than stay solely in the grasp of modernity's influences, repeating patterns of development that replicate managerial and psychotherapy professions. Post-modern sensibilities suggest that hybridity and diversity will triumph over conformity and standardization, and rather than mimicking the practices of other (modernist) professions to gain credibility, coaching may do well to stay ahead of the field, and create it's own hybrid and diverse path.

Suggested Reading

Barley, S. and Kunda, G. (1992) 'Design and devotion: surges of rational and normative ideologies of control in Managerial Discourse', *Administrative Science Quarterly*, 37: 363–399.

Baudrillard, J. (1988) 'Simulacra and simulations', in *Selected Writings* (Mark Poster, ed.). Stanford: Stanford University Press, pp. 166–184.

Bell, E. and Taylor, S. (2003) 'The elevation of work: pastoral power and the New Age work ethic', *Organization*, 10 (2): 329–349.

Casey, C. (1995) *Work, Self and Society after Industrialisation*. London: Routledge.

Castells, M. (2000) *The Information Age: Economy, Society and Culture, Vol. I: The Rise of the Network Society*. Cambridge, MA/Oxford, UK: Blackwell.

Hirschhorn, L. (1998) *Reworking Authority, Leading and Following in the Post-Modern Organisation*. Cambridge, MA: MIT Press.

From Friendship to Coaching:
A Brief Genealogy of Coaching

Conclusion

Figure II.1   Sphinx of Tahargo 680 BC Egyptian: from British Museum
2011 (photograph taken by author, London 2011)

The Coaching Sphinx

Coaching has emerged from a multitude of personal dyadic helping relationships, beginning with friendship. Like a mythical sphinx, a coach has the head of a friend, the body of a psychotherapist, the feet of a manager, the tail of a consultant and the face of a priest. As the psychoanalyst Wilfred Bion points out, in ancient myths a sphinx asks questions of us, and this arouses primitive anxieties:

the enigmatic, brooding and questioning sphinx from whom disaster emanates ... being the object of inquiry arouses fears of an extremely primitive kind ... (Bion, 1961: 162)

The beauty of coaching is that unlike the shaman, confessional priest or psychoanalyst, the coach does not hold the same symbolic power as these former 'helpers'. The coach has the same kinship lineage, an expert who questions and listens, but with a difference; the post-modern sphinx is not the one from whom disaster emanates, but the one from whom new hope emerges.

In the church confessional, the fear of disaster comes from facing the omnipotent all-powerful God; in psychoanalysis it comes through the analyst having the interpretive power to reveal to us our unconscious fears and unwanted truths about ourselves. Yet in coaching, the power relations are transformed. There is a closer link to the pre-modern utilitarian friend and to the Soul Healer than the omnipotent priest or psychoanalyst. However, this coaching stance is becoming eroded.

Reviewing Friendship

Friendship offers us a lens to understand the relations between coach and coachee.

Aristotle's ideas about utilitarian friendships prove useful here. Any engagement with emotions and the psyche/soul will take coaches beyond purely utilitarian professional engagement, and coaches have to be aware of what this means. Coaching rarely works unless the coachee likes the coach (and vice versa). We often call this compatibility but it is a kind of utilitarian friendship by another name.

Spiritual friendship in monasteries offers some useful guidelines and makes us aware of the dangers of these close yet 'professional' relations. The dangers of friendships developing in coaching are that they can inhibit the coach from speaking openly and in role. Unlike psychotherapy, which has developed very clear boundaries to protect friendships and non-professional relationships, coaches have less rigour about boundaries and roles. This leaves them open to form different types of relationships that can be warmer, less stifled and with less power situated with the expert.

The dangers are that this opens the door to potentially more opportunities for friendship that could undo professional relations and the coaches' focus. One of the big dangers with coaching is collusion, while another is utilitarianism. The coach has a utilitarian goal to keep the sessions going and this may undermine 'courageous integrity' and honesty in feedback. The sessions can also become too conversational, too convivial, and collusion can occur for transactional reasons and for reasons of newly developed personal friendships, which may inhibit the work.

When sensing a friendship occurring, the coach has to work very hard to stay on task and in role. Mentors, and in particular those working for a number of years in the same company as the mentee, will also have to pay attention to the dynamics of friendship, both within their relationship and within the workplace as a whole. Aristotle identified different types of friendships, which can give us insights into contemporary coaching relationships. A particular type of relationship we might call coaching-friendship may act as a bridge between our authenticity and humanity and the work we do as coaches. One key to successful coaching is to focus on 'correct distance' between the emotional and 'professional' – this is never static but is flexible as relationships, change. Modernity brought a more dyadic and intimate friendship, and then post-modern friendship became increasingly important and migrated into the virtual realm alongside traditional friendships. This points to new collaborations in coaching – mimicking friendships that enable 'autonomous-relationality' (Mackenzie and Stoljar, 2000) where intimacy is coupled with safe distance and utilizes technologies to practise coaching in new ways.

Reviewing Soul Healers

Soul Healing from the pre-modern to post-modern connects the journey from shaman to coach. There is always a soulful side to the work of a healer, even when it is framed in the most secular way. Wilber (2000) claims that we are all on a psycho-spiritual path whether we like it or not. The term 'spiritual', however, is a very evocative phrase and I would rather use the word 'soul', which encompasses the secular, as in 'soul music' feeling soulful, as well as its spiritual and religious connotations and meanings. Soul is also used by other academics when discussing the transition of shaping and working with the identity and 'self' (Bettleheim and Janowitz, 1950; Rose, 1990).

The expert who is socially sanctioned to work with our psyche and soul is not a new phenomenon, as it goes back to our earliest social communities and institutions. The path travelled begins at a more communally based, ritualistic healing and continues through a more rationalistic, dyadic work that focuses on the individual in the modern setting.

Contemporary links between psychotherapy and Soul Healers are well documented (Rose, 1990; McLeod, 1997) and the links are also made between pre-modern mythic figures such as the ferryman and modernity's expert psychic-healers.

The psychoanalyst is primarily the ferryman who receives and transports the excess weight of heavy loads to the opposite bank. ... someone you meet once and who accompanies you up to the point where you know the way. (Clement, 1987: 73)

Clement goes on to remind us of unconscious and mythic associations of the ferryman and of transfer(ence):

Transference onto the psychoanalyst: the transfer (ence) of populations; the crossing of streams, adrift, at the mercy of the waves of the river. (1987: 74–75)

Coaching perhaps is the post-modern version of the ferryman. Coaching evokes this unconscious and cultural meaning of transportation; its meaning originally derived from a horse-drawn coach. If the psychoanalyst's work is to pick up the transference and carry the baggage for a while and then transfer it across the river to the place where their client can find their own way again, then what is the coaching work? Perhaps to guide the coachee on a journey, across inner-landscapes, and to transfer this journey to the networks in which they live and work, i.e. transporting them from where they are to where they need to be.

The modern move from communal to individual, from ritual to a methodology, came initially through the monastery and then the institutional church. It transformed social relations and the modern subject. The modern subject required a modern Soul Healer. Sigmund Freud opened up the therapeutic paradigm, and what emerged was an array of Psy professionals, and later, coaching. Freud broke new ground that changed the way mentally ill and psychologically disturbed people were treated, as the insane asylum and physical treatments of the neurotic were moved to the clinic and the couch. Whilst not perfect, this was a more humane and insightful approach. The 'talking cure' is therefore the foundation of coaching today.

The modern period, drawing on science and rationality, produced instrumentalization, functionalism and methodological approaches to soul healing.

This scientific-rational approach still carries weight in the post-modern period but is juxtaposed between another drive that returns to friendship and shamanic types of spirituality. Life-coaches and the discourse of coaching can claim the territory of the priest, the shaman and the scientist at the same time. The hybridity of 'Californian' New Age Life-coaching approaches have become increasingly mainstream in the workplace. A Life-coach for example may claim scientific attributes by using NLP or positive psychology; however they may then turn to non-scientific reiki healing or crystal healing.

The contemporary coach it seems draws on a vast array of influences and, true to post-modernism, says, 'Yes, we coaches are a bricolage, yes the field is fragmented, yes my practice draws on multiple sources … what's your problem?!'

Reviewing the Work Realm

The work realm has changed and with it expert helpers and work-based training. From the medieval apprentice to the modern MBA there has been a huge shift in emphasis. The emergence of the coach is linked to the rise of subjectivity in management techniques and work itself. The worker shifted from a manual labourer who brought the body to work and was controlled by sanctions and incentives overseen by a foreman, to the cognitive labourer who is expected to bring their soul to work (Deal and Kennedy, 1982; Casey, 1995). Our identities become ever more associated with our job, and employees' identities become fused with their work roles. In what Sartre (2001) would term 'Bad Faith', he challenges this fusion as a loss of autonomy and loss of our deep humanity.

The rise of the coach can be traced in parallel to the changing face of the workplace. Technical training became ever more specialized, and the role of the sports coach emphasized that each individual needs technical and motivational coaching, which then became a metaphor for coaching in the workplace. Management consultants and business schools worked on human relations, teamwork and dynamics. Later, in the twentieth century, the 'subjective turn' meant that the outward bound 'team building' approaches were replaced by inward bound training (Bell and Taylor, 2004). Identity, emotional intelligence and self-awareness became core to management training and to organizational theorists. The move was to create workplace cultures that were communities of solidarity, with transformational leaders who had visions and values that employees could follow with passion (Peters and Waterman, 1982; Barley and Kunda, 1992). Employees had to bring more of themselves to work, while managers had to manage people's emotions, and show leadership through their enthusiasm and authenticity. These changes demanded more specialist inputs to support the emotional work that is far from being 'soft'.

Costea et al. highlight that the 'softness' of this new discourse of capitalism should not be confused with an ease in its burdens on the managerial self, as it 'denotes the expansion and intensification of demands on the self to become ever more involved in work with its whole subjectivity' [2008: 672]. (Cullen, 2009)

Psy professionals entered the workplace; career counselling and employee assistant programmes offered one-to-one counselling support, and mentoring became more popular. Psychometric testing, 360-degree feedback and other forms of measuring employee engagement became popular. Coaching emerged initially as a remedial form of support for those who needed to improve, but very quickly became the only management development activity that could offer both tailored individual emotional support and at the same time act as a bridge between the individual psyche and the organizational demands. Coaches worked in this gap – between the individual and the organization – and their task was to build the bridges that would make both more successful.

The Coach as a Post-modern Nomad

In the post-industrial, knowledge-based workplace, coaching has a collective function beyond one-on-one coaching practice (the macro-social influences, see Chapter 12). One metaphor for coaching might be the post-modern nomadic workers. Pre-modern nomads went from village to village, picking up and passing on news, sharing narratives and stories, offering a service of knowledge transfer, news updates and a general function of engagement and sociability.

In the post-modern workplace the coach can be compared to the nomad. Working from organization to organization, from department to department, picking up knowledge, transferring it, passing on tips, insights and stories. Coaches have a collective function – they are important actors in the global workplace, nodal points of communication in the networks of organizations.

Coaching falls into a paradox in that it is both post-modern and new – a hybridity of energy, and yet at the same time it returns to orthodoxy, regaining something that was lost in modernity's striving for efficiency through rationality. At times coaching seems to challenge and break up the dominance of reason, science and functionalism, whilst at other times is seduced by these forces.

The pre-modern and post-modern influences have impacted on the hybrid, adaptive and creative nature of coaching that transcends micro-techniques and searches the soul and the cosmos for a more humane world (Soul Guide Discourse). Coaching also needs a broader perspective that takes itself into the networks of power and influence, into a strategy beyond operationalism and functionalism (see Network Coach Discourse).

Coaching is a turn to the past whilst engaging with an exciting future.

Coaching speaks without fear, saying: 'Yes, let's embrace the spirit. We are the new Soul Guides learning our craft from the ancients and the moderns; we are applying them in a new hybrid spirit and in new forms for the world we find ourselves in today. We are the contemporary confessional, yet without the persecutory elements. We turn to modernity's psychological and managerial approaches yet our search is for resilience, finding ways in which we can adapt, find joy and generosity in our lives and work.'

The hybridity of the coaching sphinx – merging friendship, therapy, managerialism, consultancy and priest – is a great strength, but only if each coach and coaching school finds a way of working coherently in this potential space. Problems can arise when coaches jump between discourses, between modernity and post-modernity, between priest and friend, without the conceptual tools to find coherence in their approach.

What this brief sojourn through the past reveals is that coaching draws from many sources, and should not be pigeon-holed too quickly. Referencing the past to inform the future is important, as coaching can too easily get caught up in its own newness, without reference to history and past helping relationships that reveal something new in each generation.

Coaching's hybridity and plurality – its sphinx-like being, drawing on the past to be awakened to the future – is a strength, not a weakness.

Part III

The Dominant Discourses of Coaching

Introduction

Part III examines the four discourses that underpin coaching as set out in Figure III.1.

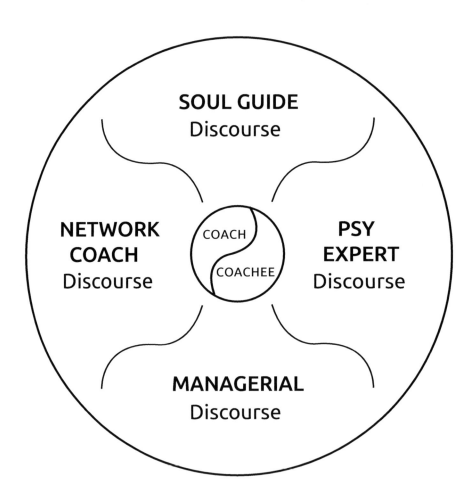

What is Discourse?

Discourse is an institutionalized or normative way of thinking that defines the 'limits of acceptable speech' (Butler, 2004: 64). A discourse determines what can be said and also what cannot be said. Michel Foucault (1972) applied discourse to the social sciences, transforming it from a purely linguistic formulation. Johnson explains:

Michel Foucault (1972) ... rigorously identified and typologized the structures of discourses, emphasizing how discourses affect everything in our society while remaining nearly unobservable. ... For Foucault, discourse is necessarily tied to systems of power insofar as the elite is able to maintain power by controlling what can be said. ... Foucault identifies three types of exclusion that can be used to control discourse: rules that prohibit what can be said, rules that distinguish reason from madness, and rules that determine truth and falsity. (Johnson, 2005)

It is not possible to escape the discourses that shape our inner and external worlds; we are produced and reproduced by society, we are immersed in language and culture. Even our gendered and sexual selves, which are usually considered biological or natural, are bound by the social discourses that create us as subjects (Foucault, 1977/1991; Butler, 1990; Rose, 1996) – binary gender difference and normative heterosexuality are examples of normative discourses that create us as subjects. When we speak of our subjectivity, we speak of our individual and social selves, as the two are inseparable. We are 'subjected' to discourses that produce us, that naturalize and normalize our ways of being. As autonomous subjects we feel, we experience, we follow and we resist these discourses. Heterosexuality is privileged and naturalized in our society for example; and as subjective, emotional and thinking beings, we react to these norms in individual as well as socialized and regulated ways. If we break from the normative discourse, we are disciplined by society in order to attempt to maintain conformity (Foucault, 1977/1991).

We embody the discourses that exist in our culture, our very being is constituted by them, they are part of us, and thus we cannot simply throw them off. (Sullivan, 2003: 41)

Discourses are 'socialized' ways of thinking. However, they are not fixed or static, but fluid and multiple. They are particularly powerful when they work within institutions. Foucault's work shows how the medical discourse not only shapes the institution of medicine, but also has widespread social impact on how society subsequently regulates itself in other realms – how we construct our sexuality or how we interpret sanity and mental illness.

Discourse is closely related to power. However, as Foucault points out, there is not one discourse that excludes or dominates in a hierarchical way:

To be more precise, we must not imagine a world of discourse divided between accepted discourse and excluded discourse, or between the dominant and the domi-nated one; but as a multiplicity of discursive elements that can come into play in various strategies. (Foucault, 1978: 100)

Discourses act in multiple and plural ways. They are not planned by some elite power, yet powerful elites do shape and reproduce those dis-courses which support their power; the discourses of patriarchy of the past century have been reproduced by church, business and state in order to favour the existing male elite in power. Discourses can be an instru-ment of power, creating limitations as to how we act, yet at the same time being:

... a point of resistance and a starting point for an opposing strategy. Discourse transmits and produces power, it reinforces it, but it also undermines and exposes it, renders it fragile and makes it possible to thwart it. (Foucault, 1978: 101)

Foucault reveals that rituals work within discourses to give some voices credibility and power above others. For example, medical professionals are called as expert witnesses and he cites religious, juridical and thera-peutic discourses that have rituals that create elite voices; these voices are given credibility and legitimacy independent of what is being said. Remembering this as we go through the coaching discourses is important. By revealing the discourses that shape our coaching practice, we are able to understand how they influence us, and by revealing them we regain some agency as to how we act within them, as individuals and collective bodies.

A Critical Discourse Analysis of Coaching

The power that is hidden in discourses produces knowledge, 'truths' and norms, placing limits on critical and reflexive thinking. These discourses shape coaches, the coaching profession and the individuals being coached. They need to be explored and revealed so that the power they exert, the way they shape practice, and the inequities and the tensions they hold can be scrutinized and openly contested.

The following four chapters outline themes emerging from a critical dis-course analysis. The methodology for the analysis is outlined below. Critical discourse analysis is not a unified field, but with diverse inputs from different social science and linguistic backgrounds. The discourses outlined in this text are a result of theoretical, social and textual analysis. Norman Fairclough (1995), a leading figure in the development of critical discourse analysis, identified three dimensions of analysis:

- Analysis of discourse carriers (e.g. speech/texts)

- Analysis of discourse production (e.g. how texts are produced and consumed)

- Macro-level analysis (e.g. societal and wider contexts)

The critical discourse analysis utilized here draws on Fairclough (1995, 2001) and Foucault (1977/1991) and also utilizes psycho-social and ethnographic methods. Taking a participant-observer stance whilst practising as a coach, a coach trainer and supervisor (and coachee) enabled me to get an insider perspective from multiple angles, drawing on psychoanalytic methods to analyse the emotional life and unconscious processes that occurred within coaching settings.

This critical discourse analysis was taken over a period of four years, from my time as Director of Coaching at Lancaster University, and it applies the four critical frames discussed in Chapter 1 to this process.

1 Emancipation – examining whether underlying themes within coaching serve to produce autonomy and liberation or whether they promote oppression or conformity (however benign).

2 Depth analysis – drawing on psychoanalytic and hermeneutic frames, the unconscious and under-the-surface themes within coaching texts and practice are reviewed.

3 Looking awry – brings our awareness to new possibilities, to bring new resources to examine existing texts and practice, for example, taking a genealogical approach to use historical material to reveal how contemporary coaching is emerging.

4 Network analysis – provides the frame to examine the social structures, the wider systemic implications of what seems normative or a good thing when looked at from a reductionist perspective.

These frames are applied to:

a Written texts: academic texts, websites, brochures, institutional texts from professional coaching bodies, advertising, conference papers, journals.

b Spoken texts: in coaching sessions, supervision, conferences, informal coaching dialogues, teaching sessions/lectures.

c   Coaching micro-practices: analysis of the form, the techniques and methods of what happens in the micro-practice of delivering coaching; from the dialogues around contracting, to the architectures and materiality of the coaching process.

d   The macro-social: analysing and observing how coaching companies, regulating bodies and educational institutions engage with and produce coaching discourses.

I worked with colleagues, clients and academics to discern meaning from this analysis, and did not use discourse analytic software.

Core to this particular critical approach is to bring one's subjectivity to the research, and to begin from the experience one has. As Miller (2011) writes:

The first time Lacan tried to speak of psychoanalysis, he didn't start from Freud at all, but from his practice. This is what you find in Lacan's text of 1936: 'Au-delà du Principe de realité' ...

He proposed a phenomenological description of analytic experience; thus from the beginning it was a matter of identifying the data of experience. Beginning from experience is a different starting point than beginning from theory or knowledge, yet in reality they are inseparable, as we come to our experience with knowledge and culture.

Experience is particularly relevant to practices such as coaching and psychoanalysis; the critical theorist Bhaskar 'could not really talk about psychoanalysis as a potential science of emancipation without actually having experienced it' (Bhaskar, 2010: 94). To understand and talk about coaching is the same; it has a powerful experiential method and form that needs to be experienced in diverse settings to gain insights into it. Having experience of overlapping professions, such as therapy and counselling, enables a comparative analysis to take place – to know what it feels like to be in the coaching seat as opposed to the therapist chair. To fully understand a discourse, one needs to inhabit it as well as critique it from an external position, whilst guarding against being colonized by it.

This initial discourse analysis sets out four discourses that will require development and further research.

Coaches and coaching theorists, having focused on gaining information about coaching knowledge and technique, also need to observe themselves and their practice from new perspectives: to look at the discourses, structures and mechanisms that inform the 'thinking behind the thinking'.

This analysis reveals that within coaching four discourses currently exist:

• The Soul Guide

• The Psy Expert

- The Managerial

- The Network Coach

These discourses apply to both coaching and mentoring, both are shaped by them, and the way each is practised or taught will depend on which discourses dominate each coaching context. It will also depend on the coach and mentor, on their background, training, skills, experience and capacity to theorize and practise different approaches. Mentoring and coaching, as previously stated, cannot easily be separated or categorized, so it is better for those working in these fields to think about their specific and local application of coaching and mentoring in order to theorize and make sense of what is underpinning their work, and if they should be working in another discourse.

The next four chapters will explore each of these discourses and how they influence and shape coaching. Chapter 10 follows this, discussing not only how coaching approaches work within these four discourses, but also how the discourses interrelate and how coaching works between them.

6   The Soul Guide Discourse

A Mirror to the Soul

Figure 6.1   **The Soul Guide Coaching Discourse (original artwork by Maia Kirchkheli)**

Introduction
Mirror to the soul: coaching the inner self
Spirituality and coaching
The soul at work: humanity, ethics and workplace spirituality
Health warning!
Coaching as a new confessional space
Conclusion
Suggested reading

Introduction

We arrive at truth, not by reason only, but also by the heart. (Extract from Blaise Pascal's *Pensées*, 1670, published posthumously)

The term 'Soul Guide' indicates coaching that transcends the rational and material – it enables a playfulness to explore deep human experience in the unique space created by the coaching pair. The coach holds a 'mirror to the soul' creating a reflective, contemplative space that opens up the realm of wisdom rather than knowledge, being rather than doing, and ultimately is part of the human search for truth, meaning, authenticity and love. The Soul Guide Discourse comes from the past (Soul Healers in different guises) and yet is the most contemporary approach, taking coaching beyond the discourses of modernity (Psy Expert and Managerial Discourses) and into the post-modern realm. Soul Guide Coaching offers a counter-cultural point that claims a different territory, another possibility: beyond the dash to become modern, efficient and productive, beyond 'homo-economicus' and also beyond the therapeutic, whereby the client becomes 'a patient' or a client with a problem. The Soul Guide Discourse represents the aspect of coaching that has emerged from other 'Soul Healers' over the centuries, those in socially sanctioned roles who have worked with the interior aspects of the self – meaning, emotions, identity, the unconscious, the conscience, the human spirit, values and beliefs, existentialism, how to live, how to face loss and ultimately how to face death. Of all the coaching discourses it has the longest continuity and is therefore of special importance.

The soul space is indefinable, yet is accessible through one's experience. Soul Guide Coaching works in this experiential space. The word 'soul' itself is problematic; naming this discourse the Soul Guide is knowingly to risk misunderstandings. Each person will project onto this term their own passions, prejudices and perceptions. To some it evokes a particular religious or spiritual meaning, to others a secular reference to our deep humanity. Soul Guide Coaching enables engagement with these, while how the 'soul' is explored depends on the coach's stance and experience, and the coachee's beliefs and life experiences.

Soul music is a good analogy for this work: music that touches our souls, that comes from spiritual/religious/cultural roots (African American Gospel music), but has merged with many other musical sources. Soul music is not necessarily spiritual, but can certainly touch our spirit. The same is true for Soul Guide Coaching. Let me be clear: the Soul Guide Discourse is not limited to the religious and spiritual; it encompasses secularism, humanism, existentialism, phenomenology, theology and many other ways of exploring the inner self. Essentially this book follows Socrates and Plato to whom the soul was the essence of the person.

Soul Guide Coaching at its best focuses on the inner self, free from utilitarian goals and outcomes. At its worse Soul Guide Coaching uses this approach as an instrumental device to attain high performance performativity. Spirituality, humanity and soul work are then utilized as an instrument or tool towards purely productive performative ends. Surprisingly when these links are made in the coaching literature, rarely are ethical questions asked.

Nancy Kline, author of *Time to Think* (1999), works from within this tradition, whereby her focus on silence and creating a space, rather than chasing goals from the outset, is refreshing. Kline is not explicitly spiritual in her approach but her work is influenced and resonates with her Quaker background, and promotes a thinking environment that comes from the capacity to not rush into action. From an analytic discourse perspective this emerges from religious contemplative traditions.

What happens in the silence? The real art of coaching

'Must we speak?

And if we do, what might we destroy?

How can we know?'

Out of a particular silence comes clear thinking – choice, courage, change. (BACP, 2011)

Soul Guide Coaching is not confined to specific approaches – its discourse is alive and continually present within coaching; yet it often goes un-named, unnoticed or happens in a covert way. Coaches advertise and work in the domain of an Executive Coach; however, they often find themselves doing 'soul work' with their coachee.

Bachkirova (2011) has a chapter entitled 'Coaching the soul' where she explains that this is coaching in relation to the spiritual in its broadest sense focusing on three groups:

1   Potential clients who demonstrate capacities beyond those available to individuals with unformed, formed and reformed ego ... this group can include people who are called mystics and sages ... who can bring their organisms on a regular basis to an unusual state of 'no-self'...

2   Clients who have unusual (spiritual/mystical) experiences and wish to integrate these experiences ...

3   Clients who have a deep interest in the spiritual ...

Bachikrova writes that 80 per cent of the world's population fit into the third category which is why coaching the soul is an important if not an easy subject. I take a broader view that Soul Guide Coaching transcends those who claim no-self, or have unusual spiritual experiences or who have a deep interest in the spiritual. Soul Guide Coaching is a place of refuge from materialism, from instrumentalism; the soul can speak from diverse, unexpected places, connecting our deep humanity that may be described in spiritual terms or in purely human emotional terms. As Deleuze expresses below, even the non-spiritual have souls, just not the archetypal religious/psychological soul we are accustomed to thinking about. Gilles Deleuze claims that the soul is found in a discontinuous surface, a multiplicity of spaces, relations and divisions that are established through a kind of in-folding of exteriority, rather than existing in a psychological system that lies deep within us (Deleuze, 1988: 94–123).

The Soul Guide coach works with a person's experience, and Deleuze's description is helpful in clarifying that whilst the coach works with the inner self, this is not separate from the external, from the 'in-folding of exteriority'. Many coaches work on the premise that within us there is a whole authentic person, a soul to be found, yet as Deleuze says, the soul is found in a 'multiplicity of spaces'. One of these places however is often conceptualized by the coach and coachee as the 'inner self'.

Mirror to the Soul: Coaching the Inner Self

Epiphany, revelation and love: coaching beyond Homo-economicus

The Soul Guide coaches from a place of 'not-knowing', coaching with an openness that allows soul-coaching to take place. This is not about 'therapizing' a coachee; the coach is not looking for unconscious defences or to regress the coachee. However, it is possible to harness the brilliance of Freud, and work with an applied form in a coaching setting that uses the methods of psychoanalysis for a coaching approach that develops an 'associative intelligence' in the coaches and their coachees (this is discussed in Chapter 13 on coaching education).

If coaches learn how to use free association and paternal and maternal containment working with counter-transference and interpretations, then the coach has a working methodology and theoretical base for coaching in the Soul Guide Discourse from an unconscious perspective. This approach differs radically from the Psy Expert approach that focuses on behavioural change rather than a depth analysis that works with the unconscious, existential, deeply human and spiritual concerns using non-directive, non-technique-driven approaches. The outcomes are not to create a more productive employee, but to help the coachee 'locate themselves', to discover their inner and authentic self, which means facing the demons as well as discovering their hidden talents. By discovering themselves in depth, the coachee creates a solid ethical and values base to work from and thereby becomes more grounded and works from a place of grounded authenticity.

The unconscious, the soul and the existential self

Coaching in this open-ended way allows both the unconscious and the soul to come to life in the coaching room. Bettleheim's book *Freud and Man's Soul* discusses how American psychology has become all analysis, to the complete neglect of the psyche or soul (1982: 19).

Let us recall Freud's edict, 'Where Id was there Ego shall be', meaning the task was to make the unconscious more conscious, allowing individuals to liberate themselves. If we follow Bettleheim (1982) and recover the soul work, a coachee can become more aware and able to shape their future selves. Other approaches to Soul Guide Coaching come from philosophical, humanist and theological approaches, a diversity which is welcomed, for example in Jean-Paul Sartre's exploration of 'good faith' and 'bad faith' (Sartre, 2001). This can be very helpful in explorations regarding life's meaning, how it is lived and how we make choices. These are central to the coaching work of the Soul Guide.

This coaching stance opens a space to explore the essence of the self – the existential self, the meaning of lives, angst and joy, fear and frailty, hopes and desires, freedom and confinement, values and meaning.

To coach as a Soul Guide means to work within a cultural and unconscious symbolic order. Working in the space of Soul Guide can take place within any coaching approach, although it is less common in business coaching which focuses more on role and output, and delves less into the deeper inner-work of the Soul Guide coach. Executive and Leadership coaching can set out on a path of goal-focused pragmatism, but in my experience, Soul Guide Coaching very often emerges in an unplanned way and becomes central to the coaching work.

Life-coaching and transpersonal coaching

Life-coaching and transpersonal coaching are the clearest coaching areas in which the Soul Guide Discourse is seen. The website statement below captures the Life-coaching stance that works in the Soul Guide Discourse. It clearly states that spirituality is about 'inner-fulfillment and your true desires', and separates itself from institutional religion.

> *How can Life-coaching help me to explore my spirituality?*
>
> A Life-coach may help individuals to:
>
> Establish their inner dreams and goals
>
> Explore what is really important in their life
>
> Develop a relationship with their inner self
>
> Identify any obstacles in their way and find out how to overcome these
>
> Grow spiritually
>
> Live in accordance with their beliefs and inner values
>
> Learn to live in peace and acceptance
>
> Gain a deeper understanding of where they are now and where they want to be. (Life Coach Directory, 2011)

Transpersonal coaching focuses on personal development that transcends psychological and emotional form and applies transpersonal psychology (also applied to therapy) to coaching:

> ... it is devoted to the idea of development, and holds that we are all on a path of psycho-spiritual development whether we know it or not and whether we like it or not [Wilber, 2000]. (Rowan, 2010: 148)

Stephanie Sparrow writing in *Personnel Today* cites John Whitmore (2002), a leading proponent of transpersonal coaching:

> Transpersonal coaching is useful for coachees who need more than just a framework (such as the GROW model) for a coaching conversation. ... 'They may wish to explore existential or spiritual issues, and this is where transpersonal coaching can be helpful. They may feel something is missing in their life but they are unsure what it is.' (Sparrow, 2007)

The Soul Guide Discourse is represented clearly within this tradition.

Spirituality and Coaching

If a coach explicitly states they are working within the realm of spirituality, this adds a further dimension. Spirituality is a confused category and very difficult to define. It carries meanings that are socially constructed (Gergen, 2001). For some, spirituality may signify a fluffy west-coast idealism or it might be more threatening – 'Is this person looking into my soul?', 'Do they have mystical powers?', 'Are they whackos?' Spirituality may also remind individuals of experiences they have had in religious institutions where they experienced powerful transformative experiences or, conversely, they may feel coerced where power has been abused.

Spirituality remains a contested term (see Box 6.1).

Box 6.1   Spirituality

The term 'spiritual' needs to be problematized and critiqued in order to help make sense of it, as it is not a clearly defined or agreed term. 'Spirituality' is an especially challenging term when used in the context of the secular workplace.

When spirituality is discussed outside of specific spiritual contexts such as different faith communities or religions it becomes challenging because there is not a shared language or normative assumptions to express and define it.

Good secular leadership practice involves ethics, humanistic compassion and creativity, so what differentiates spirituality in leadership? Mitroff and Denton claim that spirituality is interconnectedness:

> If one word best captures the meaning of spirituality and the vital role it plays in people's lives, it is 'interconnectedness'. (Mitroff and Denton, 1999: xvi)

But if it is interconnectedness, how does spirituality differentiate itself from systems theory – biology, network theory and eco-systems? Zohar and Marshall describe spiritual intelligence (SQ) as 'the intelligence with which we access our deepest meanings, values, purposes and highest emotions'. They write:

> In understanding SQ and Spiritual Leadership it is important to list the twelve transformative processes of SQ: Self-awareness, Spontaneity, Vision and Value led, Holistic, Compassion (feeling with), Celebration of diversity, Field-independence, Asking why?, Reframe, Positive use of adversity, Humility, Sense of vocation. (Zohar and Marshall, 2011: 78)

(Continued)

(Continued)

It can be argued that not one of these 12 processes could be separated from the characteristics of a leader with a value-based, humanistic stance. This begs the question, what separates the spiritual leader from an ethical 'good' leader? Being religious or spiritual doesn't always lead to positive outcomes as many a spiritual leader has failed owing to their immoral and unethical acts.

Kierkegaard claimed that the ethical and spiritual are closely connected but not the same. One can be ethical without being religious or spiritual. However, one cannot be spiritual or religious without some commitment and relationship to the divine source or God.

Spirituality is easily then confused with ethics and morality that many non-spiritual people share. Spirituality hopefully leads us to act upon these values 'by their fruits yea shall know them' (this can apply to all spirituality beyond the Christian realm) but this doesn't mean that these values are in themselves spiritual. Conversely the opposite can also be true – spirituality as a tool at work can also lead us into further narcissism:

> Zohar and Marshall use the term Spiritual Intelligence. ... Spirituality paradoxically becomes linked to cognitive intelligence and rationality. ... I was listening to a leadership lecture recently on spiritual development for business leaders, where participants were offered 'executive yoga' in the morning and 'executive meditation' in the evening. I wondered how 'executive yoga' differs from 'yoga'. The paradox is that these techniques are supposed to move leaders away from narcissism and ego, and yet making yoga and meditation 'executive' attempts to make it elite in some way, for the 'special executive'. (Western, 2008a: 179)

Spirituality is differentiated from institutional religion by some people, but the categories are not so clear and further language needs to be used to separate them (Heelas and Woodhead, 2005).

Spirituality signifies something of immanence, transcendence and mythos, as opposed to secularism which is signified by science, rationality, materiality and logos. Spirituality can be inclusive of the latter, but cannot exist without signifying in some way the divine that transcends time and the material world.

It is important to hold these complexities in mind when considering spirituality and coaching. Taking a spiritual stance, the coach needs to be aware that they will stimulate powerful positive and negative transferences and unconscious projections from their coachees. These projections are not about the person, but about the person-in-role: *'my spiritual coach'* who can take on the primitive desires we either want to be saved from, or we unconsciously desire; i.e. a perfect caring mother: *'She's amazing ... so insightful, and such a good person, it's like she can read my soul.'*

A coach, like a therapist, can be seen as a secular form of the priesthood, and a coach who acknowledges their spirituality moves closer to this idea of the secular priest. There are far too many examples of priests, pastors, therapists and coaches who fall from grace when they become seduced by idealized projections and transferences. Therapists are highly trained and supervised to increase their capacity to be self-knowing while priests work in institutional settings that provide some containment and safety for them.

Coaches are much less well protected. The training and self-work is much more limited than therapy and they work in a more informal setting with a less rigorous division of roles (coaches may go to dinner with clients whereas therapists don't). Supervision is also limited in coaching.

When a coachee seeks a 'spiritual coach' they bring with them a set of expectations and perceptions both about themselves and about the coach. Taking a critical view of spiritual coaching is therefore vital in order to safe-guard and learn from this important practice as there are too many examples of spirituality and power being abused or misused.

Coaching from a spiritual place can overlap with secular coaching from a deep ethical and humanist space. Table 6.1 (Western and Sedgmore, 2008) shows a coaching framework that can be interpreted from a spiritual or secular place. This may also be a useful framework for pastoral care, pastoral counselling and for spiritual directors, as well as Soul Guide coaches.

The Soul at Work: Humanity, Ethics and Workplace Spirituality

This section examines the Soul at work, taking an ethical perspective and critiquing how organizations, theorists and managers can utilize the soul, spirituality, subjectivity, emotions and identity in explicit and subtle 'coer-cive' ways to increase productivity and profit, at the expense of authentic human development. Reviewing this work with coaching in mind, there is an important 'health warning' for coaches, that is, to refrain from being seduced to partake in coaching that espouses 'soul' or depth work, yet in practice is helping to produce what Casey refers to as 'designer employees' with a 'capitulated sense of self' (Casey, 1995).

Soul hierarchies

Alan Seiler (2005) promotes soul work and writes in *Coaching to the Human Soul* (Vol. 1):

The concept of soul can sound elusive and esoteric, either a religious notion or a 'touchy feely' concept that is unrelated to the practicalities of everyday living and the functioning of organisations. To take this approach closes off a dimension, and a higher order, of learning that is relevant to both personal and organisational learning. (Seiler, 2005: 10–11)

Table 6.1   A secular and spiritual coaching framework

Secular		Spiritual
Silence. Reflection. Free association. Stream of consciousness.	**Thinking space**	Silent contemplation. Meditation. Prayer. Grace – opening to the divine.
Pairing with coach – bringing hope through the birth of new ideas. Recognizing strengths and achievements. Holding the space when painful and anxiety provoking. Future focused. Finding exceptions to problems. A humanistic optimism.	**Hope**	Pairing with coach – pairing with the divine, bringing hope through engaging the spirit. Recognizing charism – God's gift to each of us. Holding the space when in 'the dark night of the soul', offering spiritual hope! Accessing the good news of different religious/ spiritual teachings. A faith in a better future.
Playing with ideas. Fun – art – creativity. Getting in touch with the unconscious and the body.	**Imagination**	Engaging with the infinite creativity of the divine. Tapping into one's spiritual nature and source.
Connectivity across boundaries, building relationships, stakeholders' awareness.	**Network**	Connectivity of all things. Divine or cosmic unity and holism. Deep ecology. Finding God in and through relations with others.
Identifying who to speak to next. The move from thinking to action. Application of coaching process to the workplace.	**Knowledge exchange**	Finding the truth through listening to others and to the divine. Moving from contemplation to action. Application of coaching to 'spiritual life', ethical behaviour and social justice.

Seiler talks about higher order of learning, following Maslow (1976), Wilber (2000), Torbert (1993) and Beck and Cowan (1996), who tend to insert hierarchic stages into their popular 'theories', stages such as spiral dynamics and integral psychology. The popular interest in Wilber's and Beck and Cowan's work has its critics, who write that whilst the theories claim inclusivity, they can be seen as socially elitist and authoritarian. In his spiral dynamic theory Beck characterizes developmental tiers for individuals, and suggests that 'Spiral Wizards' have the capacity to make superior decisions and manufacture consent at lower levels. This rhetoric of tiers, levels and wizards reflects the hierarchical nature and worryingly the 'magical' qualities of these special people. This language feeds narcissistic personalities with big egos who can easily misuse spirituality in the workplace.

Spirituality and profit

> The notion of the soul is connected to enduring organisational concerns of performance, productivity, organisational success and competitive advantage. (Seiler, 2005: 11)

There is a distinct lack of critical thinking in this domain. To develop spiritual/human awareness in whatever form is usually related to states of humility, the loss or overcoming of ego-states, and is certainly non-materialistic according to the great philosophical and religious teachings. When Seiler links the soul to gaining productivity the warning bells sound.

The links between spirituality and profit are clearly separated by John Whitmore, who sees that people want more in their lives. Spirituality and religion have both always promoted social justice, but at the same time they can act in a coercive way.

Case and Gosling discuss the instrumentality of spirituality at depth in their excellent article 'The spiritual organisation: critical reflections on the instrumentality of workplace spirituality' (Case and Gosling, 2010). They trace how religion/spirituality and work focus on the task of improving employee's working conditions:

> ... the relationship between the organization of work, religion and spiritual life is hardly new to social science. Indeed, analysis of this relationship is foundational to the social theorizing of Weber, Marx, Durkheim and Freud in considering the emergence of Methodist, Calvinist and Quaker corporations during the Industrial Revolution. (Case and Gosling, 2010: 258)

However, religion and work were never a straightforward altruistic act. Religious morality inspired positive changes that were influential in humanizing the workplace, but they also carried an ideology that underpinned a paternalism that accompanies the philanthropy. For example, the Quakers made exceptional progress in workplace conditions but this was also aligned to profit and to imposing their Quaker morality:

> What convinced Quaker magnates of their approach, however, was not so much the moral strength of their position but its commercial results: managing the labour force decently was good for business. (Walvin, 1997: 183)

Walvin continues:

> The Quaker magnates tried to maintain a distinct moral tone at work. ... The Rowntree family insisted on decorous behaviour to and from the factory ... recruited workers from 'respectable homes' ... and refused to

employ married women in the belief that they should care for hearth and home; single mothers were never employed. (1997: 191)

Walvin concedes however that:

> it is not to diminish the motives or achievements of Rowntree, Cadbury or other industrial philanthropists to suggest that their pioneering welfare projects should in fact be judged as contributions to [a] new style of industrial management, rather than as exercises in Quaker inspired benevolence. (1997: 190–191)

The links between workplace and spirituality have always been multilayered with multiple agendas, some designed to harness the soul to maximize profit, others to offer employees opportunities to be fully themselves at work, and sometimes both.

There is now a renewed interest in workplace spirituality, which is influenced by 'New Age spirituality' and the 'unchurched' movement (Wexler, 1996; Bell and Taylor, 2003; Heelas, 2008), whereby spirituality is taken out of religious institutional settings, and becomes personalized and immanent rather than transcendent. Workplace spirituality follows the 'turn to subjectivity' (Woodhead, 2004) and the shift from manual labour to cognitive labour. Utilizing the subjective and cognitive self at work means engaging with emotions and the identity. Employees are expected to bring their whole person to work, and this inevitably leads to the interest in workplace spirituality.

Whyte indicated this trend as early as 1956 when writing about the new 'organization man':

> No one wants to see the old authoritarian return, but at least it could be said of him that what he wanted primarily of you was your sweat. The new man wants your soul. (1956: 365)

Emotions and identity, and the spirit/soul, are now harnessed for the purpose of ever greater productivity. Popular publications in this field include:

> Barrett (1998) *Liberating the Corporate Soul*, Conger (1994) *The Spirit at Work*, Howard and Welbourn (2004) *The Spirit at Work Phenomenon*, Jones (1996) *Jesus, CEO*, Klein and Izzo (1999) *Awakening Corporate Soul*, Lodahl and Powell (1999) *Embodied Holiness: A Corporate Theology of Spiritual Growth* ... (Case and Gosling, 2010: 277)

Bringing the whole self to work

Humanists, diversity and inclusion experts, and spiritual and faith leaders, talk about bringing the 'whole self to work', claiming this to be a good thing. This allows someone to bring their sexuality, their faith and their 'whole person' to work, creating a better environment for them and for the company, the idea being that if the employee can be 'whole' they will feel happier, and also be more engaged and therefore more productive for the company. The individual, society and the company then benefit.

This 'holistic' approach is commonly regarded as part of the coaching territory. Coaches can help an individual integrate themselves to the company values. On the flip side, it is argued that this 'bringing the whole self to work' is a colonization of the self by the company, which wants your soul purely to increase productivity and profit. Tourish and Tourish (2010) argue that:

> ... the workplace is not a useful medium for people to find the deepest meaning in their lives ... [l]eaders of business organisations are not spiritual engineers or secular priests, charged with responsibility for the human soul, and business organisations are not a suitable forum for exploring such issues. (Tourish and Tourish, 2010: 219)

Health Warning!

There are dangers that management techniques attempt to create organizational cultures that harness the employee's 'soul' to the company in order to maximize productivity. Coaching then can become a 'tool' to help achieve this. Messiah Leadership (see Western, 2008a) explicitly attempts to engineer strong cultures by setting out visions and values that followers identify with in order to foster a tight cult-like company culture that 'frees' employees to act (Kunda, 1992; Tourish and Pinnington, 2002). Collins and Porras, in their best seller *Built to Last* (2000), claim that 'the most difference in having an enduringly great company was the greatness of the leader'. In their chapter titled 'Cult-like cultures' they write:

> In short, understanding that cult-like tightness around an ideology actually enables a company to turn people loose to experimental change, adapt and – above all – act. (2000: 123)

Peters and Waterman in their bestselling book *In search of Excellence* describe excellent companies with strong cultures as:

> Fanatic centralists around core value ... yet as one analyst argues,
> 'the brainwashed members of an extreme political sect are no more
> conformist in their central beliefs'. (1982: 15–16)

These authors praise 'cult-like' totalizing cultures that may score high on employment engagement surveys, but they also prohibit dissent and promote uncompromising conformity.

Sometimes these leadership styles and cultures refer explicitly to spirituality and the soul, and at other times it's implicit. Much of the transformational leadership literature (Burns, 1978; Bass, 1998) links goodness, authenticity and self-actualization to leadership without specifically referring to spirituality (Bass, 1998: 171).

Yet as Grint points out, this leadership carries in its language images of prophetic religious leaders:

> During the 1980s, charismatic leadership returned with a vengeance,
> complete with all the accoutrements of biblical charismatics including
> visions missions and zealot like disciples. (Grint, 1997: 13–14)

In this scenario, coaching drawing on soul work shapes the self to the demands of the organizational culture. The coach is working on an agenda to colonize the self to fit the company. A false self is created, a performative, purely productive self that 'performs to the norms' in order to keep job and career on track. Coaches working in this area then become a part of the socialization process, using the language of liberation but working unthinkingly towards a process of domination.

Coaching then can become a part of the management apparatus to colonize the soul. There is a big drive in corporations to align personal and organizational values, which has the obvious danger of creating homogenized and totalizing workplaces. Coaching around company values, behaviours and leadership competencies needs to develop robust critical insights in order to resist being used to create conformist cultures.

In defence of Soul Guide Coaching

Having critiqued workplace spirituality and the use of culture control in organizations, there is something vital and intrinsic to our humanity, identity and experience that is closed off if we ignore this Soul Guide Coaching Discourse in the workplace. Without Soul Guide Discourse, coaching becomes purely a materialistic process focusing on efficiency, performance and productivity.

To coach in the Soul Guide domain it is important to be aware of the dangers. If you are coaching on performance, choose your approach! Move away from Soul Guide Coaching and into the Psy Expert Discourse; do not contaminate or bastardize the work with the soul! This is not to compartmentalize, but to allow soul work to take place without reducing it to utilitarianism or economic gain.

Having set out the critical position and the dangers, the next section will express how Soul Guide Coaching can be beneficial and how the coach works within this discourse.

Locating ourselves: a Soul Guide Coaching exercise

In my work as an executive and leadership coach I experience coachees from diverse backgrounds, many of whom feel dislocated. I share this 'countertransference' with them, this generic state of displacement. Many coachees respond immediately as it speaks to their emotional condition; they are not desperately lost, nor are they necessarily very unsettled, alienated or disorientated, yet they don't feel located or grounded. They are displaced, they don't know their place, they do not have a place. They feel ungrounded and dislocated from place. The coaching work here is to 'locate the self'. One coaching exercise I do is called 'Locating Ourselves' where I take coachees to an art museum, usually the Tate Modern, and offer them a series of questions as they wander the vast space of the Turbine Hall, and then associate with the artwork in the gallery (see Box 6.2).

Box 6.2 Locating Ourselves: Coaching Exercise in Art Gallery

You have one hour to wander the gallery, with the objective of using the art and the space to reflect on how you locate yourself in the world of work. To locate ourselves means different things to different people as it raises questions of identity, of perception, of hope and aspiration, and of family and cultural inscriptions upon our bodies and thoughts.

Questions to reflect on as you wander, look and experience

- Who are you?
- What is your place?

(Continued)

(Continued)

- Where are you from?
- Where is your home?
- Who are your people/community?
- How does work define and relate to your identity?
- How much do you estimate, as a percentage, your identity is defined by your work/profession?
- How does technology play a part in constructing who you are, as a professional and as a person?
- (As you wander the gallery jot down notes in relation to the art and its impact on you.)

Probing questions for reflection

- What makes you feel 'located' and grounded?
- What dislocates you and makes you feel fragmented or alienated?
- (When looking at the artwork and also at the space, try to be open and responsive to what emerges.)
- What thoughts are triggered?
- What pictures/art do you distance yourself from and walk away – why?
- What feelings does the art work stir? What memories? What shadows?
- What associations?
- What is your body saying?
- What connections are you making?
- What are you left curious about?
- What are you left preoccupied by?

We work on who they are and what their place is. The aim of this work is to locate the coachees in a material world, to develop an associative intelligence, and to help them develop an ethical self.

Gary Snyder writes:

> ... place, and the scale of space, must be measured against our bodies and their capabilities ... to know that it takes six months to walk across Turtle Island is to get some grasp of the distance. (1990: 105)

To be located is to find our place – geographically, in our family, at work, in kinship groups, in community, in faith, in ourselves. Finding our place and locating ourselves as individuals and collective groups is, in my experience, one of the greatest challenges of our times, and Soul Guide Coaching provides the space to do some of this very important work. The flexibility of relocating the coaching pair from a desk to a virtual place, or to an art gallery, is an example of how coaching can usurp the more static/modernist therapeutic approaches. In this emergent space, coachees are achieving different insights and transformations through unexpected ways, without focusing on goals. An authentic self is explored, and the results are powerful. I coached a senior leader in the banking sector working in a new international regional role: our work began in the Managerial and Network Coach Discourse, focusing on role and how to influence change in a large geographical network, but soon we found ourselves in the Soul Guide Discourse, working on his inner self; so I took him to the Tate to do the locating exercise, which completely opened up new perspectives and allowed a new exploration of his work/life.

Coaching beyond function and utility is what Soul Guide Coaching is; yet at the same time, as the above shows, the executive makes important links to their work. But measuring this empirically would be very problematic, and I would argue a waste of resources. Qualitative research, however, might be very useful.

Coaching as a New Confessional Space

Western man has become a confessing animal. (Foucault, 1978: 59)

I will now turn to how the confessional links to the Soul Guide Discourse, claiming that coaching is the post-modern confessional. This does not refer to a sinner–priest relationship, as the confessional has been transformed into a space that allows a multiplicity of confessions, of desire as well as sin, as a place where the coachee can confess and at the same time discover our doubts, anxieties and preoccupations, and in doing so discover and explore our authenticity and the making of the self.

Confession is deep rooted in the Western cultural psyche, and has taken on new populist forms in the past two decades. Coachees find themselves often unwittingly confessing their desire and/or anxieties to a coach, even when the coach may be contracted to do performance-focused work. This is somewhat true in mentoring relationships as well, although the external coach offers a more confidential and specific context for the confessional to take place. The coach has the option (if trained and able) to take up the role of Soul Guide, to stay with the coachee on this journey.

Modern and post-modern society stimulates the desire for confession, to tell 'the other' about our desires and fears, to disclose our secrets. We confess

Figure 6.2   **Confession box, Krakow, Poland (photograph taken by author, 2011)**

privately and publicly to friends and to TV cameras. The talk show became a vital instrument of confession:

> Oprah Winfrey, Jerry Springer ... and all their imitators were evangelists of the talking cure who believed that secrets are a slow-working poison to the soul, and that confessing them in a public forum has a healing effect. ... Whatever their motives for appearing they acquiesced to the idea that disclosing to a national audience their misdeeds and emotional afflictions would cleanse their soul. (Cobb, 2005: 255)

Confessing in the popular media, in magazines, TV radio talk shows, and also in 'high' culture too, autobiographies are filled with confessional stories. Confession can be liberating for two reasons: firstly because it unburdens an individual, and secondly because of the symbolic meaning of the confession – within it resides a redemptive promise 'to be forgiven'.

Coaching is inscribed by contemporary culture and produces a new confessional space for the coaching pair. To coach as a Soul Guide is to listen to the confessions of the coachee, to hear their hidden desires, fears, angst and anxieties.

The new coaching confessional is a conversational place freed from the baggage of having to achieve goals, regressive reflection or unnecessary guilt. It is ultimately where *human* meets *human* in the coaching relationship, replacing a more transactional engagement where *technocrat* meets *employee*.

Confession can have negative connotations of being sinful or of being judged. However, in contemporary society, it transcends this perspective and the confessional becomes also a place of discovery, a place where the self-examination takes place in an open way; where our shadow side is revealed, where insights and revelation take place.

The confessional journey

In a coaching session, the confessional discourse takes on meaning with wider and more constructive outcomes than a religious or psychotherapeutic 'confession' because of the different parameters at work. Under religious confession the penitent (the modern day coachee) undergoes self-examination and confesses sins (deeds and thoughts) to the priest who is authorized on behalf of the Church and God to give absolution and penitence.

Foucault wrote that psychoanalysis was the inheritor of the religious confessional (Foucault, 1978), while in psychotherapy, the secular priest (analyst, therapist or counsellor) holds a socially sanctioned ritual where the client undergoes a self-examination, revealing their interior selves. 'Bad' deeds and hidden and forbidden thoughts are spoken in therapy that aren't spoken elsewhere: *'I cheated on my wife and feel really guilty* [or *don't feel any guilt]', 'I have a fantasy about sleeping with other men', 'I hate my home life but my partner thinks we are getting on fine and wants to get married.'* Therapy offers psychic and emotional reparation in place of the religious absolution.

Coaching now provides a new privatized space for the confessional to occur. Foucault recanted his earlier work on confession where he realized that confession could work without the repressive hypothesis, i.e. confession went beyond governance, domination and control (Foucault, 1980; Butler,

1990: 164). Confession had another aspect whereby the confessant could 'constitute a truth of oneself':

> ... the self constitutes itself through discourse with the assistance of another's presence and speech ... the point is not to ferret out desires and expose the truth in public, but rather to constitute a truth of oneself through the act of verbalization itself. (Butler, 1990: 163)

A particular 'speech act' – the making of the self

The act of coming to a coach is to make a particular kind of 'speech act'. Verbalizing one's inner thoughts to a professional confidential listener, a socially sanctioned witness (the coach) changes conversation into another form of speech that acts upon us in a different way. Just speaking in this context is itself an act of transformation. Speaking in a coaching session is to speak oneself into existence. The speaker is also the listener. The coachee often doesn't know what is going to be said until it is spoken, and can be surprised by the content as if listening to another person speak. The transformation happens when thoughts are materialized into sounds and words made by the throat, voice and tongue, so that the witness and the speaker physically hear what they say. In this way the coachee materializes themselves; and they discover and produce themselves through this 'speech act'.

To achieve this, a confessional site is required, with a speaker and a listener/witness (a credible socially sanctioned person), and the best site is one that is freed from a repressive (religious) or pathologizing (psychotherapeutic) hypothesis. In coaching, the coachee is more in control of their confession and also of their redemption and reparation. They are not forgiven by a religious or secular priest, as the coach doesn't inherit the same level of symbolic power as the priest or the psychoanalyst whose words carry a sacramental power, supported by ritualistic form. The coach and coachee collaborate to work on the reparation; some of it happens through the act of confession, sometimes through acts outside the session. Sometimes the reparation is based simply on insight, and has nothing at all to do with sinning.

Private and public confession

> We have become a singularly confessing society. The confession has spread its effects far and wide ... the confession became one of the West's most highly valued techniques for producing truth. (Foucault, 1978: 59)

The religious confessional began as a public act before becoming a private act, taking place for centuries in the religious confessional booth. By becoming a private act, taking place between the new powerful dyad – penitent and priest – it paradoxically became increasingly powerful as a social form of control in England. In the twelfth century a law was passed making confession obligatory. Foucault writes how this had the impact of re-enforcing individuality.

> The truthful confession was inscribed at the heart of the procedures of individualization by power. (Foucault, 1978: 59)

The impact of the private confessional helped produce the new modern subject – the reflective, individualized self, who internalized a 'Big Other' (God). This ensured that each individual examined their conscience, developing a strong super-ego and conscience, self-policing and monitoring their behaviour and thoughts.

The reflective, individuated thinking we take for granted today in the West was not always the case (nor is it universal, though becoming more so with the expansion of capitalism and modernity). When the modern person confesses their sinful and desirous selves to a professional confidant(e) (counsellor, priest, coach) many argue that this reinforces a privatized, capitalist, individualized and atomized society (Putnam, 2000; Furedi, 2003). Yet in the past two decades the confessional has become once again a public event, a spectacle for the masses, a form of entertainment. The confessional has permeated the social in such a way that there is a social compulsion to confess, both privately and publicly, and a huge desire to be a confessional voyeur. Perhaps it is because we learn about ourselves through other people's struggles and perhaps there is an element of sadism, where people enjoy observing another's pain.

Oprah specializes in star confessions, and she leads from the front.

> Oprah confesses that she's fallen off the weight loss wagon. The medical and emotional issues that contributed to her weight gain. Plus, how she's getting back on track with the help of Bob Greene and making a commitment to live her best life .... (Oprah Winfrey Online, 2011)

Jackee Holder, a Life-coach, follows this pattern and writes on her website:

> Like many of the clients I see, behind the scenes of my public life there was a whole other drama. There was a huge secret that I carried. What you saw on the outside wasn't always reflected on the inside. ... From the outside looking in, you wouldn't have known that

> I was often living a life that was in chaos. Sometimes barely meeting my bill payments, procrastinating on things that would help my business, managing my time ineffectively and so it went on. (Holder, 2011)

She then shows the path to redemption:

> Along the way I learned how important it was to practice self-care, to nurture my creativity, which is so often the source of my productivity.

Celebrities such as Ricky Martin, 'who confesses that for most of his life he faced an inner struggle', are invited onto Oprah shows to confess their inner struggles, and be it sexuality, drink and/or drugs, they come to Oprah and to publicly confess, to tell all. The masses love to identify with the emoting star, who receives huge fees to publicly cry, to show remorse and then to disclose how they have overcome their struggle, to wild audience whooping and applause.

At another level, Jerry Springer shows us how the spectacle of the public confession replaces the past fetish of the public hanging; poor and marginalized people come on to confess their sins before a baying crowd. Publicly confessing seems to achieve three things:

- It makes the immortal mortal, bringing the celebrity into our own world of messy emotions.

- It rehabilitates the star – they make public reparation and in return regain the public adoration.

- 15 minutes of fame – it creates a celebrity status for individuals who are marginalized outcasts.

The desire for the confessional seems insatiable in today's society.

Forgiveness, absolution and penitence

To be absolved, the Catholic Church teaches that the religious penitent should:

1 Be contrite (feel sorry)

2 Confess (speak the deed/thought)

3 Offer penance (put right – by prayer or deed)

The coaching version of the confession also offers a space where these three conditions apply, and the path to redemption is followed through offering penance by deed and self-acceptance.

Self-forgiveness

In coaching, forgiveness (absolution) and penitence come in two ways. Firstly self-forgiveness and self-acceptance are part of the physical process of coming to the coach and verbally confessing – '*It is such a relief to finally speak about this to someone; I have been hiding from myself for years.*' By the very act of turning up and speaking of their emotive lives in the session the client confesses and demonstrates contrition: '*I am being open with myself, facing myself, doing what is right.*'

The other way a coachee is forgiven is through the socially sanctioned coach accepting their account without passing a negative judgment upon them. The contemporary professional 'ear' is trained to be non-judgmental. Simply being accepted as who you are, with empathy and without negative judgment, seems to have a powerful 'soul healing' impact that triggers forgiveness. Being accepted by the coach often precedes the personal acceptance and forgiveness. Atonement may follow if the client chooses to change their behaviour, apologize to an injured party, make reparation for their deeds or indeed their neglect – '*I never told my father I loved him. I think I will write to him.*'

A skilled coach working in the domain of the Soul Guide also has an active role. They must initially create the space for the confessional (paternal and maternal containment) then take up the role as guide for the conscience. The Soul Guide is not a spiritual director as they do not speak on behalf of a greater power or try to interpret the coachee within any specific religious tradition (unless this is specifically agreed between coach and coachee who share a belief/ faith system). The Soul Guide can be a very challenging role – it does not have the protective rituals, uniforms or setting of a priest/psychoanalyst, and can therefore only be undertaken when a lot of trust has been achieved. Knowing when to confront the coachee about their authenticity, duplicity or the dissonance that exists between their feelings and their speech is skilled work.

The coaching site is a new post-modern confessional, an important part of coaching that requires more attention. It is a cultural phenomenon, and produces personal growth, subjective truth, and seems to be an important part of how individuals create their selfhood and identity in today's society. The Soul Guide Coaching Discourse is the coaching space where the confessional, alongside other 'inner self' work, takes place.

Conclusion

> The Freudian Pair enables the analyst and (client) to feel the echo of his or her being. ... It is like seeing one's soul in a particular type of mirror. (Bollas, 1997: 40)

The coaching pair can also enable the coachee to feel the echo of his or her being, to see their soul in a particular type of mirror, yet the coaching mirror is very different to the psychoanalyst's mirror. The Soul Guide 'mirror to the soul' is a more diverse mirror, bringing different reflections to the coachee. What differentiates Soul Guide Coaching from other discourses is that the Soul Guide coach does hold a mirror, moving it to different angles, to show the coachee different perspectives of themselves, whereas other discourses are more active and externally focused in their approaches.

With Soul Guide Coaching, something strange happens in this coaching space. The truth speaks itself into this space, often surprising both parties.

When training and supervising new coaches they are often surprised and can be overwhelmed at the material the coachee reveals, as one coaching supervisee put it:

> ... we were working on his career goals then there was a pause, and the discussion suddenly changed; Mark (the coachee) said he didn't really like his job, then he elaborated and said he detested it. He went on to say his whole life was a mess and I was dumbfounded ... he looked stunned too, and there was a tear in his eye.

A confidential coaching conversation creates a potential space for many diverse conversations; the strategic, the business, the organizational, the team, and also a confessional conversation that opens the way for Soul Guide Coaching.

The social speaks through us

The Soul Guide coach is an unconscious carrier of culture, inheriting aspects of the social role of the shaman, doctor, priest and psychotherapist, all of whom enact and embody the Soul Guide Discourse. It has passed through many incarnations, it has morphed and changed, and the coach is the latest post-modern receptacle of this discourse. The coach is a new incarnation of the professionalized listener, the 'socially sanctioned ear'. The experienced and 'in tune' coach becomes accustomed to this soul work; they feel the stirrings of the soul and make a space for it, respecting it. They hesitate before offering a 'clever coaching question' to fill the space, to show their efficacy, instead pausing with an inner stillness that allows the coachee to reveal themselves. Coaching in the Soul Guide Discourse is to create this potential space, offer emotional containment for the coachee as they locate themselves, and to offer Soul Guidance to the coachee as they work in the space of 'becoming'.

The Soul Guide Coaching learns from what Burrell (1997) calls 'retro-organization' and draws upon the pre-modern soul healing traditions, and

acts as a bridge between the pre-modern and the post-modern. It is developing a hybrid coaching approach that delivers a post-modern confessional, a
space for lightening the burden of the world and contemplative reflection –
for exploring meaning, identity, emotions and experience.

It is post-modern in the sense that it draws on the therapeutic yet it is not a
therapeutic intervention; it draws on religious heritage and yet is very clearly
a non-religious practice; Soul Guide Coaching is a post-modern hybrid practice. Religious and therapeutic approaches impose meanings onto confessional,
pastoral and psychological relationships, whereas the post-modern coach has
a new freedom, and moves between approaches, whilst treating modernity's
insistence on rationality, utilitarianism and scientific reductionism with disdain.
The Soul Guide holds an important place on the coaching map that counters
the excesses of other discourses, and places truth, personal experience and the
soul as central to coaching work. It has particular resonance in today's world
as it allows the self to be explored, free from the therapeutic search for the
wounded self, and free from the striving to achieve goals and outputs.

Strengths

The Soul Guide offers a unique place in coaching; it holds with the traditions of the shaman, the monk, the healer and the 'wise counsellor'. It
challenges modernity's obsession with rationality, progress and order.
The Soul Guide is vitally important owing to the increasingly marginalized spaces in society for such conversations and explorations to take
place, free from the burdens of religious dogma or therapeutic pathologizing tendencies.

The Soul Guide opens a liminal space, pauses and hesitates, listening to
the heartbeat of the conversation rather than only its content. It is the coaching space where the post-modern confessional takes place; a site that wel-
comes disorder, where the unconscious is liberated to speak, where the soul
itself finds its voice, where desire is heard, and an individual's subjective
truth is found. This is not easy work but takes courage from both parties.
The Soul Guide then coaches the individual to help them live their life with
more meaning, desire, generosity and authenticity. The consequences of this
work can be profound, often in subtle and unexpected ways, to the coachee
and to those around them.

Challenges

The inexperienced or inauthentic Soul Guide may use the rhetoric of spirituality, soul work and the authentic self, whilst actually reproducing narcissism.

Asking a coachee about their desire does not mean working without the 'reality principle' (see Chapter 13), avoiding responsibilities in relationships, or offering unreal coaching advice such as 'You can be anything you wish to be.' Promoting narcissism and false choice is a weakness that undermines deep soul work. 'Love-ins' can take place in Soul Guide Coaching, when a collusive mutuality forms, where both parties unite against a bad external world, enjoying their time together but not doing the real soul work. Spirituality can also be used subtly and coercively to align an individual to a corporate vision in order to make the coachee more conformist and more productive.

To be a Soul Guide coach is to coach from a place of life experience, insight and maturity of spirit, and Soul Guide Coaching cannot be taught through techniques and skills training. Soul Guide Coaching requires the coach to undergo a personal formation process. Training can help develop the coach but it's a longer term and more challenging process and therefore coaching courses often omit this discourse when offering the quick-win coaching technique approaches.

Suggested Reading

Bachkirova, T. (2011) *Developmental Coaching: Working with the Self*. New York: Open University Press.

Bell, E. and Taylor, S. (2004) 'From outward bound to inward bound: the prophetic voices and discursive practices of spiritual management development', *Human Relations*, 57 (4): 439–466.

Case, P. and Gosling, J. (2010) 'Wisdom of the moment: pre-modern perspectives on organizational action', *Social Epistemology*, 21 (2): 87–111.

Heelas, P. (2008) *Spiritualities of Life: New Age Romanticism and Consumptive Capitalism*. Oxford: Blackwell.

Rowan, J. (2010) 'Transpersonal coaching', in E. Cox, T. Bachkirova and D. Clutterbuck (eds), *The Complete Handbook of Coaching*. London: Sage, pp. 146–158.

7 The Psy Expert Discourse

Coaching the Outward Self

Figure 7.1　The Psy Expert Coaching Discourse (original artwork by
　　　　　　Maia Kirchkheli)

Introduction
The Psy Expert Discourse: a product of modernity
Therapy culture and the Psy Experts
Technicians of the psyche: Psy Expert coaching
Psychodynamic and humanistic approaches to coaching
Conclusion
Suggested reading

Introduction

Psy is a term used by Nikolas Rose (1985, 2011) and others to refer to the Psy professions of psychology, psychiatry, psychiatric social work, psychotherapy, etc. Rose relates the rise of the Psy professions to 'therapeutic governance' (Rose, 1990) and other social impacts. Drawing on Foucault, the rise of the Psy expert is both a reaction to social change (alienation in modern society for example) and also a producer of social change. The Psy expert and therapeutic culture produce a subjectivity that impacts on wider society–changing how we think and producing an increasingly individualized reflective self (some say increasingly narcissistic and neurotic). Therapeutic culture and the Psy Experts shape how we create our identities, how we make sense of our emotions, what is permissible and what is not. This is sometimes referred to as the Psy complex:

> **Psy-complex** The set of professions dealing with the psyche: psychology, psychiatry, psychoanalysis, psychotherapy, psychiatric nursing, and psychiatric social work. The term derives from the work of Michel Foucault and French post-structuralists as Jacques Donzelot and Robert Castel, who analysed the role of the social and 'psy' professions in regulating family life, sexuality, mind, and rationality. (Marshall, 1999)

This chapter will explore the links and the impact that the Psy Expert Discourse has on coaching, which draws heavily and increasingly on it. The main focus of this chapter is the coach as a 'technician of the psyche'. There is a growing movement in coaching towards psychology, expertise in techniques and evidence-based practice, all of which emanate from a particular strand of Psy Expertise, the clinical psychological and scientific (or pseudo-scientific) elements. The humanistic psychotherapies and psychoanalytic and existential approaches can fit within the Soul Guide Discourse or the Psy Expert depending on how they are performed. What we are concerned with in the Psy Expert Coaching Discourse is the rapid growth in tool- and technique-driven psychological coaching practice which is underpinned by psychology drawing on science and rationalism.

Coaching in this discourse begins with individual examination, diagnosis and assessment – 'What are your challenges, issues, problems, goals?' – followed by Psy expert interventions based on micro-change psychological technologies such as CB (cognitive behavioural), NLP (neuro-linguistic-programming) or solution-focused coaching.

Psy Expert coaches work as 'technicians of the psyche'; their aims and claims to success are based on the ability to change cognition and behaviours that inhibit success, and to encourage (and make resilient) positive behaviours that enhance personal performance.

The chapter begins by charting the rise of Psy Experts and their impact on society, revealing how Psy Expertise has an effect beyond the treatment or coaching of individual clients. Psy Experts are more than a body of knowledge or thought, and therefore the discourse produces a way of thinking in society that has entered coaching.

> Suppose we consider psychology not as merely a body of thought but as a certain form of life, a mode of practising or acting upon the world. We could then seek to identify what one might term the techne of psychology: its distinctive characteristics as skill, art, practice and set of devices. (Rose, 2004)

It then outlines how the Psy Expert coach works in the domain of the *outward self*. I use the term the 'outward self' to indicate that in Psy Expert the coaching focus is less on personal growth, depth work or on the existential or spiritual self (Soul Guide) but more on personal performance, and how we relate to others through our thoughts and 'outward' behaviour. In the case of executive coaching, the Psy Expert coach is clearly mandated to help an individual employee change their behaviour to fit with the norms of the company, often measured by competencies and values. More than other coaching discourses, the coach clearly claims credibility from the professional expertise that comes from the particular Psy discourse informing their work, including CBT, NLP, and clinical or occupational psychology.

Kilburg's definition of an executive coach neatly sums up the Psy Expert Coaching Discourse:

> Executive coaching is defined as a helping relationship formed between a client who has managerial authority and responsibility in an organization and a consultant who uses a wide variety of behavioral techniques and methods to assist the client to achieve a mutually identified set of goals to improve his or her professional performance

and personal satisfaction and consequently to improve the effectiveness of the client's organization within a formally defined coaching agreement. (Kilburg, 2000: 65–67)

Note the focus is on *identifying goals*, and using *behavioural techniques and methods* to *achieve the goals* for *professional performance* and *personal satisfaction* and to *improve the effectiveness* of the client's organization. This approach to coaching highlights some of the key words in the Psy Expert Discourse. Lewis-Duarte (2009) cites Stern (2004) to show how CBT might be useful in coaching a leader:

> To facilitate learning, a coach can help a leader better understand current behavior and communication style as well as identify alternative behaviors. Then, the coach can help the executive practice and perfect specific performance management skills (Lewis-Duarte, 2009: 10–11).

The Psy Expert Discourse is familiar and popular as it offers techniques and methods tried and tested in the fields of education, management and health. It has entered into the wider social domain through popular culture. Psy Experts are socially sanctioned and are especially welcomed into the managerial world, because the Psy Expert draws upon the same underlying premise as the manager: scientific neutrality and effectiveness through rational approaches.

The Psy Expert Discourse: A Product of Modernity

> Coaching is both a practice based in psychology and a psychological process based on behaviour change. (Zeus and Skiffington, 2002: 3)

Freud entered the scientific milieu from the outset, realizing his new profession of psychoanalysis required the legitimacy of science to be recognized. Psychoanalytic seminars are still today called 'scientific meetings', in spite of the clear lack of empirical 'scientific' evidence to support these claims (Popper, 1963).

The Psy Expert Discourse began with Freud, but became hugely influential in society after the liberal, individualistic 1960s. Psy professionals initially mimicked a medicalized/scientific way of thinking about the psyche and emotions, working within the realm of symptoms, diagnosis and treatment of a pathologized *'wounded self'*. Carl Rogers (1951) in the human potential movement then adapted and shaped the Psy Expert in line with a more positivistic, individualistic, humanistic and democratic ideal, following the United States Declaration of Independence (1776) which famously pronounced 'life, liberty and the pursuit of happiness' as being the unalienable right of all men. This was taken on board by the human potential movement who connected therapy with the idea that through working on yourself, happiness becomes possible (see the 'wounded and celebrated self' p. 1).

This is an interesting reworking of the Puritan work ethic, the American Dream, the growing individualism and the potential of therapy to be used beyond Freud's claim that it could turn 'hysterical misery into ordinary unhappiness' (Freud and Breuer, 2004). Sachdev identifies how some therapeutic models are more suited to the happiness project than others, and coaching has adopted these with relish:

> The idea of therapy being used to increase one's happiness may sit better with some therapeutic models, such as Cognitive Behavioural Therapy (CBT) which is based on the assumption that our attitudes can be changed to improve our affects and emotions (Neenan and Dryden, 2004), or the person-centred approach, which posits self-actualisation as the ultimate need of all humans (Rogers, 1961). (Sachdev, 2011: 7)

Other therapeutic approaches such as psychodynamic and existential are present but are much more marginal in coaching. Sachdev cites Van Deurzen (2008) who argues that all therapists need to be 'realistic' and not to focus purely on pathology or on happiness but to be able to stride the whole spectrum of human existence. The preference in coaching leans to positive happiness and particular Psy Experts who are more technique focused than holistic.

The idea of the 'self' was changing in the post-1960s culture; a new subject was being produced where happiness became possible through 'working on the self' as well as through 'working in the world' for material gain, satisfaction through work, relationships, achievements:

> The therapeutic has expanded into popular culture at every level, which is permeated with its messages: trust your feelings, have faith in yourself, follow your bliss, do your own thing, listen to your inner-child, do what you feel's right, be true to yourself. These messages are offered as formulas for salvation. (Cobb, 2005: 252)

Strong links appear between the therapeutic and emergence of coaching. Coaching developed the notion of expanding the 'therapeutic values that one could organize one's life around' (Cobb, 2005: 252) and imported them into the workplace through the new Psy Expert, the coach, carrying with them their coaching toolkit, psychometric tests and psychological credentials.

Zeus and Skiffington (psychologists) clearly reveal how psychology is influencing coaching:

> Coaching like therapy is clearly a psychological process. When a coach is dealing with the inner psychological world of the coachee, he or she is functioning within the realm of therapy. (2002: 10)

Linley (2006: 2) supports this view and says the Psy Expert influence is increasing as it is 'moving to a new generation with psychology and evaluation becoming a new force in coaching'.

Coaching imported and drew upon the Psy discourse because of the success of the techniques found in the Psy professions. Ives makes a common assumption about the differences between coaching and psychology/therapy:

> While therapy primarily addresses feelings, coaching is focused on changing actions (changes in feelings are a consequence). (Ives, 2008: 100)

This repeats a coaching mantra that is an over-simplification, because there is no unified therapy or psychological approach, nor is there a unified coaching approach. The differences between a behavioural or CB (cognitive behavioural) psychologist and a psychoanalyst is much greater than between a CB therapist and a CB-trained coach. A CB psychologist may work in clinical practice and as a coach; and whether working in therapeutic milieus or in coaching, they bring the same toolkit and theories with them. It is the challenges facing the 'client' or coachee and the context of the work that differ (although even here there are overlaps).

Those pushing for psychology-informed coaching (led by psychologists) are bringing coaching ever closer to the psychological mindset that focuses on the individual, with little focus on the team, the organization and other social aspects. The Soul Guide, Network Coach and Managerial Expertise Discourse can become marginalized when the focus is on individual change, behaviour and performance, although coaches with broader skills and experience will work in other coaching discourses, and make the important connections between them. However, the emphasis is on the individual and this skews coaching towards an atomizing, individualist and reductionist view of the social world.

It is important to note that influences are never uni-directional but are reciprocal, and coaching in turn influences the Psy professions and therapy, bringing a new focus of working with well-being and positive change. Coaching has been strongly influenced by Psy professions (Peltier, 2001), a factor that has been contested within coaching circles, mainly because the Psy Expert approach focuses too much on reflection and individuals rather than on activity and the organization. Gray (2006) argues 'it is far from clear why coaching should necessarily so often adopt a psychotherapeutic approach' and (Ives 2009: 109) says that psychotherapeutic approaches are actively discouraged by some coaching training organizations as it blurs the line between coaching and therapy.

The Psy discourse shows however that a) there are many reasons to draw upon and learn from psychotherapy b) that even those coach training programs that try to avoid psychotherapeutic influences use them unconsciously or by default, i.e. there is no escape from the Psy discourses influence in coaching, c) the dualistic polarised debate, coaching versus therapy, is an outdated and tired debate; the questions now should be about correct and appropriate use of therapeutic influence, and balance between the Psy discourse and the other discourses that differentiate coaching.

Therapy Culture and the Psy Experts

To understand the importance of the Psy Expert Discourse in coaching we must first look at how the therapeutic permeates all aspects of the social. Psy Experts intervene in our lives and are closely associated to 'therapeutic culture' (Lasch, 1979; Furedi, 2003). Rieff (1966) wrote *The Triumph of the Therapeutic*, identifying the dominance of therapeutic culture in our society. Since the 1960s therapy culture has expanded exponentially, permeating all spheres of our life-worlds (Habermas, 1987). Rose explains how the influence of the Psy Experts has an impact on how individuals become self-governed, and how they produce a self that is explained through therapeutic language:

> It is against this background that we can locate the emergence of a second cluster of technologies for the government of the autonomous self: those associated with the 'psy' knowledges of human individuals, groups and the determinants of conduct. ... Today, psychologists elaborate complex emotional, interpersonal and organisational techniques by which the practices of everyday life can be organized according to the ethic of autonomous selfhood. (Rose, 1999: 89–90)

The coach as a 'Psy Expert' is a further development in the expanding therapeutic regime. The Psy Expert Discourse is a particular aspect of 'therapeutic culture', focusing on the expert technical aspects of psychology rather than the more diffuse, humanistic and psychodynamic approaches.

These Psy Experts draw upon a myriad of therapeutic and psychological approaches, but they share in common the rhetoric of science and rationality, claiming the same moral neutrality as scientists and managers (MacIntyre,

1985). The dominant Psy expertise in coaching comes from the technique and methods adapted from psychological interventions that are reductive and focus on micro-cognitive and behavioural change. Lewis-Duarte highlights a common view that coaching has become a behavioural science, that is delivered through the technique:

> Simply put, the key impetus and fundamental assumption behind executive coaching is to create behavioral change in the workplace ... (Lewis-Duarte, 2009: 18–19)

Yet to achieve behaviour change via communication over a few coaching sessions is very difficult and is often overstated. As researchers point out, coaching's empirical evidence is lacking to support these claims.

> The current literature on executive coaching identified a lack of empirical research regarding all facets of the industry. With the rapid expansion of executive coaching as an organisational intervention, there is a great need for empirical research that helps coaches succeed [Goldberg, 2005; Lowman, 2005; Sperry, 1993; Thilo, 2004]. (Lewis-Duarte, 2009: 103–4)

If the Psy coach claims to be effective by influencing behavioural change that impacts on organizational efficiency, they work in the same mode as MacIntyre's manager. The Psy coach often works together with the Managerial Discourse, which when used together link personal performance to organizational productivity. The two clearly fit well, as they are underpinned by the same modernist and scientific theories.

Psy disciplines cover a broad church, but their coaching is dominated by behavioural and goal-focused approaches. Humanistic and psychodynamic approaches are very visible in coach training, literature and practice; however, the tools and technique approaches are favoured by coaching practitioners and educators because they are more concrete, and offer something tangible, demonstrable and saleable, and they are easy to train.

On the other hand, the psychology, technique and behavioural approaches do not address certain challenges, for example:

1 *Emotions and Experience.* Coaching inevitably triggers emotions and disclosures (see coaching confessional and as Kilburg (2000: 173) says, 'coaches must prepare to confront and manage these most challenging and interesting aspects of human behavior'). Breaking thinking and behaviour down is a reductive process; it can help in some areas, but more complex emotional dynamics and relational experience cannot be treated like an empirical rational experiment.

2   *Organizational Dynamics.* There is a very tenuous link between personal behaviour change and organizational change (Fleetwood and Hesketh, 2006). Role expectations, personal authority, leadership, followership, the exercise of power, team dynamics, customer relations, organizational culture, complex network relations, IT systems and socio-technical processes are not covered within the Psy Expert Discourse.

Technicians of the Psyche: Psy Expert Coaching

> The end goal of executive coaching frequently is sustained behaviour change; this is best achieved through the application of established psychological principles. Psychologists have a duty to define the competencies required to achieve sustained behavior change through the medium of executive coaching and to be proactive in conveying these standards of competence to the public. (Brotman et al., 1998)

This quotation neatly sums up the focus of the Psy Expert coach. They gain legitimacy from being 'technicians of the psyche'. They are trained in a wide variety of techniques, applying psychology and psychotherapy to different levels of competence and training. When working in executive or business coaching the Psy Expert should also incorporate the Managerial Discourse into their work, making strong connections between an individual's changes, the coachee's role and the work outcomes that are desired.

The danger with Psy Expert coaching is that it imports psychology/psychotherapy under the banner of coaching. Whilst the language of coaching may be different, the underlying logic doesn't change – it retains a very individualistic stance without connecting the person to their role or the organizational network (Network coaching). If the coach is working with an individual outside a work context, then Psy Expert coaching can focus on the goals and performative gains an individual wants to make in regards to their life and relationships. The coach will analyse the inhibitors to their success, and plan interventions to help them make progress. Interventions will vary from visioning exercises, anxiety control or cognitive coaching to overcome negative thinking.

Tools of the trade: psychometrics

Executive coaches who utilize the Psy Expert Discourse often use psychometrics and 360-degree feedback tools. Psychometrics are huge business:

the value of psychometric tests sold every year to UK organisations is more than £20 million ... In the United States, it is suggested that the value of sales of psychometric tests and inventories for recruitment, team and personal development is in excess of 100 million US dollars per year. ... More than 3.5 million people around the world annually complete the Myers-Briggs Type Indicator personality inventory (MBTI). (Briggs Myers, 2000: 5)

Harper (2008) traces psychometrics back to the earliest days of the Psy Experts: Jung's influence on archetypes were the foundation of the MBTI, and then the behaviourist Eysenck developed his Personality Questionnaire (EPQ) which was the forerunner of many of today's personality tests. Harper points to the need for psychologically minded coaches to do psychometric testing (Harper, 2008: 48).

Other psychological techniques and tools are manifold (see Zeus and Skiffington, 2002) and draw on the scientific methods of rationality, order and reductionism. They use these techniques to classify 'challenges' in emotions or behaviours into component parts, analyse them and offer remedies and solutions.

Psychometrics and other Psy Expert sanctioned tools are the perfect fit for coaches and managers as they are tangible, they give kudos to the coach, and they give actual data and results. The usefulness of different tools and how they are used is hotly debated. However for coaches they offer a perfect entry point to executive coaching.

Positive psychology

Positive psychology is an excellent example of the Psy Expert morphing and adapting to the times. Positive psychology fills a gap beautifully – psychology was too deficit focused, and there grew a need for positive emotions, meaning and engagement to be studied under the psychology umbrella. By focusing on empirical scientific methods and language, 'the science of happiness', the legitimacy and attention gained has been a big success. Positive psychology is, however, critiqued by psychologists themselves, for many reasons – for being too 'one-size-fits-all', for not being inter-relational, for missing cultural and contextual insights into happiness, for focusing too much on the individual, for being 'separatist' between happiness and the rest of the emotions, and for being negative about negativity (see Christopher and Hickenbottom, 2008; Fernández-Ríos and Cornes, 2009 for a full critique).

That is what positive psychology is about – it goes beyond the treatment of depression and anxiety to ways in which we could all live more rewarding lives. The exercises it offers include the systematic practice of kindness, gratitude to others, counting your blessings, and exploiting your strengths rather than attacking your weaknesses. It also teaches resilience and optimism. (Layard, 2011)

Box 7.1   Applying Positive Psychology to Coaching

Coaching is a practice in search of a backbone, two backbones actually: a scientific, evidence-based backbone and a theoretical backbone. I believe that the new discipline of positive psychology provides both of those backbones ...

First the theory: positive psychology is the study of positive emotion, of engagement and of meaning, the three aspects that make sense out of the scientifically unwieldy notion of 'happiness'. Positive psychology attempts to measure, classify and build these three aspects of life (Seligman and Csikszentmihalyi, 2000). Practising exactly these three endeavours may bring some order into chaos by limiting coaching's scope of practice.

Second, the science: positive psychology is rooted in empirical research. It uses traditional methods of psychometrically established measurement, of experiments, of longitudinal research, and of random assignment, placebo-controlled outcome studies to evaluate whether interventions work. It discards those that do not pass these gold standards as ineffective and it hones those that do pass (Seligman et al., 2005). Coaching with these evidence-based interventions and psychometrically established measures will help set the boundaries of responsible coaching practice. (Seligman, 2007: 266)

Solutions-focused coaching

Another popular approach from the Psy Experts is solution-focused coaching. It is easily taught as a method and its popularity again is its focus on the 'positive' and because it is a brief intervention, is goal focused, claims quick success and has a simplicity that is great for coaches to learn quickly:

Change what's not working; do more of what works; scaling and the miracle question are all useful coaching interventions.

Solution-focused approaches, for example, originate in the observation that significant change occurred in clients when they talked about their 'preferred futures' (O'Connell, 2006: 339), so this approach already incorporates a focus on goals in terms of desired states. ...

The 'miracle question' is a key technique within this model, where clients are prompted to 'generate a description of life without the problem' (O'Connell, 2006: 341). This helps to clarify what clients really hope for, what they may have already done towards improving the situation and what strategies are likely to be helpful. (Sachdev, 2011: 9)

Solution-focused (SF) therapy has been directly imported into coaching as it fits easily with the ideas of well-being at work, technique-driven change, and it is brief and claims high efficacy. In practice the SF approach can provide useful additions to other coaching approaches, but on its own does not suffice, as it is self-limiting and repetitive if over-used. Techniques and methods such as SF coaching have a place, but when they override the breadth of human experience and holistic insights that include the context, and the underlying causes of a persons behaviour, they tend to miss the important things. Psychoanalysis teaches us that we often enjoy our symptom (Zizek, 2001) we even fall in love with our symptom – and whilst our ambivalence takes us to a coach or therapist to change it, the paradox is that we defend our symptom to the death (sometimes literally). The only way to get real or sustainable change can be to understand what the symptom signifies, not to simply seek to remove it, as a symptom is so often a symptom of something else. This is not just about pathologic states, but about how we live in mundane, everyday life. The idea of describing 'life without the problem' as posed by the miracle question, therefore, is so often the wrong question; and like many coaching questions that focus on happiness and solutions, they start from the wrong place. When you start from the wrong place you nearly always lose your way.

The dangers of positive psychology and the happiness imperative

Barbara Ehrenreich critiques this positive thinking, in her book *Bright-Sided: How the Relentless Promotion of Positive Thinking has Undermined America*, not only claiming 'that on a personal level it leads to self-blame and a morbid preoccupation with stamping out "negative thoughts". ... On a national level, it has brought us an era of irrational optimism resulting in disaster' (Ehrenreich, 2009). In her introduction she offers a view that contradicts the idea of American 'happiness', in spite of the cultural 'happiness imperative':

Surprisingly, when psychologists undertake to measure the relative happiness of nations, they routinely find that Americans are not, even in prosperous times and despite our vaunted positivity, very happy at all. A recent meta-analysis of over a hundred studies of self-reported happiness worldwide found Americans ranking only twenty-third, surpassed by the Dutch, the Danes, the Malaysians, the Bahamians, the Austrians, and even the supposedly dour Finns. In another potential sign of relative distress, Americans account for two-thirds of the global market for antidepressants, which happen also to be the most commonly prescribed drugs in the United States. (Ehrenreich, 2009)

Put succinctly, Beradi writes:

Depression is deeply connected to the ideology of self-realization and the happiness imperative. (Beradi, 2009: 99)

Cognitive behavioural coaching

Cognitive approaches aim to change coachees' 'irrational' core beliefs into 'rational' beliefs (Neenan and Dryden, 2004). This approach is clearly desirable in workplaces because it 'is direct, straightforward and results-orientated' (Peltier, 2001: 96). Workplaces like to focus on 'management by objectives', goals and targets. Cognitive Behavioural coaching is used to challenge self-limiting beliefs. Peltier, referring to cognitive coaching, believes a strength of coaching is that 'the coach could (and should) tell you that you are thinking poorly. ... A coach can teach you how to improve the quality of your thinking' (Peltier, 2001: 81). Cognitive coaching approaches make use of imagery, mental pictures, visioning. The claims are that coaches using CB approaches identify with the coachee, faulty thinking and irrational beliefs, and coach to make a cognitive adjustment.

CBT offers coaches techniques, empirically tested methods and claims to success. Its supporters are many, including health systems and national governments. The government of the UK in 2009, for example, invested £173 million to train and employ 10,000 CBT therapists. However, whilst CBT claims great success, Oliver James (2009) finds disagreement:

Work by the eminent US psychologist Professor Drew Westen et al. (2004) found that two years after treatment, two-thirds of those who had CBT have relapsed or sought further help. Findings for anxiety are similar; a large Scottish study, published in 2005, found that only 18 per cent of patients who had received the therapy for anxiety still had no symptoms two years after treatment. If given no treatment, most people with depression drift in and out of it. After 18 months, those given CBT have no better mental health than ones who have been untreated.

Apart from the efficacy of CBT versus other coaching or therapeutic interventions, there is a long-standing antipathy to this psychologically designed
formula for working with people. Jacques-Alain Miller, the Lacanian psychoanalyst, discusses in a journal:

> *Le Point*: And how would you define cognitive behavior therapies?
>
> *J Alain Miller*: As for CBTs, they are training and conditioning
> techniques and not at all psychotherapies. They only take observable
> behavior into account and when they integrate psychic functioning,
> it is only in terms of the treatment of information. In times past an
> eminent mind, the Soviet Pavlov, revealed the efficiency of condition-
> ing, in the dog. To influence humankind using the same means, is
> horrible ... (Miller, 2005)

A similar critique is made by Laing about behavioural therapy, he claims
that 'An inhuman theory will inevitably lead to inhuman consequences'
(1967: 45) and explains:

> Behaviour therapy is the most extreme example of such schizoid
> theory and practice that proposes to think and act purely in terms of
> the other, without reference to the self of the therapist or the patient,
> in terms of behaviour without experience, in terms of objects rather
> than persons. It is inevitably therefore a technique of manipulation
> and control. (Laing, 1967: 44–45)

The over-riding critique is that cognitive behaviourist approaches separate
the person from their whole experience, treating them as a separate object,
rather than an authentic person in relation to others.

Psychodynamic and Humanistic Approaches to Coaching

The Psy Expert Coaching Discourse is dominated by psychology, usually
drawing on psychometrics and cognitive behavioural techniques, yet
from psychoanalysis there is another tradition that is closer to a contemplative practice, and overlaps with the approaches from the Soul Guide
Discourse.

   Aaron Beck, one of CBT's founding theorists, differentiates the circum-
scribed goal approach of CBT from the open-ended 'evocative therapies' of
psychoanalysis and client-centred therapy (Beck, 1976: 320). Psychoanalysis
can be very pathologizing, ultra-clinical and elite, giving the analyst a lot of

power (that at times is misused – see Masson, 1990), yet at its purest and best, psychoanalysis offers coaching a different and creative coaching path. Gilles Arnaud writes of the psychoanalytic trained coach:

> It is a matter of letting oneself fall into that particular state that Lacan (1970) termed 'semblance', which entails creating a silence within and becoming deeply persuaded that, relative to oneself, one knows nothing. ... Indeed, were the executive coach to aim at instantly instigating improvements in the client's management and to conceive the goal of psychoanalytically oriented executive coaching in terms of change or solution, we feel that the chances are high of his or her missing the mark. ... The client tends therefore to be considered as an object to be modeled rather than as a subject. (Arnaud, 2003: 1147–1150)

This is similar to how Bion, from the Tavistock psychoanalytic tradition, drew on Keat's use of the term 'negative capability':

> man is capable of being in uncertainties, Mysteries, doubts, without any irritable reaching after fact and reason. (Keats, 1970: 43)

Bion regarded the analyst's role as to find an inner space that allowed that 'Patience should be retained without "irritable reaching after fact and reason" until a pattern evolves' (Bion, 1984: 124).

Semblance and negative capability signify a move back to the contemplative traditions of the desert monks. The monk creates a physical space (a monastery or cell/cave in the desert) and also in themselves, away from the world's noise and disturbance to empty themselves in order to be filled with the Holy Spirit (other, Eastern meditative traditions have similar practices). In psychoanalysis a space is created, whereby the emptying is of the neurotic noise and activity of the ego and super-ego, to allow the unconscious to speak. In coaching, there is a capacity to hold a space, to manage the anxieties, to dash to action, to contain the anxiety of not knowing, and to listen. This can release something far more profound and creative than dashing for goals and results.

The psychodynamic Psy Expert approach is a polar opposite in many ways to the scientific-rationalism of CBT and clinical psychology approaches imported to coaching. Yet psychoanalysis traditionally loses itself by trying to claim scientific efficacy, yet it is struggling to find a different sort of truth, other than scientific truth.

Arnaud highlights two points. Firstly 'semblance', the art of holding silence and a state of not-knowing, realizing that the coaching work is neither in the coach or the coachee, but between them. Secondly, the route to coaching success is through a meandering path, rather than a direct route. This takes me back to the beginning of the book, which discusses 'Looking Awry' – to get to the truth one has to look from a different place. In coaching, the perceived wisdom is that the coach's gaze is direct, the goals are set out, and the coach targets them with the coachee; it is rational and hopefully measurable. In contrast the psychoanalytic approach is to create blurring, to offer a disruptive intervention by saying, 'Let's forget goals for a while; just breathe and when you're ready talk … speak about what's on your mind, your preoccupying thoughts. What's present in the here-and-now?' Psychoanalysis shows us that there is another path in coaching. Differing from therapy, the coach doesn't contract to coach for many years, and attempt to regress the patient or create dependence, but works with associative intelligence and containment, providing a very special space for the coachee to become fully a subject, rather than an object to be changed. Western (2006), in *Coaching at Work*, identifies that the psychoanalytic method can apply to coaching in the following ways:

- *The Coach as Container* – offering structural and emotional containment to coachee.

- *Not Knowing* – the coach fosters an attitude of open curiosity and the ability to tolerate the unknown.

- *Free Association* – encouraging new ideas and thoughts to emerge from the unconscious.

- *Hope* – arises from the coaching pair (Bion, 1961) working together and giving birth to new ideas. This can be frustrated by the interference of too much technique, where the coach takes expert lead.

This article goes on to discuss how other insights, such as defence mechanisms, projections, transference and counter-transference, parallel process learning, splitting and the reality principle, are all helpful to coaches to understand the relational dynamic and to support developmental learning. The 'reality principle' is a very important concept that coaching can learn from, particularly for the coaching approaches with a hyper-positive energy claiming that 'individuals have all the answers and resources within them' – the reality principle helps balance this, and gives the coach the reminder that others in the world exist, that economic and material worlds exist, that everything is not possible, and that to learn developmentally, to make any gains, means facing and overcoming loss and frustration as well as utilizing self-belief.

When applying psychodynamic approaches to coaching the key difference to therapy is to apply them without a pathologising lens or creating regression and the dependency culture of the classic psychoanalytic method.

The coaching aim is to work with the coachee collaboratively, to engage with the unconscious, to increase insight and creativity, and to work in a hopeful pairing. This is in contrast to the psychoanalytic goal which is to regress the patient, then repair and rebuild through increasing personal insight over the long term.

Those practising psychodynamic coaching are often influenced/trained as therapists and carry a 'pathologizing tendency' that attracts and produces a 'wounded self' coachee. The psychodynamic coach works more on the inner self, and if used creatively, the psychodynamic coach works between the Soul Guide Discourse and the Psy Expert Discourse, working on how the inner self, the inner theatre, is enacted in outward behaviours, thoughts and relationships.

The same applies to humanistic approaches to coaching. Carl Rogers and existential approaches used in coaching are anti-technique and aim to 'follow the coachee', and when used in a more 'purist way' they fit into the Soul Guide Discourse, working with the inner self to try and find the authentic, true self. Contradictions occur when these approaches are mixed with technique-driven approaches, so non-directive theory is mixed with directive approaches; then the discourse switches to the Psy Expert Discourse. Moving between discourses is clearly something that happens, and when done thoughtfully can be excellent coaching practice. However this is different from confusing theoretical ideas that are contradictory; then the coach and coachee end up in a mess.

Underpinning psychodynamic approaches and person-centred humanistic approaches are the effects of 'therapeutic culture'. In my experience, some therapists/counsellors from psychodynamic traditions make excellent coaches, if they manage to transcend pathologizing and clinical world views, and use the insights and methods in new ways.

Conclusion

The Psy Expert Discourse is currently flourishing in coaching, which is becoming increasingly instrumental in its use of tools and techniques, its focus on short-term goals and its claims to transform people. Clients come with a desire to be happy, to perform better at work and in life, and the Psy Expert claims efficiency in this domain. Coaching bought by managers means that the Psy Expert Discourse is dominated by those approaches that mirror the Managerial Discourse, claiming science, rationalism and measurable goals.

Coaching is about working with people, and inevitably draws upon the traditional territory of the psychologist, helping coachees manage anxiety, overcome fears, and discuss interpersonal relationship difficulties whilst working on building confidence and improving performance.

Psy Expert coaching 'to produce an improved outward self'

To improve personal performance in work and life through behavioural and cognitive modification is the aim of most Psy Expert coach interventions (the psychodynamic/humanistic traditions may work beyond these aims).

Organizations use this method to produce the employees that conform and meet their requirements, competencies, values and behaviours and specifically improve their performance. HR functions set out company values, and then identify behaviours to match those values.

The promise of coaching is dual: for the individual it promises to help them discover and reach their true potential in performance, whilst reducing the problem areas. For the company it aims to align the employee's behaviour with the company's values and raise their competencies and performance.

Mentors draw much less on these Psy expertise skills as the mentor is less likely to be an externally trained expert in Psy disciplines than a coach.

> Unlike coaching where psychological methods often migrate to informing practice and brands of coaching (see for example Solution Focused Coaching or Cognitive Behavioural Coaching) mentoring draws on this literature to inform and challenge rather than create practice. (Garvey, 2010: 350)

There is a strong argument from Psy Experts that *all* coaching should fall in line with the Psy Expert Discourse. Bluckert adds his voice (2006: 92), suggesting that 'psychological mindedness' should be a standard proficiency in executive coaching. There is a 'turf war' going on for the heart of coaching, and for the economic benefits that accompany the winners. Psychologists are a well-organized body, and are moving in on the coaching territory and having a big impact. Gable and Haidt (2005) cite President Robert F. Kennedy and contend that psychology too offers an incomplete picture of human life.

> 'The gross national product does not allow for the health of our children, the quality of their education, or the joy of their play. It does not include the beauty of our poetry or the strength of our marriages; the intelligence of our public debate or the integrity of our public

officials. It measures neither our wit nor our courage; neither our wisdom nor our learning; neither our compassion nor our devotion to our country; it measures everything, in short, except that which makes life worthwhile'. ... It is our contention that the gross academic product of psychology as it exists today provides an incomplete picture of human life. (Gable and Haidt, 2005: 106)

If coaching follows Martin Seligman's (2007) aims to 'limit the scope' of coaching to the narrow ends of the Psy Expertise Discourse, then much will be lost from the profession. Psychology, and Psy expertise with the scientific method, would not just provide Seligman's backbone for coaching, it would provide an 'iron cage'. The moves towards this state are already happening, as can be seen in the constant calls for standardization, evidence-based practice and psychology-trained coaches.

Strengths of Psy Expert coaching

Psy Expert coaching is technique driven and promises short-term interventions that have an impact on personal behaviour and performance. Coaches can learn basic techniques in short time frames, therefore saving money, and it makes the entry to becoming a coach more accessible. Using techniques is also a container of anxiety (for both the coach and the coachee) as it gives a clear framework for the coaching work, which alleviates the anxiety of not knowing what to say in a session. Psy Expert coaching aligns easily with managerial thinking, offering psychometrics, behaviour change and improving competencies. Psy Expertise coaching also aligns coaching with the kudos and legitimacy of other Psy professionals, to make it more acceptable in the market place. Psy Expert coaching is goal focused and behavioural, and the focus on the outward self means the changes are visible (or should be) to others and if measurable fit with evidence-based practice, which, in turn, fits with HR teams to 'prove' efficacy.

Psy Expert coaching, from humanistic, existential and psychodynamic approaches, also offers a way into the unconscious and holistic experience of the coachee and creates a useful bridge for the coach working between the Soul Guide and Psy Expert Discourses.

Challenges of Psy Expert coaching

The technique-driven approaches are less likely to have the depth of impact of approaches that work in a deeper existential way through Soul Guide Coaching. The approach is by necessity reductionist, therefore issues that are complex and relational are missed. Whilst many of the techniques can be quickly learnt by coaches, the Psy Expert coach may unlock powerful emotions and psychological dynamics for which they may not be well trained to handle. The Psy Expert coach often has limitations in their capacity to effect change in the work domain, as they are focused on the individual rather than role and the work. There is no engagement with strategic or systemic thinking in the Psy Expert Discourse. Therefore any changes will be personal. The greatest danger of the Psy Expert Discourse is that at its worst it repeats the mistakes of the past. Laing claims that if we use techniques that treat humans as if the person is 'an object to be changed rather than a person to be accepted' then 'an inhuman theory will inevitably lead to inhuman consequences' (Laing, 1967: 45). The workplace can and does often become inhuman, and coaching must not align itself to this by focusing on high-performance through thought–behaviour modification at the cost of understanding wider causation, ethical questions and systemic power relations. The Psy Expert Discourse is part of coaching – yet within it there must be room for more than just the short-term, behaviourist and goal-focused approaches.

Many psychologists and therapists make excellent coaches, and many do not. A therapist wearing a coaching mask is doing poor therapy and poor coaching. Coaching will be informed by the Psy Expert Discourse but must not be totally colonized by it.

Suggested Reading

Brunning, H. (2006) *Executive Coaching: Systems-Psychodynamic Perspective*. London/New York: Karnac Books.

Ehrenreich, B. (2009) *Bright-Sided: How the Relentless Promotion of Positive Thinking has Undermined America*. New York: Henry Holt and Company.

Furedi, F. (2003) *Therapy Culture*. London: Routledge.

Kilburg, R. (2000) *Executive Coaching*. Washington, DC: American Psychological Association.

Newton, J., Long, S. and Sievers, B. (eds) (2006) *Coaching in Depth: The Organizational Role Analysis Approach*. London: Karnac.

Peltier, B. (2001) *The Psychology of Executive Coaching: Theory and Application*. New York: Brunner Routledge.

Rose, N. (1996) *Inventing Our Selves: Psychology, Power and Personhood*. New York: Cambridge University Press.

Zeus, P. and Skiffington, S. (2002) *The Coaching at Work Toolkit*. Roseville, NSW: McGraw Hill.

8 The Managerial Discourse

Coaching the Role Self

Figure 8.1   **The Managerial Coaching Discourse (original artwork by Maia Kirchkheli)**

> Introduction
> The coach's gaze: role and output
> The Managerial Discourse: a critical perspective
> Coaching and the Managerial Discourse
> Role actualization
> Conclusion
> Suggested reading

Introduction

This chapter reflects on how the culture, rhetoric, practices and assumptions that underpin the Managerial Discourse influence coaching. Managerialism is a way of thinking and doing that transcends the workplace and enters into all aspects of modern life. Coaching appropriates this Managerial Discourse for its own use, whilst recognizing that coaching is also colonized by 'managerialism'. Coaching and management are mutually implicated in each other's development; however, coaching is very much the younger and weaker sibling in this relationship.

I am not claiming that coaches lose their coaching role and take on a managerial role, but that the thinking and practice of coaching become infused and underpinned by the logic of managerialism.

The Managerial Coaching Discourse has evolved through three key influences:

- Coaches working with managers in organizations are influenced by the Managerial Discourse that dominates organizational culture.

- Many managers become executive or internal coaches, importing their managerial assumptions, skills and knowledge into coaching.

- Management consultancies and business schools that deliver coaching and train coaches also import their existing 'managerial' knowledge, skills and assumptions to coaching.

The Managerial Discourse brings a positive contribution to the knowledge and skill-set of coaches, whilst at the same time imposes managerialist models and mindsets on coaching. Henry Mintzberg writes that contemporary management is:

> mostly about the *soft stuff* – working with people, doing deals, processing vague information, and so forth. But the fact is that business schools have been trying to teach the soft skills for years,

yet the calls for more never cease. What is going on? The soft skills simply do not fit in … they get lost amid all the hard analysis and technique. (Mintzberg, 2004)

The paradox of contemporary coaching is that it entered the managerial world to bring expertise to deliver this 'soft stuff', yet in doing so, the Managerial Discourse has colonized and shaped much of coaching, whereby the coaching focus is becoming ever more focused on 'hard analysis and technique', thus repeating the mistakes that Mintzberg points to in managerialism in general.

The Coach's Gaze: Role and Output

Managerial Discourse coaching takes the focus away from the coachee's personal identity, and focuses instead on the *person-in-role*. No longer is the coach working on the inner self (Soul Guide), or the outer self (Psy Expert) – the coach is now working with the *role self*, for example the person as finance director or CEO.

The other key aspect is the focus on efficiency and output. The gaze of the coach shifts towards how the person-in-role impacts on productivity. Coaches working with executives claim they can improve individual role performance in order to support the manager in their task of achieving the managerial ends. The website BusinessCoaching.co.uk is a good example of Managerial Discourse coaching:

> Our Business Coaching is designed to accelerate your performance and improve your Business's bottom line results. … Our primary focus is organisational growth, or helping an organisation to achieve significant performance improvements, and therefore we design programmes that align the executive's individual goals with the organisational commercial goals. (BusinessCoaching.co.uk, 2011)

The Managerial Discourse is both important and also problematic to coaching. It is important, as coaches working in this discourse will keep the coachee focused on role and organizational output. However, this approach is also problematic because the Managerial Discourse has limitations that impinge on contemporary organizational effectiveness. There is a wholesale paradigm shift in thinking taking place around organizational management that aligns with wider social change. Twentieth-century management control is slowly being replaced by new thinking on distributed leadership, self-managed teams, systems and networked approaches to managing and leading organizing which surpass the Management Discourse that focuses on efficiency through control. A minority of coaches are working well in this domain (those working within the Network Coach Discourse) yet the majority of business and executive coaches are repeating the Management Discourse of the past century, and focusing on micro-change, short-term results and goal-orientated outputs, at the expense of developing the distributed leadership and systemic thinking that is required.

New business models and opportunities to adapt quickly to new openings or challenges are rarely seen by managers or coaches who focus on operational issues without connecting these to wider social, technological and environmental changes.

Managers *per se* are not the problem, nor are coaches working within the Managerial Discourse. Both are important and bring many benefits. There are good managers and good management systems that aim to be socially responsible and go beyond instrumentalism and functionalism. However, the Managerial Discourse is underpinned by a logic of knowledge gathering, reductionism, rationality and efficiency that produces a particular subjectivity and mindset in the workplace. The manager and 'the managed' create a control and dependency culture. Gary Hamel in his *Harvard Business Review* article 'First let's fire all the managers' says that 'Management is the least efficient activity in your organization' and wonders 'If only we could manage without managers' (Hamel, 2011).

This chapter begins by bringing a critical eye to the Managerial Discourse in general, in order to establish the underpinning dynamics that managerialism brings to coaching. Managers are the main consumers of organizational coaching, so it is important for coaches to appreciate:

1   How managers are institutionalized into 'a way of thinking and doing' determined by the Managerial Discourse and its underpinning logic of control and scientific rationalism, to attain efficiency. Coaches will then be better placed to coach, see the underlying patterns and stand aside from the discourse to influence change.

2   How coaches themselves are influenced by this discourse. Many coaches are also institutionalized into the Managerial Discourse that can blind them to alternative ways of conceptualizing challenges, and seeing new ways of doing things. Coaches can echo the Managerial Discourse, pushing for ever greater efficiency and productivity or alternatively they can 'unlearn' old habits, and learn new ways to lead and organize, bringing new thinking and adding real value.

This chapter now examines the Managerial Discourse before applying it to coaching.

The Managerial Discourse: A Critical Perspective

Managerialism is a product of modernity, particularly of the Enlightenment values of science, rationality and progress that entered the economic sphere through urbanization and industrialization. The Managerial Discourse gains authorization and legitimacy from science/rationality, but also from an emotional and unconscious perspective. The word 'manager' inspires confidence and reassurance; it offers the fantasy that the irrational forces of nature, of the human hordes and our unconscious inner selves, can be rationally managed and are therefore controllable. Since the Enlightenment, man has sought to dominate nature (including the dark forces of human nature) and the Managerial Discourse aspires to this, making all things universally manageable. Finally, the Managerial Discourse gains legitimacy from holding the democratic ideal. Management claims to be meritocratic and transparent, making democracy and managerialism the best form of governance and organizing. Martin Parker corroborates this, stating that 'Management is clear, is accountable, is precise' (Parker, 2002: 4).

However, it seems that even in the West which fights wars for the democratic ideal, managerialism tops democracy when times are tough. In the recent 2000s owing to the financial crisis, Italy and Greece both abandoned democracy and found themselves governed by 'neutral' technocrats working within the Managerial Discourse, with the aim to manage the crisis more efficiently – as the *New York Times* (2011) put it, 'roiling financial markets have upended traditional democratic processes'.

David Skelton (2011) writes in the *New Statesman*:

> Government of the technocrats, by the technocrats, and for the technocrats is hugely undesirable and, by its very nature, bad for democratic legitimacy … Rule by technocrats has replaced rule by the people – with unelected, economically orthodox international bodies like the European Commission and the IMF working with unelected technocrats now heading up national governments to implement tough austerity measures that have never received public backing.

The abandonment of democracy in favour of managerial technocrats – without a whimper from European politicians or the electorate demonstrates how the Managerial Discourse is totalizing and dominant in Westernized culture. It is therefore not surprising to find it a powerful discourse within the emergent coaching movement.

The dominance of the Managerial Discourse

Parker comments that we find managers everywhere – in 'football clubs, hotels, railways, museums: they are universally essential' (Parker, 2002: 6). Managerialism permeates all workplaces and society beyond, becoming such a normative way of thinking that it is difficult to imagine a world without managers.

Alasdair MacIntyre (1985) cites the manager as one of the three main 'characters' of the twentieth century. A character fuses role and personality to emphasize a particular social and moral idea of a culture. He takes a philosophical view and explains the essence of the manager's claim to expertise and dominance:

> ... their skills enable them to devise the most efficient means of achieving whatever end is proposed. (1985: 74)

Their technique is an 'aspiration to value *moral neutrality* and the claim to *manipulative power*' (1985: 86). MacIntyre summarizes management expertise as drawing upon three core themes:

- Moral neutrality

- Manipulative power

- Efficient means to achieve ends

MacIntyre's view is that the manager's authority and claim to effectiveness are through the manager's ability to manipulate employees to become compliant to company requirements:

> The manipulation of human beings into compliant behaviour; and it is by appeal to his own effectiveness in this respect that the manager claims authority within the manipulative mode. (1985: 74)

MacIntyre's view of the manager plays out in coaching in two distinct ways. Firstly the focus on efficiency and output can be a positive driver of (short-term) success, and coaches working within this discourse are welcomed as they support these ends. Secondly, managers privileging the ability to achieve the ends most efficiently claim that in this pursuit they are morally neutral (our role is to deliver the primary task of increasing output). For example, the technocrats running Greece and Italy imposed by the European Union are deemed as morally neutral and above political allegiance; yet this is absurd as the EU is a political entity with political aims and ideology that imposes severe social cuts to maintain their particular political and economic system of neo-liberal capitalism.

The coach working from the Managerial Discourse therefore has contradictory aims. The welfare and best interests of their coachee, who may be overworked and stressed, may be in direct conflict with the Managerial Discourse that demands increasing workloads to achieve ever greater efficiency and output. The moral obligation of the coach working from the

Managerial Discourse is clear: to achieve the efficiencies on behalf of the sponsoring client, sometimes at the expense of the individual whose welfare the coach also purports to support.

MacIntyre's well-respected views have far-reaching implications. Milton Friedman, who dominated economic and management thinking in the latter part of the twentieth century (through his neo-liberal theory), claimed that the manager/executive has only one moral purpose, and that was to make profit:

> The executive is an agent serving the interests of his principle to serve the stockholders and thus there is only one social responsibility of business – to use its resources and engage in activities designed to increase its profits. (Friedman, 1962: 132–135)

Friedman's views have led to a catastrophic state of affairs for the environment and for social equity, and are now largely rebuked. The Managerial Discourse is a twentieth-century phenomenon, and in the twenty-first century it needs re-examining. Managers and organizations are being challenged to take a wider view realizing that with profits come corporate social and environmental responsibilities. There is growing realization that what is good for the environment and for society is also good for sustainable business (see Network Coach Discourse, Chapter 9). Paul Polman, Chief Executive, Unilever, claims:

> There is no conflict between sustainable consumption and business growth. .... Quite the opposite, in fact. There is a compelling case for sustainable growth – retailers and consumers demand it and it saves us money. (BBC News, 2010)

Whether or not we agree with MacIntyre, it is clear that the current Managerial Discourse has gaping holes in its logic. Yet the fact remains that the discourse is universally applied to workplaces, and has inserted itself into governance and bureaucratic control within the public sphere.

'That which can be measured gets attention'

The growing coaching turn towards the Managerial Discourse can be seen through goal setting, targets, evidence-based coaching and measurable outcomes. This changes the very co-ordinates of coaching.

The focus of coaching becomes adjusted to what can be measured, rather than evaluating performance and leadership capacity more holistically. Coaches begin with small measurable targets and goals, which limit their vision around connectivity, strategy or a systemic perspective. Coaches, too, feel the weight of the measurement and efficiency gaze: they too are being measured against ROI targets and on measures such as 'improved 360-degree feedback' to use two examples. As with any audit the coaching outcomes are under pressure to be positive; and science is not as clean or neutral as it claims.

Audit culture: control and measurement

Control and measurement are important facets of the Managerial Discourse. In early industrialization – and still in the emerging markets and some manufacturing – control of the human body was paramount as the manual labourer was tied to the rhythm of the machine. Frederick Taylor's (1947) ideas of 'scientific management', known as the 'efficiency craze', were taken up by Harvard MBA and dominated much of managerial thinking in the last century. Whilst predictions were towards a diminishing role for this approach, it seems through audit culture and target setting, that the 'efficiency craze' has re-emerged, and is imported into coaching through 'coaching by goals' and trying to measure coaching's financial impact through ROI and the focus on evidence-based practice.

Through industrialization, based on this management science approach, productivity increased. Managerial processes included control of human and material resources, standardization, the division of labour, and processes epitomized by 'Fordist' industrialized production lines. Industrialization improved productivity and enabled the mass production of cheap goods. New management techniques constantly sought efficiency and productivity improvements. However, from the earliest days of Taylorism, there have been questions about the ethics of treating humans like 'cogs in the wheel of a machine'.

Whilst contemporary managerialism offers a more humanistic face, the Managerial Discourse has not completely decoupled itself from its roots in the machine metaphor. The dehumanized efficient machine is still a metaphor in the workplace, even if toned down and rebranded as 'lean manufacturing'. The Managerial Discourse remains very resilient and adaptive, and inevitably coaching has become infused with it.

In the UK education sector for example, managerialism led to a drive in efficiency and attainment, but with huge costs to staff morale and with little improvement in education. Professor Gunter, from the Manchester University School of Education, writes

'Remodelling is being legitimised as practice through organisational efficiency and effectiveness, and not teaching and learning.' Modernisation and re-modelling in particular have tyrannical tendencies. (Gunter, 2007)

Michael Power in *The Audit Society* (1997) writes of the consequences of the explosion of using targets and audits across all sectors, and he points out that even nation states are audited. He says that audits are not just technical applications, but they are also ideas that colonize and distort because audits and targets favour that which can be measured over true effectiveness and improved performance. This distorts what is focused on in order to hit targets that are not essential. In the health sector, targets to reduce waiting lists in accident and emergency departments meant that patient welfare was of secondary importance. Patients were moved from A&E and left on trolleys in corridors for hours, in order to meet the time targets of treating them and moving them. The goal of improving health care efficiency missed the point that people are not machines, and a hospital is not a factory production line; there was no space for clinical decisions and the human factor.

Power's claims that when we set goals and targets, they have unforeseen consequences and the data is never value free. Social science is not clean or neutral; it also has to account for human influences, power and politics. The conflict for managers is an internal pressure to produce comforting audits that reassure senior executives and shareholders, whilst actual results may not be aligned to this:

> We can expect to see acute problems for anxious managers who, much like their former Soviet counterparts, will need considerable creativity to manage auditable performance favourably in the face of objective decline. (Power, 1997: xvii)

Coaching and the Managerial Discourse

Coaches working within this discourse are invested in the idea that they mirror managers and they too bring their coaching expertise and work with a moral neutrality to help produce more efficient workplaces, aligning themselves with HR and managerial rhetoric.

There remains the challenge of articulating the full value and worth of coaching, when the uniqueness of each coaching relationship makes this all the more difficult. A coachee who emerges in any way more capable, curious, sensitive, self-aware and humane is able to engage in the organization with improved confidence and personal authenticity, and can offer more thoughtful engagement; however, this may not be measurable in empirical or behavioural terms. Coaches aligned too closely to the Managerial Discourse will be more likely to comply with the search for output without helping the manager develop his or her critical capacity.

Goal setting: the shock troops of the Managerial Coaching Discourse

The rise of target, audit and 'goal culture' has permeated much of coaching. GROW Coaching has a huge following, and setting goals is key to its success, yet as Garvey et al. note:

> 'coaching' goals can limit what is covered and prevent broad development of the person or prevent getting into deep and difficult issues that require a nuanced entry following lengthy dialogue. (Garvey et al., 2009: 156)

Not only do goals and targets limit what is covered, they also define how we think about organizational and personal challenges and dynamics. Goals and targets are the 'shock troops' of the Managerial Discourse in coaching – they break challenges into sizeable chunks taking a modernist managerial approach, while suggesting progress through a linear mindset. The word 'goal' becomes a key master signifier for the Managerial Discourse in coaching. Goal setting applies to Life-coaching as well as Executive, Performance and Business coaching, and the instrumentalization of our lives, our happiness and even spirituality are all part of the Managerial Discourse and its extended web of influence.

Mentoring too imports a goal approach, but it is less prevalent in the literature, which still recognizes more tacit and supportive relationships, while traditionally mentors have fewer short-term goals and longer-term relationships.

Division of labour: the split between the manager and the coach

Key to the Managerial Discourse is the division of labour and breaking things down to component parts. When external coaches are engaged, this too can be a division of labour. The manager in effect outsources a key part of his/her role to the coach, namely developing and giving feedback to their team-members. The manager then loses contact with this part of their work, as coaches working confidentially do not provide feedback about issues emerging in the coaching relationship. A split then emerges; the 'target expectations' are held inside the organization without an awareness of the human limitations (held by the coach); this can reinforce the 'production line mentality'. Also where coaching remains in a private space the coach and coachee can both lose the wider context. When this occurs, there are two parallel realities and the split widens ever more – the manager pushes his/her demands and the coach and coachee work in their private space, soaking up the pressure.[1]

Coaching dilemmas

An advanced coaching task is to become aware of the contradictions in the Managerial Coaching Discourse. Working towards efficiency and company success is vital, but not if this undermines morale, or creates blind-spots with serious human consequences, which have devastating consequences as in the 2008 troubles in the financial sector.

The relationship between the Managerial Discourse and coaching is problematic. Coaching prides itself on helping individuals discover themselves and become more positive, 'happier' people, yet at the same time coaches are expected to promote efficiency and improve output by coaching the organization's 'human resources'. These two agendas are not necessarily in conflict, but they can be. Garvey et al. explain:

> We see a tension between, on the one hand, the focusing of benefits of control, and on the other hand, the energizing advantages of liberation and personal responsibility. (Garvey et al., 2009: 160)

Put another way, there is a tension between conformity and creativity, and between autonomy and dependency. The coaching rhetoric of liberation is contested by an overtly heavy Managerial Discourse that focuses on control, performance and efficient output.

Role Actualization

Another side of the Managerial Discourse in coaching is the focus on person-in-role rather than the inner or outer self of the Soul Guide and Psy Expert Discourse. This coaching work is very valuable, and applied wisely can create a reflective space and a conversational process that can be clarifying, and can develop the executive in a subtle and yet powerful way that does impact on their individual performance and organizational output. Role coaching is therefore a vital part of coaching, and offers a way of utilizing the Managerial Discourse effectively.

Taking Maslow's 'hierarchy of needs' (Maslow, 1976) self-actualization is the peak experience an individual strives for. Managerial Discourse coach-

---

[1] I thank Reka Czegledi-Brown for these points about the split between the manager and coach.

ing has a different aim: to help the executive attain 'role actualization', i.e. so that the *role self attains peak performance,* and therefore the individual gains personal satisfaction and career success whilst also impacting on the organization's success.

When working on a role self, it is also important to think about role relationships and relatedness. This goes beyond personalities and involves authority, power, followership, leadership, resource control and influence, while most importantly how the coachee, as their role self, relates and influences others in this network of roles (Newton et al., 2006).

A coach is required to look at the person-in-role in terms of function and its relatedness to other roles, but also to 'attend to and interpret emotional experience' (Armstrong, 2005: 6).

Most managers have multiple roles in organizations that can be confusing and at times contradictory, especially as some roles are explicit and others implicit. Therefore a coach working from the Managerial Discourse will focus on how the person inhabits or fits the role, while looking at how they can coach the person to help them adapt to their role/s. Undertaking a role analysis and linking this to task accomplishment is core to the work of the coach in the Managerial Discourse. One of the roles a manager/executive may have is to take up a leadership role, have is which is briefly explored below.

Leadership coaching and Managerial Discourse

When we talk of management we also must reflect on leadership, which is gaining in currency in the field of coaching and organizational thinking. I have not dwelt on leadership here because whilst 'leadership' is a popular term in coaching, much of what happens within leadership coaching comes within the still dominant Management Discourse; that is, a lot of popular leadership theory is based on the Managerial Discourse that substitutes the leader for manager in terms of the goal 'always to be more efficient', yet they are attained through slightly differing means – leadership and culture control rather than managerial control (Barley and Kunda, 1992; Western 2008a). When leadership coaching takes place, the Soul Guide Discourse works on the individual leader, on their values and authentic self, and the Network Coach Discourse works at a more strategic and network level.

Coaching leaders from a more progressive perspective than repeating the outdated ideas about heroic and transformational leadership is the challenge for contemporary coaching. Coaching often uses the language of transformational leadership when trying to sell its wares, claiming to coach leaders to reach their full potential, to lead with passion and vision; yet this repeats the ideology of heroic individual leadership, which can undermine collaborative teamwork and misunderstands how change takes place through networks of activity rather than heroic individual charisma. Coaches working with leaders are encouraged to educate themselves in the latest leadership theory in order to critique the simplistic ideas of Messiah or Control Leadership, and work in more contemporary ways. It is the ends that need changing, not just the means.

The manager/leader as coach

Managers coach rather than control. (Peltier, 2001: xvi)

Managers and leaders now desire and are demanded to have coaching skills, and there is a new rhetoric around the manager as coach (Hamlin et al., 2006; Hunt and Weintraub, 2007).

This reverses the position of coaching drawing from managerialism, and demonstrates how coaching is also influencing the Managerial Discourse itself. This is in recognition of workplace changes where cognitive labour, knowledge work, identity and emotions are ever more important in managerial work. Differentiating between internal coaches and managers with coaching skills is important: an internal coach is a trained coach working as an employee within an organization, whereas all managers and leaders require coaching skills if they are to be successful in the domain of managing people.

Conclusion

The Managerial Coaching Discourse has distinct strengths but when the discourse itself becomes exclusive or excessive, the strengths soon become weaknesses. Even the most devout business coaches, whilst espousing the Managerial Discourse, often undermine their own rhetoric, and many stray from the path of efficiency and work in the 'softer', more personal areas of coaching. Garvey et al. (2009: 153) wonder in coaching and mentoring if 'the goal setting ideology reflects lived practice and presents the whole story of conversational learning'. Whether the rhetoric of the Managerial Coaching Discourse exceeds what happens in practice is unknown, and research in this area is much needed. Such is the currency associated with the Managerial Discourse, however, that even those coaching approaches that do not relate easily to it (psychodynamic, existential approaches) often adopt the language of efficiency, output and goals almost as an obligation. What happens in practice and how coaches work across other coaching discourses requires some ethnographic research to evaluate espoused and actual coaching practice.

Coaching has both appropriated and is being colonized by the Managerial Discourse in four ways:

1 *Coaches align their aims with the management aims* to improve efficiency and productivity through coaching interventions.

2 *Coaches claim the same expertise in universal effectiveness as the manager.* Coaches claim their coaching 'methodologies, tools and techniques' influence individuals and organizational change. They claim an expertise that is not reliant on knowing an industry but that is universal in supporting coachees to be more efficient, to perform better in their roles and therefore become more productive.

3 *Coaching has become the chosen signifying term* that has taken over from other terms – 'soft skills', 'people skills' are now called 'coaching skills'. The Managerial Discourse is becoming 'softer' and more people focused, and coaching and mentoring are playing an important part in shaping and supporting this process.

4 *'Managers as Coaches.'* To have coaching skills is part of many managers' annual review. Having coaching capabilities as a manager is now commonly accepted as a desired management/ leadership competence.

The Managerial Coaching Discourse is here to stay for as long as managerialism dominates the organizational landscape. An adaptive coach will draw upon this discourse to resonate with the manager's concerns and language, yet they will not exclude the other discourses, or disregard a broader perspective. Role and output are essential focus points for the coach to work effectively with executives, and yet as Deetz identifies:

> the modern business of management is often managing the 'insides' – the hopes, fears, and aspirations – of workers, rather than their behaviors directly. (Deetz, 1995: 87)

The coaching pair have an opportunity to shape the management domain, working on the 'insides' as well as the context and the organization, rather than just react and respond to the colder, machine metaphors of efficiency at all costs.

The strengths of the Managerial Coaching Discourse

The explicit focus on role and output, improving efficiency and productivity, defines a clear role for the coach. Coaching makes connections between the person-in-role as it focuses on the exploration of how individuals take up their role, how they exercise authority, how they access creativity, and how they become team players appropriately. The coach then makes the link between individual role performance, and team/organizational performance and output. This clear coaching focus is very helpful to many executives.

The challenges of the Managerial Coaching Discourse

The dangers are that coaching becomes value free, that the focus on output and efficiency over-rides other ethical and strategic concerns. Managerialism has, at its heart, control and efficiency and is reductionist. The discourse can reinforce short-termism and a silo-focused culture. Coaching then also becomes limited in its scope and reductionist in its outlook. There is a real need for a critical coaching perspective to challenge the limitations of this Managerial Discourse that on the one hand has supported organizational and social success, but on the other has also led to creating a society that hasn't valued natural resources or social equity and has dehumanized many workplaces. Its technocratic approach lacks a natural ethical and humane sensibility. The challenge for coaches is how to work in the Managerial Discourse without succumbing to it. The blind-spot is to follow a narrow path, rather than draw from the breadth and creativity that coaching can offer to executives and organizations.

Suggested Reading

Garvey, B., Stokes, P. and Megginson, D. (2009) 'The goal assumption', in *Coaching and Mentoring: Theory and Practice*. London: Sage, pp. 151–161.

MacIntyre, A. (1985) *After Virtue: A Study in Moral Theory*, 2nd edn. London: Duckworth, Chapters 3 and 6.

Parker, M. (2002) *Against Management: Organization in the Age of Managerialism*. Cambridge: Polity Press.

Rostron, S. (2009) *Business Coaching International: Transforming Individuals and Organizations*. London: Karnac Books.

9 The Network Coach Discourse

Influencing the Network

Figure 9.1 **The Network Coach Discourse (original artwork by Maia Kirchkheli)**

Introduction
The new zeitgeist
The coaching response: the emergent Network Coach Discourse
Network Coaching in practice
Conclusion
Suggested reading

Introduction

> Our growing sensitivity to the natural ecological context, rightly
> understood, should inspire a new focus on our social institutions;
> natural and social ecology are, profoundly, mutually implicated.
> (Bellah et al., 1992: 15)

Network Coaching is an emergent coaching discourse that captures the
zeitgeist of our times. It is coaching's response to our increasingly networked, global, digitized and interdependent world. The twentieth-century
'machine metaphor' for organizations is changing to a twenty-first century
metaphor of the network. This reflects the increasingly connected world,
where organizations are more global and have complex stakeholder relationships and global interdependencies with transnational finance, transnational trade and regulation, and also with the environment and wider
political contexts.

> The new zeitgeist reflects the increasingly connected world, where
> organizations are internally more networked, with flatter hierar-
> chies and less compartmentalized, departmental boundaries.
> Employees are more self-managing, taking multiple and flexible
> roles, working often in fluid international, virtual teams, put
> together for specific short-term projects. The stability of formal
> roles and tasks is being eroded, and replaced with the nomadic,
> knowledge worker. Companies work with complex stakeholder
> relationships, that means collaboration with competitors, and
> relationships with customers and clients that transcend business
> and encompass personal identity. (Glaeser, 2011)

The Network society is not just about the global, it impacts at the local level too.
Mobile phones in Africa are transforming local business/trading, as they offer
new information on market prices, so local traders get fair prices; and new
banking and credit systems are evolving using mobile technology, making it

possible for credit and payments to take place that were previously impossible, thereby enhancing new trade/business possibilities for local communities.

I coach in a hospice in the UK, working with their CEO[1] to turn the hospice 'inside-out'. Her vision is to transform hospice care through 'open access'. She wants to engage and develop the network of care in the community, so that the hospice is not seen as a building, a medical centre where people come to die; but a vibrant hub that interacts with a network of community, enabling many more to access the hospice network who cannot at the present time, and to keep people in their community as much as possible.

Coaching is struggling to free itself from the twentieth-century modernist paradigm that still dominates much of organizational thinking. Both the Managerial and Psy Expert Coaching Discourses are born from this modernist paradigm with little reference to the new zeitgeist. Despite being a relatively 'new' profession, coaching literature and training doesn't sufficiently take into account the organizational and social changes that are occurring. Much of coaching (like much of management thinking) is in denial, repeating what we know, and looking for simplistic solutions rather than face complexity and change. Yet there are beacons of change in the business world. Progressive companies are pushing the agenda, with an early leader in this area being Body Shop founder Anita Roddick:

> Businesses have the power to do good. That's why The Body Shop's Mission Statement opens with the overriding commitment, 'To dedicate our business to the pursuit of social and environmental change'. (AnitaRoddick.com, 2006)

More recently Paul Polman, CEO of Unilever, has taken an 'Eco-Leadership' approach (Western, 2008a, 2010). In an interview at the Davos World Economic Forum 2011, he explained that he was trying to break with short-termism and create a socially responsible business to deliver long-term and sustainable success. Polman states:

> People always think that to do the right thing costs you more. That is not true at all. It can actually ignite innovation and lower your costs. The alternative of not having sustainable sourcing, of having to deal with the effects of climate change, is a much higher cost on business ... It is time to change, that is why I am here. I want to live in a better world. (Davos, 2011)

---

[1] St Nicholas Hospice, Bury St Edmunds: CEO Barbara Gale.

Other progressive companies work with networks as their organizational metaphors, without being so explicitly ethical and environmental. Obvious examples are three of the world's biggest companies – Apple, Google and Facebook. All have re-thought business models in line with social transformation and technological innovation; and this has also impacted on how the companies internally organize. Coaches will be left behind, and are doing a disservice to the individuals and organizations if they limit their approaches to twentieth-century models of work and leadership.

The Network Coach Discourse reflects those coaches who are looking beyond reductionist thinking and towards more connectivity, a more holistic approach fitting with the contemporary changes.

The Network Coach Discourse offers coaches a way to help executives to assess complex systems, to look for the connections and interdependencies in networks and to analyse power relations. The coaching task is to help equip leaders to face these new realities, to develop responses that account for power and influence in organizational networks, and to actively aim to identify hidden and undisclosed conflicts of interest.

Network Coaching acts in accordance with the 'Web of Life' (Capra, 1996) in which we are all implicated as individuals, teams, organizations and global citizens. The Network Coach Discourse engages with the most challenging and exciting developments facing organizations – how to distribute leadership, how to collaborate across virtual and real boundaries, how to be ethical and successful, how to read social changes and help to create adaptive organizations. The Network Coach Discourse is marginal yet emergent and is leading coaching into the new zeitgeist.

The New Zeitgeist

Globalization, Techno-Capitalism, Digital Labour, Environmentalism

> Our zeitgeist is a new (and ancient) awareness that we participate in a world of exquisite interconnectedness. We are learning to see systems rather than isolated parts and players. ... We can see the webs of interconnections that weave the world together. (Wheatley, 2006: 158)

This new zeitgeist emerges from scientific discoveries and environmental and social changes.

Box 9.1   Key Factors Influencing the Twenty-first Century Zeitgeist

1 New scientific discoveries such as quantum physics – 'the new concepts in physics have brought about a profound change in our worldview; from the mechanistic worldview of Descartes and Newton to a holistic and ecological view' (Capra, 1996: 5).
2 Environmental awareness. The rise in awareness of our finite natural resources, global warming and the destruction of the earth's biosphere has abruptly re-awakened our connectedness to and interdependence with the environment (Lovelock, 1982). Environmental and other social movements have also led to new innovations in self-managing and self-organizing systems, utilizing new information technology.
3 Technological advances and globalization have on the one hand made the world smaller, more connected and interdependent, and on the other hand increased the experience of alienation and displacement. Nomadic workers, whether as high-paid executives or as low-paid immigrant workers, mean there is an underlying disconnectedness within the modern self, creating atomized subjects within fragmenting communities.

There is an ever-growing complexity of connected networks of organizations, suppliers, producers and consumers, forming webs of interaction with no single leadership, no planned strategy, set in a constantly emerging and changing political and social environment. From this arises new organizational forms and leadership approaches.

Source: Western (2008a: 184)

By the turn of the twenty-first century the post-industrial knowledge economy became infused with social, political and environmental forces that have changed the very co-ordinates of the world order. Globalization, the fall of communism, the Arab spring, and then the rise of the BRIC economies (Brazil, Russia, India and China) challenge the hegemony of the West. New organizational forms emerged, such as the new transnational corporations that became powerful on a scale previously unknown. National regulation gave way to global financial infrastructures, and global networks of communications mean that trade and distribution all transgress national boundaries. Business is global, ideas and culture become global, weather systems are global, climate change is global, and social movements become global. We are all connected in ways we are just beginning to comprehend.

From my personal experience of coaching and consulting in many organizations and sectors, I have observed a struggle between two competing agendas. Thoughtful leaders realize that change has to happen in light of this new zeitgeist or their organizations will ossify and die; at the same time the immediate pressures driven by short-term demands mean they often turn a blind eye to this knowledge and continue with their heads in the sand.

The change demanded is counter-intuitive and leaders haven't yet got a map to find their way. This is why the emergent Network Coach Discourse is so vital, to support leaders find their way in this new emergent environment and to challenge the hegemony of short-termism and managerial control. I will briefly outline the contemporary workplace before addressing the coaching response to these changes.

The contemporary workplace: digital labour and techno-capitalism

Luis Suarez-Villa (2009) describes 'techno-capitalism' as capitalism that draws on digital labour and futuristic accumulation. It arose from the post-Fordist strive for a new commercial domination linked to the revolution in technological advances. Financial markets take on a hyper-real quality, where untold wealth is created in virtual dealings, external to links of real-time labour and production. However, the impact on real lives and communities when these markets collapse is profound. Our networks are infused by technology, our communications are immediate and mobile; we are computerized beings, digital workers in a brave new world that promises both new freedoms and new oppressions.

Alongside the rise of techno-capitalism is the rise of nomadic global labour. Nomadic/immigrant workers fill service jobs in wealthy countries. Manufacturing jobs are outsourced to developing countries, and new technology allows low-skill 'call centre' jobs to be outsourced to India. Low-cost global workers support the global network of business whilst at the same time highly paid global CEOs and financial experts are hot property. *The internet is our mirror*, a vast distributed network where binary divisions and linear structures dissipate and the real and the virtual blur and merge.

Employees are faced with new complexities, having to bring their cognitive and subjective selves to work, and this demands time to think, to reflect, to integrate and to process the multiple and fast-changing tasks they face. I completed writing *Leadership: A Critical Text* in 2007, and argued that a new form of leadership was required to address the challenges of the twenty-first century:

> Leaders of multi-national corporations are also finding that they have to find ways to increase the emergent capabilities within their companies to have any chance of keeping pace with change and the de-centralised forces impacting on them. Within organisational leadership there are attempts to find ways of working with the unpredictable and uncontrollable patterns ... (Western, 2008a: 185)

In 2008 the financial crash shocked the world, and its repercussions are still with us. There was not enough emergent capability in the system to predict the potential collapse. The US Senate issued the Levin-Coburn Report on the 2008 financial collapse and the report concluded:

> ... the crisis was not a natural disaster, but the result of high-risk complex financial products, undisclosed conflicts of interest, and the failure of regulators, the credit rating agencies and the market itself to rein in the excesses of Wall Street. (US Senate, 2011)

The complex and virtual financial systems that led to 'unpredictable and uncontrollable patterns' mixed with a lack of ethics and regulation led to this contagious collapse. Banks, corporations, nations and regulators all have to respond to the challenges thrown up; a new leadership is required, and coaching has a responsibility to support these leaders and to find coaching responses.

The Coaching Response: The Emergent Network Coach Discourse

The Network Coach Discourse is the emergent coaching response to the contemporary workplace and social changes. Network Coaching responds to our contemporary social conditions; it unapologetically pushes an agenda, aiming to help coachees think spatially and connectedly, and also to be socially aware and ethical in their approach. The coachee is encouraged to create a new conceptual map of their workplace, stakeholders and society beyond. This illuminates the network (and their thinking) exposing where power lies, where communications are blocked, and helps the coachee to be sensitive and responsive to patterns, relationships and connections that are key to understanding change.

Leadership coaches must guide, facilitate and sometimes cajole leaders to analyse ethics, power and resources within their organizational network. A coach is not an ethically neutral player: coaches are not counsellors taking a non-directive, individualistic approach; they too are implicated in the social world. Corporations have social as well as business responsibilities, and so do coaches. Coaches can no longer repeat old mantras about transformational leadership and achieving short-term measurable results, at the cost of abandoning their ethical responsibilities. Network Coaching is to take a stance, working to align individual and organizational success with social responsibility and sustainability. This brings new pressures to managers and leaders who require new support mechanisms, and coaches are excellently placed to provide a sanctuary where networked and connected thinking can take place. The Network Coach also brings ideas and proactive energy to the coaching relationship, to help leaders map their networks, in order to think more connectedly and influence change that promotes progressive strategies, aligning social and environmental concerns with organizational long-term sustainable success.

Systems coaching approaches

Coaching utilizing systemic approaches move towards the Network Coach Discourse. These approaches usually focus on human systems within organizations, but little attention is paid to the social, political and environmental challenges facing organizations. Systemic and ecological ideas about organizations, to their detriment, often marginalize important structural issues, such as power and resources. Coopey (1995) critiques Peter Senge and other systems approaches that 'idealise community and overplay the importance of dialogue without adequately addressing power'. Other examples of systemic coaching approaches are Team Coaching (Hawkins, 2011), and approaches that utilize coaching as an OD intervention; however these are very marginal. Stern discusses an 'Essential System's Perspective', saying that executive coaches should read organizational dynamics, psychology, business and leadership development, beyond popular journals, with which I fully agree. She then defines a systemic coaching approach:

> The professional coach needs to understand and work within an organisational system ... These key stakeholders include the following: the executives' manager; the HR department; executive development professionals within the organisation; and the executive peers, employees and others. (Stern, 2004: 158),

This systemic coaching approach is an important transition from focusing on an individual's psychology by bringing into awareness other organizational stakeholders. This approach, however, still conceptualizes the organization as a closed system, as it leaves out wider systemic influences. To expand the systems approach we need to view the network from three key areas:

1 *Social, political and economic*: how external systemic influences impact on the organization and individuals.

2 *Power, knowledge and discourse*: how power, language and culture from within the organization and from external social influences impact and constrain organizational change.

3 *Nature and technology*: taking account of systemic forces beyond human actors, i.e. how local and global natural environment impacts on organizations (use of natural resources, toxic waste, etc.) and how technology impacts.

Actor Network scholars demonstrate how humans are not the only actors in a network, and the dominant human-centric view minimizes how technology and machines and nature participate in our social networks (Law, 1993; Latour, 2005).

Psychodynamic systems coaching approach

This psychodynamic systems approach emerged mainly from the Tavistock Organizational Consultancy tradition (Menzies Lyth, 1960; Hirschhorn, 1988; Miller, 1993; Obholzer and Roberts, 1994; Armstrong, 2005; Kets de Vries, 2006). This coaching approach attempts to bring together psychoanalysis and open systems theory (von Bertalanffy, 1968).

Clare Huffington in *Organizations Connected* (Campbell and Huffington, 2008) discuss how coaches work with an individual, yet bring 'the system into the room' exploring systemic impacts and thinking with the coachee. Western (2008b), in the same text, cites an example of Organizational Development coaching that moved from individual to the system, working initially with the CEO, then the senior team, before finally intervening with the whole system working to 'democratize strategy'. David Armstrong develops the 'organization-in-the-mind' in reference to coaching, bringing together the individual's emotional life with the organizational culture. Armstrong differentiates the organization-in-the-mind from a mental construct or idea about the organization, saying it is an emotional reality. Using this method, the coach interprets the coachee as both an individual and as someone presenting a particular representation of the organization (Armstrong, 2005). Applying organizational role analysis (ORA) to coaching

(Newton et al., 2006) makes psychodynamic links between an individual, their role and the organization system.

The strength of this psychodynamic systems approach is the application of object relations theory to coaching. In brief it applies the individual psychodynamic insights of Melanie Klein, developed by Bion to groups (1961) and to organizations by Menzies Lyth (1960), amongst others. Psychodynamic coaching helps individuals make sense of their internal worlds in the theatre of work, how their 'object relations' play out with others through projection and introjection, and how group defence mechanisms are formed; this approach can be extremely helpful in coaching.

The limitations of this approach are that these individual psychoanalytic understandings derived from an 'individual on the couch' are contested in groups and organizational settings, and the application of this approach struggles to reach a mainstream audience in the business world or business schools (Kets de Vries' work is the exception). The other limitation is that coaching with a psychodynamic systems lens can often work with an undercurrent that is pathologizing, consistent with the psychotherapeutic search for the 'wounded self'. However, it is not always a bad thing to counter some of coaching's more gung-ho adherents from positive psychology, NLP and solution-focus traditions, as it addresses some of the malfunctions of organizational life. Professor Mark Stein, writing from within the psychoanalytic tradition, says:

> While I do not like (or use) the term 'pathology', one important area of attention for a number of scholars is organizational failure (this is a term that I do use) and, especially at present, those organizations that were involved in the credit crisis. … I feel this is precisely the moment to be focusing on such organizational malfunctioning. (Stein, 2011)

Finally another limitation of psychodynamic systems coaching is that, like other systemic coaching approaches, it focuses mainly on human relationships. As Brunning (2006: xxii) states, 'The systemic aspect of the model therefore attempts to create an understanding – one could say it conducts – an ecological survey of human relationships.'

This ecology of human relationships is at the expense of exploring the wider 'ecology of the network', which includes technology, discourse, power and the natural environment, as well as humans. A Network Coaching approach extends the eco-system beyond humans as it includes analysis beyond organizational boundaries into the social realm (see the Appendix for a description of a coaching approach that moves from individual depth work to the wider network).

Network Coaching in Practice

The Network Coach Discourse impacts on coaching practice in seven key areas:

1   Contracting and scoping

2   Guiding the coach in sessions

3   Coaching the networked self

4   Ethics and values

5   Developing strategic agility

6   Connecting to the wider network

7   Collective coaching wisdom

Contracting and scoping

The Network Coach stance is essential at the pre-coaching stage of contracting and scoping. Costs and efficiencies can be saved if scoping and contracting are done through the prism of the Network Coach Discourse. The scoping and contracting process becomes the first Network Coaching intervention, rather than being simply a legalistic/contractual process. Network Coaches will ask, 'What part of the network should the coach/es intervene in and what impact will this have on other parts of the network?' For example, if coaching a select elite, does this set up a hierarchy of haves and have-nots that impacts on morale? What begins with a request to coach middle managers to improve their performance can go in two directions:

1   *From the Managerial Discourse*: a contracting and scoping discussion about how measurable, performance targets and goals can be established. What competencies are the managers working towards? What are the affordable time, engagement and costs of a coaching intervention?

2   *From the Network Coaching Discourse*: a contracting and scoping discussion takes a different trajectory. Is coaching the best solution for these managers? How are the managers going to pass on their coaching gains to others? What coaching approach is required, from which discourses should the coaches work? What are the unspoken challenges in the network? Can these managers learn from internal mentors rather than external coaches? How to build in internal capacity from a coaching/mentoring intervention? How does knowledge exchange take place after the coaching? Perhaps an approach integrating internal mentoring and external coaching

will save the company money, embed learning and create capacity-building opportunities. How does the coaching intervention link into other OD and leadership development interventions?

Guiding the coach in sessions (in which discourses/areas to coach)

The Network Coach stance takes an overview of the four coaching discourses, informing the coach from which discourse they should be working at any given moment depending on the context. Network coaching is to take a third position outside of the immediate coaching relationship. Very often in coaching there are misunderstandings and tensions that go unspoken; should we be working on the inner self, the outward self, the role self or the networked self? It means that the coach shifts from a reductionist stance to take a much more strategic position, working to understand the network, the interdependencies, the entanglements and connections that impact on the work. The coach needs to be both present in the session, and also present in the network .

Coaching the networked self

Network Coaching is to locate the coachee in their organizational network, learning how they are influenced by, and can influence, their network. The coach helps the executive connect to their network, and become more eco-literate, to read situations more strategically and systemically, seeing connections, interdependencies, nodal points of power and blocks to change. They coach executives to think more spatially, to distribute leadership within their team, and to think about engagements with customers and stakeholders. This mapping of their network goes beyond traditional organizational boundaries to encompass stakeholders, supply chains, customers and competitors. The coach asks them to conceptualize whether they feel emotionally connected or disconnected, located or dislocated. Our networks are filled with emotions, feelings and power dynamics, alongside material resources and technical communications. How the leader interacts with all of these, and influences change, is the work of the Network Coach.

Ethics and values

The Network Coach works from an explicit ethical stance, aligning themselves with leaders, managers and organizations working from a value base, and challenging those who do not. Organizational networks are not benign networks of activity, but networks filled with competing agendas and tensions. To take a network approach is to use network analysis to take an ethical stance. They collaborate to work towards the *ethics* of sustainability and creativity; organizations are networks set within wider eco-systems, which include the natural environment. The coaching task is to 'humanize' the workplace and take a socially responsible position with the stakeholders and the supply chains in which they work. The Network Coach works with organizations towards sustainable and ethical practice, making the ethical links to organizational success as shown in Box 9.2.

Box 9.2   The Ethical Business Case

- *Protecting the Brand* against social activism and negative consumer voices.
- *Efficiency Savings* by reducing energy bills and waste.
- *Retaining and Attracting Talent*. Ethical and socially responsible companies are more attractive to bright minds. Individuals want to be proud of the companies they work for, as work and personal identity are connected.
- *Employee Engagement and Brand Loyalty*. Employees and customers want to be identified with successful companies/organizations that align good business with 'doing good'.
- *Anticipating Regulation*. As natural resources decline and climate change increases, international and national regulation will also increase. Eco-leaders lead rather than follow these moves, anticipating change.
- *Building Emergent Capability*. Engaging all employees in tackling the big issues creates unexpected opportunities. Distributing leadership is to see the patterns and opportunities that emerge from the unexpected.

Source: www.simonwestern.com, accessed June 2010

Coaching can bring ethical dilemmas to life, noticing how gender, race, sexuality and disability issues are played out in the workplace – who has a voice and who doesn't – and supports the coachee to take an informed and courageous stance to begin to influence dialogues of change. What are the systemic and structural power issues that go unspoken but hold back women in the boardroom for example?

Network Coaching means not only to raise obvious moral questions, but also to question what Zizek (2008) calls 'systemic violence' in organizations. This is the unspoken, but destructive, systemic forces of discrimination, subtle bullying, and decisions that impact on environmental sustainability and on downstream impacts that may exploit labour in developing countries.

Developing strategic agility

Coaching to develop an eco-literate sensibility in the coachee develops a macro-view that enables and encourages a new strategic agility, utilizing feedback and data in new ways to see the emergence of where the next business opportunity might be, or where the next challenge might arise. The coach helps the coachee to make connections across boundaries, to find nodal change points in a system. The coach works to support distributed leadership, encouraging diversity and facilitating leadership from the edges. Strategic agility means that individual coachees are more able to strategically adapt to emergence, and that distributed leadership and technical and social systems and processes are in place to support strategic agility throughout the organizational architecture.

Connecting to the wider network

The Network Coach does not limit the perspective to in-house thinking or take their direction from the organization's 'said' way of doing things. They broaden the canvas to take a wide-angle view, to 'look awry', to observe trends in other industries, learn about new technologies and how new business models are changing the way business looks, and how environmental concerns are driving change. This is particularly important when coaching at a senior level. Coaching is a rare opportunity to engage leaders in thinking about the bigger picture, sharing with them and learning from them, and together moving beyond the status quo of repeating the same thinking and same mistakes from previous cycles.

Collective coaching wisdom

To develop its potential, Network coaching also needs to find ways to harness the collective wisdom held by coaches. Coaching emerges from an oral tradition and continues this tradition. In the past, nomadic traders, travellers and storytellers passed on news and knowledge between villages. Coaches likewise play a role in passing on news and knowledge between the organizations and companies they work in. Coaching conferences, workshops and research papers share knowledge in a formal manner, but further developments would really benefit coaching. Coaches hold important and 'privileged' information about what is happening in the workplace – the emotions, the changes and the experiences at work. New research approaches are required to gather and analyse this knowledge, and to collate the coaching wisdom that lies dormant or hidden. Organizational developmental coaching approaches are also required to use coaching as a collective and systemic intervention into organizations.

Conclusion

Coaching is dominated by reductionist language and goal-focused approaches and in the margins the Network Coach Discourse struggles to find its voice. Mentoring has even less in the literature about taking systemic or networked approaches, an exception being Keller (2005) who offers a coherent mentoring approach that draws on systems thinking:

> This article presents a systemic model of mentoring depicting the interdependent network of relationships established between mentor, child, parent/guardian, and caseworker against the backdrop of agency policies and procedures. (2005: 169)

The Network Coach Discourse consists of coaching approaches that bring systems, networks, ethics and sustainability, and organizational development into the coach's sphere. Other influences that will develop the emerging Network Coach Discourse come from the influx of approaches that are entering managerial and coaching worlds, for example, integral, complexity and holistic approaches (see Bateson, 1972, 1979; Beck, 1976; Senge, 1994; Wilber, 2000; Wheatley, 2006.)

The by-product of this coaching approach can be profound. The coachees develop their own capacity to think beyond the confines of their department; they begin to locate themselves emotionally in a wider space, and become more adaptive, generative and strategic.

Organizational networks must account for power

Organizational networks do not replicate natural eco-systems that operate without political and power dynamics. Capra (1996) writes, 'The new concepts in physics have brought about a profound change in our worldview; from the mechanistic worldview of Descartes and Newton to a holistic and ecological view' (1996: 5). However, these 'biological' metaphors and environmentalists have drawbacks too: 1) nature is seen as a benign and neutral force and the metaphor omits the structural and discursive power and politics that are involved in organizational and social life; 2) there is a Luddite tendency and an inherent utopianism – 'the garden of Eden' lurks in the shadows, where a fallen world is described with the idea that nature can be our 'perfected teacher', and the language of environmentalists and integrative thinkers (Beck,1976; Naess, 1989; Wilber, 2000; Senge et al., 2004) can be evangelical in these terms, bringing spiritual, transcendental and nature together in an unholy alliance.

Actor Network theory (Latour, 2005 and Law, 1993) brings new ways to understand networks and organizations that counter this trend and account for non-human actors in our workplaces. It is striking that in a computerized, digitized age, one of our greatest struggles is to make sense of the relations between humans, technology and nature. The social is made up of the inter-dependent aspects of all three. How human emotions are shaped by material objects and technology, and how our bodies and social relations are changed by them, are profound. As Sherry Turkle says:

> It's not what computers do for us but what they do to us, to our ways of thinking about ourselves, our relationships, our sense of being human. (2011: xi)

If the organizational eco-system consists of humans, nature and technology, coaches have to engage in all three domains if they are to make a truly Network coaching intervention; and it is in this domain that coaching is least developed.

Pascal's wager

Blaise Pascal set a philosophical wager that even if the existence of God cannot be determined through reason, a rational person should wager as though God exists, because living life accordingly has everything to gain, and nothing to lose.

This can be applied to the emergent Network Coach Discourse. The rational coach should wager that we need to be more ethical and sustainable and to think in a more networked way about organizations. By doing so we have everything to gain and nothing to lose.

Strengths

The Network Coach Discourse takes coaching to a more advanced level, and will be applied by advanced practitioners. It brings the organizational and the social into the coaching relationship, and at the same time encourages the coachee to take a more strategic, ethical and networked approach to their work. Network coaching reflects the new zeitgeist and responds to a more interdependent, fast-changing and technical world facing social and environmental challenges. From the contracting and scoping work the coach brings the network into play, and with it the actors and their agency into view: Who has power? Where is the influence? What impact does technology have? What are our costs of waste and using natural resources? What new business models and strategies can impact on this? What are the future trends we have to plan for?

If coaching is to continue to have a creative, ethical and sustainable impact on the contemporary workplace the emergent but marginal Network Coach Discourse will need to develop and grow, to balance the other discourses that are disproportionately dominant in relation to it.

Challenges

As with any networked, systemic approach, Network Coaching cannot offer easy or reductionist answers. You cannot capture Network Coaching in an acronym, or teach it through techniques, tools or specific skills. Network Coaching means to think about connections, to be more nuanced, to see patterns and be more adaptive to the emergent. This is counter-intuitive to 'managerial control' and coaching approaches that offer more simplistic approaches such as 'GROW coaching'. It is therefore harder to teach and to sell than the other approaches. However, in the business world, people buying coaching are becoming wary of over-simplistic approaches, and more aware of the need for coaching approaches that go beyond individual change and address how leaders influence change in the wider organization. There is a growing demand for approaches that address the real challenges and complexities they face, and the Network Coaching Discourse reflects the small but growing movement within coaching that attempts to address these issues.

Suggested Reading

Campbell, D. and Huffington, C. (eds) (2008) *Organizations Connected: A Handbook of Systemic Consultation*. London: Karnac Publications.

Capra, F. (1996) *The Web of Life*. New York: Doubleday.

Latour, B. (2005) *Reassembling the Social*. Oxford: Oxford University Press.

Newton, J., Long, S. and Sievers, B. (eds) (2006) *Coaching in Depth: The Organizational Role Analysis Approach*. London: Karnac.

Western, S. (2008) *Leadership: A Critical Text*. London: Sage, Chapters 13 and 14.

Wheatley, J. (2006) *Leadership and the New Science*. San Francisco: Berret Koehler.

10 Discourse Mapping

Coaching Across and Between Discourses

Introduction
Discourse mapping
Coaching across and between the discourses
Discourse mapping: situating coaching approaches
Conclusion

Introduction

In the previous four chapters each discourse is discussed as a separate entity, and each is clearly informed by a set of particular social, theoretical, discursive principles and assumptions. However, in coaching practice these discourses rarely operate in isolation from each other. The majority of coaches and coach educators work without awareness of the 'normative' assumptions and the discourses they inhabit; in coaching, a lot is taken for granted. The theory and models used reflect their training or preferred way of working, yet the under-pinning discourses often go unnoticed and entrap coaches in certain ways of thinking. Some may coach from one very dominant discourse (for example, CBT-influenced coaches are clearly working within the Psy Expert), yet whilst they may aspire to the logic of scientism and rationality, and apply expert techniques, they may at the same time slip into coaching as a transpersonal experience, with an interest in Reiki healing and spiritual aspects, coaching from the Soul Guide Discourse. A hybrid coaching approach is not necessarily good or bad – it can be effective and creative, or confusing and contradictory.

Coaches may draw on different discourses for good reason, shifting the coaching dialogue from the individual to team performance and leadership roles, drawing on the Managerial Discourse. In other cases the switch of discourses creates dissonance and can lead to confusion and poor coaching practice. For example, if the coach advertises him/herself from the Soul Guide Discourse, and in their rhetoric claim their approach is non-directive, and that

Table 10.1   The four discourses of coaching: an overview

Discourse	Soul Guide	Psy Expert	Managerial	Network-Coach
Coach Stance	*Mirror to the Soul*	*Technician of the Psyche*	*Role Coach*	*Emergent Strategist*
Coaching Approach	The coach continues the lineage of 'soul healer', where the coachee reveals their hidden 'inner' selves, desires, inner thoughts and contemporary sins (to be sad, feel weak, anxious – all that need to be hidden at work). To help coachee find their authentic selves: identity, meaning and values.	Applying psychological tools and techniques to help the coachee. Personal performance is the coach's core objective. Psychometric tests, CBT, NLP and other goal- and technique-driven approaches are used.	The coach focuses on the person-in- role and on output. Coach analyses with coachee their multiple roles: e.g. how they lead and motivate their team and individuals to get the best results.	The coach views organizations as networks. They coach to reveal connections and interdependencies. Helps the coachee to think beyond silos where power lies, and how to influence networks. Helps coachee see big picture, look at influences beyond the immediate workplace, and act strategically.
Coach Gaze	*Experience*	*Performance*	*Productivity*	*Connectivity*
Aim	To create a space for coachee to discover their desire, and to face their inner dilemmas and reflect on the meaning of life and their values. The 'true self' is both discovered and constructed in this redemptive space.	To modify thinking and behaviour to support coachee success. To improve personal performance in both work and 'living'.	To improve role performance and organizational productivity by maximizing efficiency and increasing productivity. Drawing on scientific rationality, and managerial assumptions.	To help coachee take a more connective stance, to see patterns and power in their networks. To develop strategic thinking, to work more emergently across networks, and to be more ethical.
Coachee works on	*Inner-Self*	*Outward-Self*	*Role-Self*	*Networked-Self*
Coach Expertise	Creating a space for the soul/ psyche to speak. Listening and responding with reverence, courage and insight.	To 'coachify' psychological interventions, helping coachee adapt their thinking and behaviour to achieve their goals.	Facilitation of coachee in work-role to achieve greater personal, team and organizational productivity.	The coach facilitates ways to understand and then influence the workplace. Prompts strategic and spatial thinking, and raises ethical questions.

the coachee has all the answers within themselves, but in practice they switch to the Psy Expert and use expert coaching techniques, then problems will arise. By using psychological techniques and acting as the 'all-knowing' modern expert, this can reduce the coachee to a dependent, 'unknowing' recipient of coach expertise. Moving between discourses is an important coaching skill, but it has to be done in a conscious and planned way, preparing the coachee for the shift in emphasis without undoing or undermining the overall coaching aims.

Coaches work both within and also between the discourses. This sometimes means to switch from one discourse to another, at other times to merge or work between the discourses. There are continuums along the axis between the discourses, as well as differences between them. This chapter will now look at some examples of how a coach can work along and between these axes.

The four discourses are set out in Table 10.1 and the coaching discourse map in Figure 12.2 (p.248) will help the coach to reflect and think about where they situate themselves in terms of their coaching approaches.

Discourse Mapping

When delivering coaching to an organization or planning a coach training programme, there are many assumptions about what coaching can and should deliver, and each stakeholder may have a different, often competing, assumption about what coaching is and what it might deliver. The discourses help to define what is hoped to be achieved, and what might be on offer; this is a very different starting place to setting out coaching goals. Setting goals entails inserting modernity's divisive knife, when we move from holistic thinking to divisive and reductive thinking. Challenges and contexts are reduced and dissected, breaking them down into 'achievable and measurable goals'.

Discourse mapping helps educate and inform, it generates rather than reduces, opens a thinking space, and through this process we find there are few clear divisions and a lot of blurred edges and overlaps. An excellent coaching exercise is to undertake discourse mapping in a group (of coaches or coach trainers, or in team coaching with clients) and watch fascinating discussions take place, revealing different assumptions, perceptions and expectations. The discussions are both useful for clarifying purpose and how to plan coaching in a practical setting, and also as a developmental approach; questions arise such as: What do we mean by good coaching? What outcomes are and are not measurable? How important is individual satisfaction versus client/organizational satisfaction?

It can be an important part of supervision as well, to help clarify with a coach what they are doing and why. Used with an individual coachee, discourse mapping can be helpful to identify their coaching requirements, what areas they wish to work personally (Soul Guide or Psy), or how much coaching is needed in the realm of leadership and strategy (Network Coach) or on operational effectiveness (Managerial).

In coaching supervision (or in self-supervision and reflection), discourse mapping allows an open exploration of what's happening and why. If the coach/coachee contracts to work in the Soul Guide Discourse and finds themselves always in the Managerial Discourse, is this because the coach is being seduced out of their role as Soul Guide and into safer, less individual territory?

As discussed in the previous chapter, when working in the Network Coach Discourse, mapping should be in the coach's mind at the contracting stage through to the closing phases. During contracting, it can help reveal the tensions between the client (HR or line manager) and the coachee, who may want to work in completely different areas. Discourse mapping helps the coach clarify such issues.

Mentoring and discourse mapping

Mentoring, like coaching, works from any and all of these discourses. It cannot be situated on the map as a single approach, because as discussed in Chapter 2, it is not a unified approach but incorporates many diverse approaches. However, the workplace mentor often favours the Managerial Discourse, as that embraces their agreed role to support improved productivity. A mentoring programme for senior leaders may realize that it has two aims through a discourse mapping exercise. The mentors may be charged with the double task of focusing on the mentee's role, supporting operational success (Managerial Discourse), and also supporting them to become better leaders, more strategic, able to look for emergent opportunities, connecting them to their network, and encouraging them to bring on new talent and distribute leadership (Network Coach). If this was agreed at the outset, it might change the selection of mentors, mentees and the mentor preparation/development programme.

Within mentoring, the Psy Expert Discourse is less likely to be used, because mentoring is less about being an 'expert' in personal facilitation than in coaching, so uses less psychological approaches. The mentor is often more skilled and focused on professional and technical work experience and expertise. A mentor doesn't usually get to Soul Guide work in the short term. However, in a longer-term mentoring relationship, mentees often refer to their mentors as being deeply influential on their lives, beyond workplace success, and a mentee may discuss deeply individual issues with a trusted mentor, therefore moving into the realms of the Soul Guide.

Coaching Across and Between the Discourses

Coaches work within and also between discourses, and it is important to reflect on the relationship between them. Four different pairs of discourses will now be explored, with the caveat that this is formative work, with room for other coaches and scholars to develop their own insights around how their coaching works along the axis across and between the discourses.

Four axes between discourse pairs

The axes between the discourses signify coaching work that is more fluid between discourses and not constricted to a singular discourse.
The first two axes relate to the *content* of coaching, what is being worked with.

- Axis one, between Psy Expert and Managerial, signifies *knowledge*.

- Axis two, between Soul Guide and Network Coach, signifies *wisdom*.

These next two axes relate to the *object* of the coaching, what is being worked on.

- Axis three, between Psy Expert and Soul Guide, signifies the *individual*.

- Axis four, between Network Coach and Managerial, signifies the *social*.

Axis 1. Signifier: knowledge

Psy Expert — Knowledge — Managerial

Axis 1, between the Psy Expert and Managerial Discourse, signifies knowledge gained from science and rationality, as both discourses are born from the epoch of modernity. Knowledge is the currency for improving individual performance and organizational productivity.

Coaching along this axis is about applying (and seeking) knowledge in order to improve performance, productivity, and achieving goals with economic and material outcomes. The focus is on mastering/controlling the self (Psy), and mastering/controlling the context (Managerial) through application of knowledge. Coaches can move comfortably between these discourses if they have the training and skills in both, as the underpinning logic is the same (knowledge).

Axis 2. Signifier: wisdom

Network Coach — Wisdom — Soul Guide

In axis 2, the coach and coachee aim to attain wisdom, drawing on the lived experience of the self in the world. Wisdom comes through experiential learning, and from integrating parts into the whole and connecting to the wider world. This axis is less focused on facts, knowledge, data and output, and more interested in meaning, values and the holistic system.

The Soul Guide and Network Coach axis signifies wisdom; both represent the non-linear and sit outside of modernity's rationalism. Wisdom embraces the pre-modern and post-modern. It connects to the tradition of Soul Healers, and applies this ancient wisdom with the post-modern bricolage of theories and practices, to coach the coachee to influence their networks, informed by eco-literate, holistic and networked thinking.

Coaches working across this axis link individual values and global ethics, embracing spirituality and humanism (Soul Guide), with nature and technology in local and global networks (Network Coach). Axis 2 opens the way for holism and fragmentation to sit together – aesthetics, nature and technology, emotions and spirit, life and death, community and solidarity, despair and love, and values and meaning are the 'lived experience' that requires the coach to work along the axis of wisdom. It allows for the expression of deep connections between our souls and the cosmos in whatever way the coachee expresses these. The coachee and coach work towards discovering the subjective truth for the coachee, and to express this wisdom through engagement with others. Coaching along this axis is to work with the coachee to develop the 'good life' and to build the 'good society'.

Intersection of wisdom and knowledge   The point of intersection between the two axes brings knowledge and wisdom together. Experienced coaches will support the coachee to hold onto the important and precious values in their lives, to work from a place of inner-knowing and wisdom, and to take account of the environment and social world, connecting with their networks 'wisely' and ethically. The challenge is then to pragmatically translate this into daily living, how to produce outcomes from identifying wisely what is good for the individual, group and for society. Applying knowledge with wisdom can help achieve this.

Tensions occur where the drive for knowledge clashes and competes with the different mindsets produced by the axis of wisdom. Productivity and performance, underpinned by the logic of gaining and utilizing knowledge, can sit uneasily with the search for subjective truth and ethical holism, underpinned by wisdom: logos and mythos are not always comfortable bedfellows.

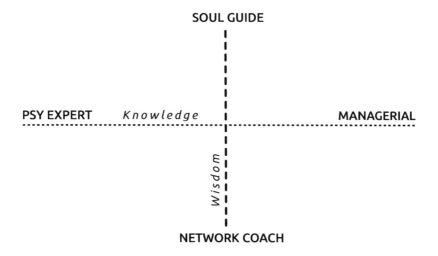

Figure 10.1   Wisdom and knowledge: coaching between the four discourses

Axis 3. Signifier: social

Managerial — Social — Network Coach

This axis between the Managerial and Network Coach Discourse relates to the social field. In both discourses and between them, the coach focuses on the coachee's role and relationship to their organization and to the social world. Coaching helps to make links between the individual role, their team, department and the wider organization, breaking down silo mentality, or taking a wider strategic remit. The coach works in the social realm, working with the individual as a 'socialized person', reflecting on how they are shaped by culture, with the organization-in-the-mind, or locating the coachee in their network. The Network Coach brings an ethical and holistic/ networked lens to the work, and the Managerial, a productive organizational focus; the coach wanders on the axis between these discourses, following the coachee, yet all the time holding a social perspective in mind.

Axis 4. Signifier: individual

Soul Guide — Individual — Psy Expert

The coaching object in axis 4 is the individual – connecting the inner and outer self, linking our inner feelings with our outward persona, to think about feelings, thoughts, body and behaviour. The coachee is offered different ways of thinking about themselves, exploring how relationships and the outward self impact on the inner self and vice versa. Coaches working along the axis connecting the discourses are comfortable working with the deep emotions, and on how they behave and perform at work and in the public realm.

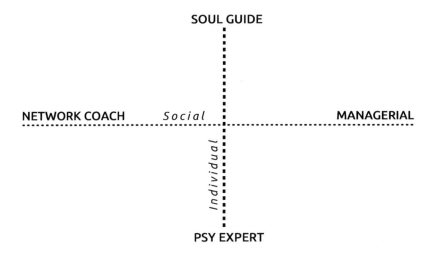

Figure 10.2   **Individual and social: coaching between the four discourses**

Intersection of individual and social   The intersection connects the individual and the social. The intersection reveals the complex levels of interaction between the individual and the social – how the inner theatre gets played out on the stage of life, and how the individual is shaped by the social. How the coach works at this intersection depends on their experience, skills and training. Unfortunately, coaching as a body of knowledge and practice hasn't developed a common language for the work along this axis, and too often focuses on the individual and the social as if two different worlds exist, when in reality there is no individual self without the social, and no individual change without social change.

Discourse Mapping: Situating Coaching Approaches

Figure 10.3 situates four coaching types onto the discourse map, showing where they might fit on the axis between discourses. It is recognized that these coaching types draw on very different approaches and discourses depending on the coach, so the example is not predictive, and each coach needs to be reviewed and placed on the map according to their specific approach.

Figure 10.3   **Mapping coaching approaches to the discourses**

Life-coach: individual

A *Life-coach* generally focuses on the individual axis working in and between the Soul Guide and Psy Expert, between the inner self and outer self, initially exploring the coachee's desire, anxieties and identity to discover their 'authentic selves' and their values (Soul Guide). The coach might then move towards how they relate to others, how their inner feelings translate to behaviours, how they perceive themselves and how others perceive them. The coach helps the coachee to change behaviours, to avoid repeating unwanted patterns, or to gain more confidence in specific areas (Psy).

Business coach: knowledge

A *Business coach* works along the axis between the Psy Expert and Managerial Discourse. They focus on knowledge, gaining data such as Psychometric testing and 360-degree feedback, which are used to design plans of action and formulate individual goals (Psy) to raise the coachee's performance, and applying this to their role in order to attain greater output. Business coaching works with the coach on team performance, drawing on HR knowledge and the coachee's expertise to try and improve productivity. Data and knowledge are converted to business plans and project management plans. The Business coach claims expertise in the capacity to translate knowledge into ordered plans; they facilitate the coachee to improve their personal performance to impact on operational efficiency.

Executive coach: social

An *Executive coach* may work on the axis between the Managerial and the Nework Coach, focusing on the social arena, between delivering operational productivity through improving their executive role (Managerial) while at the same time trying to take a strategic position, to influence their workplace network. Insights from the wider social sphere may point to where new business might come, new business models or product lines developed, how to rethink the brand, or how to become more sustainable and save on energy costs (Network Coach). The coach will also bring information and experience from the wider social realm in which they work.

Executive coaching may of course stray into Soul Guide and Psy Expert Discourses as well, but the focus of the coach who is appointed and paid for by an organization is to make an organizational (social) impact, utilizing the individual as 'human resource' in this quest.

Leadership coach: wisdom

A *Leadership coach* may work between the Network Coach Discourse and Soul Guide, along the axis of wisdom, coaching on organizational strategy and leading the organization (Network Coach), whilst at the same time making connections between their work and home life, working to enhance their emotional well-being and focusing on their deep values and how to be an authentic leader (Soul Guide). Coaching between the Soul Guide and Network Coach is to link individual belief and values and company ethics. Time spent on 'non-output' thinking along this axis can paradoxically be very productive. Companies and teams want wise leaders; and leaders who have deep insight, promote good values, social responsibility and systemic vision are in great demand.

Conclusion

There are as many variations as there are coaches, and the examples here are short because discourse mapping has to be specific rather than generic. In Chapter 12 on meta-theory, discourse mapping is used to show how coaching intersects all four axes; and it is at the intersection of all four that coaching itself becomes an identity of its own.

The coaching meta-theory (see Chapter 12, utilizing the four discourses) is the theoretical basis for a new coaching process that is being successfully tried and tested in practice, and will form the basis of a new training for coaches wishing to transcend a singular coaching approach. The aim is to expand coaching to encompass the four discourses, ensuring the coachee and client have the opportunity to work in and across the four discourses. See Appendix on Analytic-Network Coaching©.

Part IV

The Future of Coaching

11 Developing Coaching Theory

Introduction
What is theory?
Why coaching needs a meta-theory
The challenges of establishing a coaching theory and meta-theory
Developing a meta-theory: knowledge, metaphor and imagination
Conclusion
Suggested reading

Introduction

> Coaching and mentoring activities need a theory. (Garvey et al., 2009: 224)

In the final chapter, 'Towards a theory of coaching and mentoring', of their book Garvey and colleagues open with this simple but definitive statement. I agree with them although I would phrase it differently:

> Coaching and mentoring activities need theories and a meta-theory.

There are a lot of theories that already exist in coaching but most are borrowed and applied in an *ad hoc* fashion from elsewhere. Another challenge coaching faces is that models and methods can be mistaken for theory – this is true of psychotherapy and Human Resources too (Noon, 1992) – or theory is sometimes thought of only as empirical research, data and information, when it is much more. Many theories are taken directly from psychotherapy; in *The Psychology of Executive Coaching* Peltier writes, 'The purpose of this book is to translate psychotherapy theory for executive coaches' (2001: xiii). Peltier and others' appropriation and application of psychology and psychotherapy theory is useful, but this does not produce coaching theory *per se*, and definitely not a coherent meta-theory of coaching. The theoretical approaches section of *The Complete Handbook of Coaching* (Cox et al., 2010) draws directly on psychotherapy, with chapters on psychodynamic, cognitive, behavioural, solution-focused and person-centred therapy.

This coaching turn to psychotherapy theory is partly due to the influx of psychologists and therapists to coaching, and also because, in spite of a lot of debate about the differences between coaching and therapy with familiar sound bites – 'therapy is long term, coaching is short term', 'counselling is problem focused, coaching is solution focused' – there are clearly cross-over influences (as explained in the coaching genealogy and Psy Expert Discourse).

Coaching currently lacks a clearly defined body of knowledge or explanatory theory; so theory is borrowed from elsewhere. To draw upon therapy and other domains is entirely legitimate and very useful, but this shouldn't be called coaching theory. They are psychotherapy theory and models applied to the field of coaching.

Coaching practitioners do not work in a social or theoretical vacuum. Theory is present, whether it is explicit or implicit, consciously or unconsciously applied, whether it is well formed or fragmented, weak or strong. Without critical reflection on the theory or meta-theory that is being used, it leaves it to chance whether the theory is suitable for the practice taking place, and in many cases the theories used are problematic and unsuitable for purpose. For example, many Life-coaches work with the implicit and unarticulated, humanistic, non-directive theories of Carl Rogers (1961). Rogers theorized that, given the right conditions, human growth would take place. He then researched what these conditions were in counselling and other helping professions. This led to his person-centred counselling where the coach takes a non-directive approach to create the safe space for the client to grow from within (Rogers, 1961). Many coaches appropriate this theory, saying that they believe the client has the answers within, and that they facilitate this form of self-learning. However, they then become very directive and prescriptive in their interventions, drawing on a variety of tools and techniques from NLP, CB and other theoretical approaches they have picked up. The coach suddenly becomes 'the expert', and the coachee the dependent and receptive client, completely contradicting Rogers' theories and methods, as the coach taking a lead disempowers the clients. Without theoretical reflection the contradictions and tensions are not worked out, leading to poor and confusing coaching practice.

This chapter will work through a process asking, 'What is theory?', and identifying different types of theory in the first part; and then in the second part it will explain why a coaching meta-theory is vital for this hybrid coaching field. Finally, using Weick's idea of 'disciplined imagination' (Weick, 1995) the chapter will show how metaphor and imagination are equally necessary, alongside knowledge accumulation and research, for theorizing and forming theoretical frameworks.

What is Theory?

One of the big challenges facing coaching is both the lack of theory and the fact that many coaching practitioners distance themselves from theory. Theory in coaching is often confused with coaching methodologies or empirical research. Very often theory is confused with gathering knowledge and data, researching facts about the world. Theory requires one further step: discovering knowledge about the world, then formulating this into theory, perhaps through testing a hypothesis.

Fleetwood and Hesketh (2006: 1985) offer two descriptions of theory that are applicable to coaching.

Firstly, Sutton and Straw:

> Theory is the answer to the queries of 'why'. Theory is about the connections among phenomena, a story about why acts, events structure, and thoughts occur. Theory emphasizes the nature of causal relationships, identifying what comes first as well as the timings of such events. Strong theory, in our view, delves into the underlying processes so as to understand the systematic reasons for a particular occurrence or non-occurrence. ... It is usually laced with a set of convincing and logically interconnected arguments ... good theory explains, predicts and delights [Sutton and Straw, 1995: 76].

Secondly, Whetten sheds light on how theory explains causation:

> [A] complete theory must contain essential elements ...
>
> *What.* Which factors (variables, constructs, concepts) logically should be considered as part of the explanation? ...
>
> *How.* Having identified a set of factors, the researchers' next question is how are they related? ...
>
> *Why.* What are the underlying psychological, economic or social dynamics that justify the selection of factors and the proposed causal relationships?
>
> To summarize thus far: What and How describe; only Why explains. What and How provide a framework for interpreting patterns ... in our empirical observations. This is an important distinction because

> data, whether quantitative or qualitative, characterize; theory supplies
> the explanation for the characteristics. (Whetten, 1989: 490–491)

These two quotes deserve reading slowly and carefully, as they offer us a
clear way into theory. They take us into two realms of theory:

1 Predictive theory

2 Explanatory theory

Predictive theory demonstrates causal relationships where possible, producing knowledge about the external world. This is often achieved via scientific or empirical, qualitative and quantitative research (a common mistake
is to think that predictive theory excludes qualitative theory).

Explanatory theory aims at understanding phenomena, answering the
question 'why', as well as the 'what' question. As many contemporary phi-
losophers of science have pointed out, prediction in the social world is virtually impossible because there is simply too much going on and too much
constantly changing for us to be able to formulate law-like causal relationships that are possible in some natural sciences. There is nothing in the social
world remotely like Ohm's law or the gas laws – cases where one event
regularly follows another event and there are constant event regularities.
Event regularities are often used to make inductive predictions: yesterday,
event X regularly followed event Y, so tomorrow when event Y occurs, we
can predict that it will be followed by event X. Knowledge of past event
regularities is used to predict event regularities in the future. The problem
is, without event regularities, prediction based upon the idea that one event
will regularly follow another event is impossible.

> In the social world, prediction is virtually impossible although in
> some parts of the natural and man-made (e.g. engineering) world
> prediction is possible. So whilst prediction might be nice, it is not
> possible. Those that hint at prediction in the social world are almost
> always operating with an implicit idea of (some) natural science in
> the 'back of their minds'. (Fleetwood and Hesketh, 2006)

Looking at theory from the scientific angle is limited in other dimensions
too. Bhaskar argues that 'scientific knowledge' is useful but that it needs the
philosopher to put that knowledge in perspective. He reiterates the importance
of 'explanatory knowledge' situated in wisdom and values.

> Information is not explanatory knowledge; it is knowledge of the
> structures and mechanisms, of the fundamental causes of why things

are as information tells us ... for that you need explanatory knowledge, preferably explanatory scientific knowledge ... in order to use explanatory and scientific knowledge you need wisdom, which is explanatory knowledge incorporated, in the light of other values, into practice. (Bhaskar, 2010: 107–108)

This mirrors the stance in this critical text, applying what I have called *Network Analysis* and *Looking Awry*, looking beyond a reductive scientific approach at the wider social implications, and taking a *Depth Analysis*, to look beneath the surface of the 'factual' data and knowledge that scientific research finds, and finally taking an *Emancipatory Stance*, bringing values to bear on our inquiry and research to formulate probing ethical questions.

Develop coaching theory that both describes and explains coaching

Developing coaching theory is to develop knowledge about what coaching is, what micro-practices work, how they work, and also why coaching is popular in spite of a lack of empirical evidence to support it. Coaching theory should also examine the gap between coaching 'rhetoric and reality', i.e. what is claimed by practitioners and companies or coaching bodies invested in promoting coaching, and the reality. To undertake this means to analyse the quality of current research and the claims made, and to contest poor research.

Theory will also attempt to explain how coaching has a macro-social function; how coaching is used by corporations, how coaching fits into organizations as a body of practice, how it relates to Managerial Discourses and practices, and what impact university business schools and consultancy businesses are having on shaping coaching practice to meet their ends. Coaches are influenced by social and political pressures from within their own bodies and from external pressures, and these need accounting for.

Why Coaching Needs a Meta-theory

All theory (consciously and explicitly or unconsciously and implicitly) employs meta-theory ... it seems reasonable to suggest that appropriate meta-theory should be carefully considered and selected such that it is consistent with the theory rather than simply allow theory to be informed by meta-theoretical happenchance. (Hesketh and Fleetwood, 2006: 684)

Clearly, meta-theory is a different class of phenomena than theory. Theory is about substantive phenomena (such as coaching) whereas meta-theory is about what a good theory (of coaching) might look like.

Let me be clear from the outset, what a coaching meta-theory is and why it is important.

1 A coaching meta-theory is not an attempt at integration or convergence of the multiple theories to try and establish a unitary theory. This would be both impossible and unwelcome as it would begin to put limits and boundaries on coaching unnecessarily. Coaching is a dynamic multidimensional practice, emanating from the diverse traditions that inform coaching practice, and this is one of its strengths.

2 A coaching meta-theory sits over multiple coaching theories, and acts as a coherent body of knowledge that sets out the parameters of what coaching is and isn't. It enables the interrogation of those theories, and encourages explanations of coaching as both a micro and a macro social function.

3 A meta-theory will enable researchers and practitioners to ask: Are the theories we are using relevant to coaching or are they imported with little resonance? Do they help us develop understanding and explanations of coaching? Are they working towards the greater good of coaching or are they limiting coaching for other political or economic agendas? Are the predictive theories being used to promote evidence-based practice, or identify ROI, empirically solid? Do they serve or promote certain interests? What are we *not* researching, if we are focused mainly on micro-changes?

4 A meta-theory looks at the structures and processes, the wider social implications and discourses, as well as the micro-research patterns evolving.

The Challenges of Establishing a Coaching Theory and Meta-theory

Let's begin by setting out three key challenges in developing a coaching meta-theory.

Challenge 1 – practitioner anti-theoretical stance

Coaches' resistance and lack of knowledge about theory

Coaching must overcome its anti-theoretical stance if it is to develop successfully. This coaching company statement below reflects the contemporary position of many coaches:

We're probably the wrong company to ask about coaching and mentoring theory. As a matter of fact, we're not too hot on theory since we believe that you can't pigeonhole people and impose a template of how coaching and mentoring should look. (Impact Factory, 2010)

The problem is they are very likely to 'impose their template' as they haven't the theoretical resources to critique their own practice. They utilize theories and make implicit assumptions about learning, behaviour and how coaching works, yet have not developed an explicit awareness of their own assumptions, or those they are applying to others through their coaching practice.

I visited a European ICF conference a few years ago and was asking coaches from many different countries and training backgrounds about their theoretical approaches. The response I gained was similar to the above statement. There was a kind of an inverse pride in 'we are practitioners not theorists'. Speaking with Co-active coaches at a training event, they claimed, with relish, to be theory free, yet in the Co-active publications we read about the coaching relationship and the cornerstones of their beliefs:

In co-active coaching, this relationship is an alliance between two equals for the purpose of meeting the clients' needs.

Four Cornerstones

1 The client is naturally creative, resourceful and whole

2 Co-active coaching addresses the client's whole life

3 The agenda comes from the client

4 The relationship is a designed alliance. (Whitworth et al., 2007)

These statements and their approach are filled with implicitly pre-supposed theoretical underpinnings, drawn from humanistic psychology (Rogers, 1951,1967; Maslow, 1976) that make claims about individuals, wholeness and about how we learn. Each of these theoretical positions can be critiqued and contested by other theoretical stances, and if coaching is to develop, they need to be. Coaches need to clearly identify the theoretical origins that are being assimilated into practice.

For example, a critique of the Four Cornerstones might argue that the relationship is not between two equals, that the Psy expert (the coach) holds a different power to the client. Nikolas Rose, Professor at the London School of Economics, demonstrates how in counselling and therapy, power is retained in a disguised manner, and this is also true in coaching relations, although perhaps to a lesser extent:

> Therapy involves a kind of power that might be termed priestly. One person confesses and is known. The other does not, remains secret, mysterious, merely hears the confession. This kind of relation involves what Pierre Bourdieu terms 'symbolic violence'. One person is a person of knowledge, and the other person isn't. One person has the capacity to reshape the meanings through which the other makes sense of their life and their actions. (Rose, 2005)

Many coaching stances are influenced strongly from Carl Rogers' person-centred and Maslow's human potential theories which are utilized in coaching but without acknowledgement of the theoretical source; they are often used with conflicting theoretical approaches that are more directive, thereby working in two opposing ways with a client, which can be confusing.

Coaching has theories, but practitioners are in denial of, or just not aware of, the theories they are using, and practice then becomes an *ad hoc* application of techniques that can undermine consistent and good practice.

The reasons for this anti-theoretical position come from two perspectives:

1 Coaching emerged from practice rather than the academy (universities), and therefore most practitioners are both sceptical and also insecure about academic research and theorizing. One of the problems with this position is that when research or theory is discussed, practitioners (and often managers and HR teams too) are not equipped to differentiate good quality research and theory from poor quality.

2 Universities do produce elitist language, obscure theory and research that can be difficult for practitioners to access. However they also produce clear theory and research that *can* be accessed by practitioners.

Increased coaching education (that is growing rapidly) will produce more theory, and coaching theorists can make their work more accessible, yet without dumbing it down. There is also room for difference; academics and theorists influence practice (and vice versa) through reaching individual champions of change and 'communities of practice' who then go on to influence the broader coaching field. All academic work does not have to be accessible to all practitioners. There are many rooms in the house of coaching and mentoring!

Challenge 2 – integrating diverse bodies of knowledge into a common theory

To try to integrate or unify coaching theory is to try and solve the wrong problem. Garvey et al. (2009: 224) point to a challenge of theorizing coaching, saying that coaching and mentoring draw on diverse bodies of knowledge, and they select five before expanding on each to create a fuller list:

- Sport

- Developmental psychology

- Psychotherapy

- Sociology

- Philosophy

The above list alone is too diverse to be integrated in a holistic way (and others provide alternative accounts of coaching and mentoring, making the list even longer). The challenge faced when creating a coaching theory is not that of integrating or unifying diverse theories: instead, the challenge is to see what theories are relevant and which are not; which can be in relationship with each other and which cannot; and to interrogate each of them depending on the coaching approach being used in a local context.

Looking at the example of 'management theory' – it isn't unified at all. It is constantly in flux, constantly drawing upon diverse bodies of knowledge, constantly innovative, constantly in a process of becoming. Even psychotherapy and counselling theory are diverse; the theoretical assumptions behind psychoanalysis and behaviourism are widely separate, and yet there are many commonalities in therapy theory too. The task is not to integrate diverse bodies of knowledge into a holistic theory, but to offer a coherent overview and a meta-theory that is able to critique, interrogate and reflect on theory and practice, from the diverse range that currently exists and is being produced.

Challenge 3 – the growth of the wrong 'scientific' meta-theory

A current danger is that the wrong meta-theory becomes the coaching meta-theory by 'happenchance'. Hesketh and Fleetwood (2006) write eloquently about Human Resources (HR) and the question of theory and meta-theory. Their research is very pertinent to the coaching field, because HR is closely associated to coaching, and HR shares a similar interest in demonstrating efficacy and links between how by developing managers and employees – organizational performance is improved.

Hesketh and Fleetwood take a critical realist perspective, and their findings are that HR lacks the development of theory in the realm of explanatory power because it is dominated by an inappropriate 'scientific' meta-theory. This scientific meta-theory is wedded to the attempt to measure causal relations between developing people and performance outcomes. They demonstrate the inadequacy of this position, claiming that it has led to bad science and weak outcomes. Even the best research that may find a causal link is problematic because: a) it doesn't show that the simple causal link is the only causal link (there may be many others); and b) that any 'proof' of a causal link still doesn't offer an explanation of this association (Hesketh and Fleetwood, 2006: 681). Bhaskar (2010) supports this view, arguing that causal links in closed system experiments do not give 'laws' or sustainable knowledge in open (human) systems.

Hesketh and Fleetwood are not against finding causal links, but say this cannot be the endgame of HR or development activities (2006). Bhaskar is clear that science and the knowledge about the world it produces is useful, but that explanatory theories are also necessary.

In the health sector there has been huge investment in EBP (evidence-based practice) where one might assume that it is easier to measure scientifically specific health gains than in coaching, where the causal links between coaching and organizational performance are more complex and difficult to prove. However, this process of EBP has proved far from successful and in spite of it sounding very plausible and difficult to challenge, it has been counter-productive (Marks, 2002). Marks' research for the National Institute of Clinical Excellence in the UK shows that EBP is underpinned by the discourse of science, yet his research reveals it is 'opinion-based theory, a faith'.

> On the face of it, *the judicious use of current best evidence* in the making of decisions is an ideal, model procedure. Who could wish to behave otherwise? The trouble is that the majority of decisions are not based on the current best evidence, but on out-dated evidence, opinions, preferences, and routines. ... It is supremely ironic that the principles of EBP are unsupported or contradicted by evidence, that they are themselves nothing more than opinion-based theory, a faith. (Marks, 2002: 16)

Our social world is one of complex causality and open systems, so applying simplistic causality, reductionist and closed systems, science cannot explain what is going on. This requires robust explanations that may include statistics and empirical research, but that also reaches beyond statistics, to explain social causation and influence. The problems of the scientific meta-theory are that when used in complex, open human systems, it is very difficult to achieve robust results without huge investment in large studies, or by reducing research to find minute outcomes. Even when this is achieved, prediction is still impossible.

Unfortunately, coaching is following this managerial/HR tendency of evidence-based practice, using a scientific meta-theory that focuses on reductionism, deductive reasoning and emaciated explanations. The holy grail is to try and demonstrate a causal link between coaching and performance, thereby demonstrating ROI. This is chasing the wrong holy grail, and most coaches, managers, senior consultants, academics and HR leaders know this deep down to be true. To quote one CEO of a major consulting house, discussing statistical association with causality and predictability in relation to organizational performance:

> ... if you are looking for a well articulated scientific model with evidence, then unless you are prepared to listen to marketing hyperbole, you won't find it. (Cited in Fleetwood and Hesketh, 2006: 1987)

De Meuse et al. (2009) show how these arguments also apply to coaching:

> Some researchers have tried to quantify the ROI of executive coaching. For example, one case study in a Fortune 500 company reported that coaching produced an ROI of 529%. This figure was boosted to an overall ROI of 788% when including the financial benefits of enhanced employee retention. ... Another study claimed that when calculated conservatively, ROI averaged nearly $100,000 or 5.7 times the organization's initial investment in coaching. ... A close examination of these two studies indicates that the ROI numbers were derived subjectively through retrospective questionnaires and interviews. We do not criticize such methodology out of hand. It simply becomes very tenuous to draw firm cause-and-effect financial conclusions through such a perceptual-based, qualitative process, and generalize the numbers to other coaching events. ... We are not stating that it is impossible to compute ROI, but it certainly is very, very difficult to do so ... (De Meuse et al., 2009: 124)

Reductionist science equals reductionist coaching

De Meuse and colleagues highlight some of the weak science involved in researching ROI in coaching. However it doesn't address an even greater concern I have about the scientific meta-theory, which is how it reduces coaching practice to an ever-narrowing behaviourist and micro-goalfocused practice.

Theory shapes practice, and if the theory is attempting to measure causal effects, it is always 'emaciated research' and reductionist, always breaking down complex systems to look for small changes because they are more measurable.

Cognitive behavioural therapy, for example, uses this scientific meta-theory and positivism to measure outcomes and claims great success, but what it achieves is to reduce the aims of therapy to small behaviour or cognitive changes. This displaces rich human experience in favour of smaller measurable outcomes. The human and existential questions facing each of us – the deep rooted psychological, social and emotional nuances that make up our individuality, our identities, our inner theatres and the dynamic complex relations that emanate from our internal dynamic lives, the relations that involve other people and non-human actors – all vanish in the face of scientifically measurable micro-goals and outcomes. The coaching world then becomes more limited as interventions become smaller, less context and experiential and relational orientated, and more behaviourist orientated. There is clearly a place for CBT approaches but not at the expense of other approaches, as discussed in the discourses of coaching.

Following this path removes the Soul Guide Discourse, or transforms inner-soul and relational work into a technocratic approach that instrumentalizes our emotional worlds. Measuring spiritual coaching in terms of improving effectiveness at work is a good example; this transforms the whole concept of spirituality. Coaching for personal change through a series of techniques applied by a coaching Psy Expert technician without reference to the depth and richness of human experience is problematic:

> Behaviour therapy is the most extreme example of such schizoid theory and practice that proposes to think and act purely in terms of the other, without reference to the self of the therapist or the patient, in terms of behaviour without experience, in terms of objects rather than persons. It is inevitably therefore a technique of manipulation and control. (Laing, 1967: 45)

This is happening already in HR, management and other circles (see *The Audit Society* by Michael Power, 1997).

> Coalescing, after World War 2, out of the behaviour modification approach to management, the Organization Development (OD) movement was an approach that sought to engage the 'total worker', utilising the theory and techniques of applied behavioural science. The aim of these techniques was to secure involvement, satisfaction, commitment, and so on ... (Jackson and Carter, 2011: 390)

An example of this is the language and work of HR and OD teams, who are individually good people, bright people, people who want to be ethical; yet the domination of the scientific meta-theory in the workplace leads to perverse effects. A current trend is for a corporation to identify three or four core company values and then to turn these into micro-behaviours that can be assessed by tests and by line managers in performance reviews.

This process is intended to influence and coerce employees, to change their behaviours, thereby following the corporate values, to create a more ethical company with more engaged employees. There seems very little awareness that this is mimicking Orwell's '1984' surveillance dystopia. Values are personal; they can be shared but not be universally applied in a top-down process across a global company and they certainly cannot be turned into measurable objectives and behaviours that can be neutrally observed and measured objectively by line managers. The outcomes of such interventions will either be explicit resistance and cynicism (Tourish and Tourish, 2010) or implicit resistance whereby employees simply become more performative and use their emotional labour to win promotion. Those openly resisting or not conforming will be ousted, leaving a more homogeneous, totalizing workforce (Casey, 1995). The attempt to use behaviour modification techniques on a mass scale like this is simply unacceptable and also unworkable as it will not create the kind of employees it is designed to, even if the ethical is overlooked. Coaches can be asked to support this work, to coach executives to help them perform/behave according to the company's behavioural criteria, following performance reviews or 360-degree feedback reports.

I am making two critiques here. Firstly, a politico-ethical critique about how behavioural modification is used in a way that diminishes our humanity; and also claiming it has very limited impact. The OD attempts to modify employees' behaviour are often internally marketed as employee engagement 'to create more engaged employees and a better work environment'. As coaches we must remember what is behind any attempt to engage workers:

> Thus, any call to encourage worker 'engagement' assumes that the outcome will be more work. ... Managers do not have an absolute desire for their employees to be 'engaged'. If, by 'engaging' them, profits were reduced, then disengaged they would stay. We should not regard expressions of concern for workers as anything other than a desire for more work from them. For that is the purpose of the worker – to work, to *perform*. (Jackson and Carter, 2011: 392)

Coaches need to reflect on a) how they are being used by a company, taking a theoretical/meta-theoretical stance that reveals some of the ethical and political issues and b) how their coaching uses and reinforces the scientific meta-theoretical paradigm, and the effect this has on their practice and on the coachee.

The second critique is how the pervasive and dominant notion of the scientific meta-theory discourages politico-ethical thinking – science being morally neutral – by turning ethical matters into straightforward technical (i.e. statistical) problems and then solving them with the tools and techniques of statistical research.

Coaches are co-opted to work within these reductionist goals, and mostly do not question them, simply because these ideas are so widespread and normative, and coaches do not have a good meta-theory or education that helps them critique such ideas.

The task is to develop coaching theories and a coaching meta-theory that takes us beyond measurement and statistics, one that doesn't reduce coaching to a micro-behavioural project. What is required is a meta-theory that enables coaches to know what good research looks like, rather than, when they hear the word 'research', accept it as 'scientific evidence' with little critique.

Developing a Meta-theory: Knowledge, Metaphor and Imagination

Theory is not developed from a zero starting point, nor is it a static form when produced. Theory is an ongoing process – Karl Weick says he prefers 'theorising to theory' (Weick, 1995). Cornelissen comments on Weick that:

> He prefers an ongoing and creative process of metaphorical imagination and theoretical conjectures over a teleological view of theory as a fixed reference point (or truths) to attain [Weick, 1995, 2004]. (Cornelissen, 2006: 1583)

Metaphor and imagination

> Weick says that 'theorists depend on pictures, maps, and metaphors to grasp the object of study'. (Weick, 1989: 529)

Weick's idea of 'disciplined imagination' encourages the use of metaphor and imagination, in order to theorize and conceptualize theoretical frameworks.

> At the heart of 'disciplined imagination' lies the role played by metaphor as the vehicle through which imagination takes place as the source – as a simulated image for theoretical representations ... (Cornelissen, 2006: 1580)

Weick proposes that theorizing is not simply a process of logical scientific deduction, but also of heuristic and imaginative processes. Metaphor and imagination go together, and Weick uses 'disciplined imagination' to sense-make, select and schematize theoretical perspectives. If we apply this to coaching and mentoring we will begin by searching for metaphors that help us to theorize. A metaphor asserts that a is or is like b …

> Drawing on metaphors and images implies a way of thinking and a way of seeing that pervade how we understand our world generally. For example, research in a wide variety of fields has demonstrated that metaphor exerts a formative influence on science, on our language and how we think, as well as on how we express ourselves on a day-to-day basis. (Morgan, 1986: 12–13)

Coaching is like …

In this book thus far I have likened coaching to friendship, to the sphinx and to therapists. In this way each metaphor stimulates a different way of thinking about coaching and mentoring. In a teaching seminar to experienced coaches I asked them to come up with metaphors for coaching, without censoring themselves, and the result for this is shown in Box 11.1.

Box 11.1 Coaching Metaphors

Prophet – bringing good news/salvation

Lover

Ghost – seen/unseen

Remedial tutor

Doctor

Guru

Teacher

Priest

Prostitute – a paid emotional comforter

Confessor/spiritual father–mother

Therapist

Friend

Trainer

Facilitator

Advisor

Guide

Theorizing coaching is to select metaphors that inspire imagination, then to utilize 'disciplined imagination' to work these ideas, to test them against research, against the literature and experience, and then to refine them into theoretical concepts. In researching this book, the metaphors I worked with, the ideas that presented themselves in the literature and in my own coaching work and teaching, led me through a process of 'disciplined imagination' that informed the four discourses of coaching and mentoring I discussed earlier: the Soul Guide, the Psy Expert, the Managerial, and the Network Coaching Discourses.

Conclusion

Coaching currently lacks a clearly defined body of knowledge and an explanatory theory. Existing theories are borrowed and applied incoherently from elsewhere, mostly from psychology and psychotherapy (NLP, CBT, solution-focused, etc.).

As coaching theory develops, it also veers towards positivist, scientific aspirations. The 'scientific meta-theory' attempts to theorize causal relations (A leads to the outcome B), which are more appropriately used in hard science and in closed systems. When trying to find causal relations that can be universally applied to coaching (e.g. this coaching intervention leads to this outcome), huge problems arise.

Human relations are complex systems that are filled with variables and it is almost impossible to claim such causal links with universal explanations (Bhaskar, 2010). This linear approach also impacts on how coaching is conceptualized and practised. Focusing on 'evidence-based outcomes' distorts coaching practice towards micro-changes, and shapes it to become a reductionist practice. Coaching is broken down into small component parts that can be measured, such as small behavioural changes. Other systemic and subjective changes are not scientifically measurable, not 'evidence-based' and therefore de-valued. Coaching then becomes a parody of CBT or other science-based psychological practices that try to break human experience into component parts. This undermines the holistic, systemic, existential coaching approaches that go beyond behavioural change, and work with human experience in organizational and social systems. Psychotherapy and HR have both tried unsuccessfully to find the holy grail of causal outcomes (Masson, 1990; Hesketh and Fleetwood, 2006) so coaching perhaps should learn from this and try different approaches to theorizing its discipline.

Theory is an important part of cultivating the field of coaching. Both predictive and explanatory theory serve to give broader understanding and to develop coaching practice. Predictive theory is based on causal relationships that can be tested and 'proved', whilst explanatory theory aims to connect patterns and justify relationships. Both are required but in coaching, explanatory theory is currently marginalized. Explanatory theory aims to explain subjective and non-measurable/predictive qualities, but it is used to explain what factors are required for predictive theory, and to identify the weaknesses and gaps in all theoretical approaches. Explanatory theory is based on three areas of explorations:

What? What factors should be considered as part of the explanation?

How? How are these factors related?

Why? What are the underlying psychological, economic or social dynamics that justify the selection of factors and the proposed causal relationships? (Whetten, 1989: 490–491)

A more imaginative approach to theorizing is required in coaching that includes predictive and explanatory theory; one that goes beyond focusing on the micro-skills of coaching and asks the bigger systemic and structural questions as well.

This book began with a question in my mind: 'Why coaching and why now?' I was intrigued by the growth in coaching and what is actually behind the rhetoric and practice. Developing coaching theory is to develop knowledge about what coaching is, what works, how it works and also what claims are false or exaggerated. Other questions, such as how coaching fits into wider social phenomena, the discursive nature of coaching and what power relations are at play, are also part of explaining how coaching works and why it is popular.

A question that is frequently asked about developing a coaching theory is: *How does coaching integrate theories from such a diverse range of influences?* This question is the wrong question. The aim of coaching theory should not be to integrate theoretical approaches as this is a) an impossible task and b) would create a conformist, totalizing theoretical model. The question for coaching is to examine diverse theories to identify which theories are relevant and which are not, how they relate to each other, and what tensions exist between them. To achieve this we need a meta-theory of coaching that allows us to interrogate each theory, and to assess coaching approaches and how they are being used in a local context. Chapter 12 will outline a tentative coaching meta-theory based on this process.

Suggested Reading

Bhaskar, R. (2010) *The Formation of Critical Realism*. Oxford/New York: Routledge.

Cornelissen, J. (2006) 'Making sense of theory construction', *Organisation*, 27: 1579–1599.

Fleetwood, S. and Hesketh, A.J. (2006) 'HRM-performance research: Under-theorised and lacking explanatory power', *International Journal of Human Resources Management*, 17 (12): 1979–1995.

Garvey, B., Stokes, P. and Megginson, D. (2009) *Coaching and Mentoring: Theory and Practice*. London: Sage, Chapter 15.

Morgan, G. (ed.) (1986) *Images of Organization*. Beverly Hills: Sage Publications.

Weick, K.E. (1989) 'Theory construction as disciplined imagination', *Academy of Management Review*, 14: 516–531.

12 Creating a New Coaching Meta-theory

The Micro-practices and the Macro-social of Coaching

> Introduction
> Coaching micro-practices
> The coaching macro-social
> Conclusion
> Suggested reading

Introduction

Coaching emerged from a long history and has been shaped by many political, economic, religious and social influences, as discussed in Part II of the book (reflecting on the genealogy of coaching). From these influences, the contemporary practice of coaching and mentoring has emerged, and Part III theorizes that coaching and mentoring are underpinned by four discourses: the Soul Guide, Psy Expert, Managerial and the Network Coaching Discourse. These discourses help to develop a theoretical map that explains the core underlying assumptions that inform coaching practice, and in a broader sense, coaching as a social technology.

To create a meta-theory of coaching, there has to be a theoretical account of the symbiotic links between the micro-practices of coaching (i.e. how it is practised) and the macro-social of coaching (i.e. how it is organized institutionally and informally and how coaching interacts as a collective actor in the social field).

Coaching theory is weak at the present time, and in the field of the macro-social is almost non-existent. Developing a coaching meta-theory is to make links between the macro-social and micro-practices, and to give a full

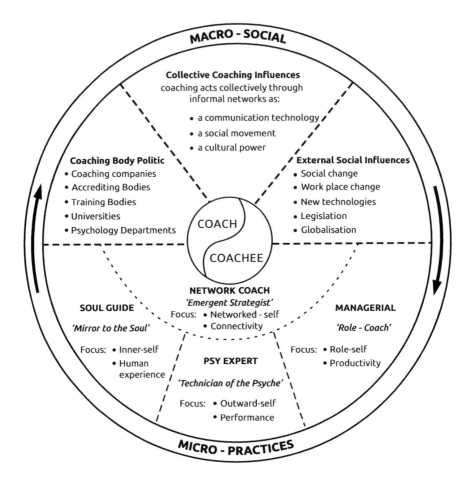

Figure 12.1   **A meta-theory of coaching**

account of coaching and mentoring beyond the limited theoretical accounts that currently exist, mostly formed from applied psychotherapy theories (Peltier, 2001; Cox et al., 2010). The meta-theory explored here offers a map of the terrain, enabling coaches to research, develop new understanding and new skills and practices, and to locate their coaching approaches within a theoretical framework.

Figure 12.1 sets out a meta-theory of coaching in diagrammatic form. The outer circle denotes that the macro and micro are in circular feedback; they are constantly producing and shaping each other. At the centre of the diagram sits the coach and coachee pairing, showing the core dynamic of coaching. The four discourses of coaching make up the bottom half of the sphere – indicating the theoretical basis of coaching micro-practices. The upper half of the sphere contains the macro-social influences, the body politic of coaching (the institutional influences), the collective coaching influences (informal rather than institutional) and the external social influences (for example, social, technological and workplace changes).

Multiple functions of the Network Coach Discourse

The Network Coach sits both within and above the other three discourses, and has three functions:

1 As one of the four discourses the Network Coach Discourse informs the micro-practices of coaching. The Network Coach helps the coachee to locate themselves within, understand the dynamics of, and then influence their organizational and social network.

2 The Network Coach takes an overview of the coaching intervention, overseeing all four discourses, helping the coach to choose which coaching discourse they should be working in at any given time depending on the client's needs, the coaching developmental stage and the changing context.

3 The Network Coach Discourse connects the micro-practices with the macro-social. It bridges the two hemispheres, connecting links between the macro-influences of coaching practice and, in reverse, how coaching micro-practices influence and engage with the macro-social.

Developing a meta-theory

To develop a meta-theory is a process rather than an end point to aim for, and it requires a collective effort. 'Communities of practice' consisting of coaching practitioners, academics, trainers, coachees and other coaching stakeholders will contribute formally and informally to develop a coaching meta-theory. This chapter builds on the work and theories of others, not just recent others, but those who over a long time period have developed diverse approaches and theories of 'helping' relationships.

This coaching meta-theory doesn't aim to provide a theoretical grand narrative of coaching, for to try and integrate multiple theories would be reductionist and confining. Instead it establishes some cohesion, and sets out parameters, mapping the terrain of coaching. The boundaries it draws are permeable; not so permeable that coaching becomes amorphous, but neither so rigid that dynamic change can't occur through the constant interaction coaches and coaching has with the social environment in which it operates.

Macro and micro perspectives

Any meta-theory of coaching must address macro-social and institutional influences by researching beyond the micro-practices of coaching. How coaching is organized, and the social–political, economic and technical changes that influence coaching practice, need theoretical resources. A macro-social approach theorizes how coaching as a body of knowledge, or practice, impacts on the workplace and in the wider social field. Let me give two examples:

1 *Coaching as a social technology.* Coaching is a social technology, meaning it goes beyond being a practice between two people; it has a social function beyond this. If coaching is to be theorized, understood and developed, the social mechanisms and processes that are involved require research and explanation. The term 'technology' as a sociological term has a broader meaning than in common usage. Technology can include the social processes as well as the 'wires and machines'.

> As a social object, technology needs to be understood not simply as the nuts and bolts, the wires and transistors, the keyboards and the semiconductors, but also as the collage of activities involved in its use. (Ackroyd et al., 1992: 10)

> 'Technology' can include social arrangements as diverse as the postal system, transportation, refuse collection, voting mechanisms, education and so on. (Woolgar, 1991: 94)

Coaching is an alignment of practices, processes, systems, discourses, texts, information and knowledge, and human and non-human interactions, and therefore is another example of a social technology. As a social technology coaching becomes more than the sum of its parts, and it can be viewed in new ways. In a world dominated by technology, humans who used to run machines, now act as social facilitators. They facilitate social and technical interactions so the technology can produce things: communications, knowledge, finance, data, virtual and material goods, etc. The employee and manager use their subjectivity to facilitate, and the social technology of coaching acts as the social lubricant to help employees utilize their subjective selves. Conceptualizing and theorizing coaching as something more than a set of techniques, or an interaction between two people, encourages a meta-theoretical stance that gives a richer account of coaching.

2 *Coaching mimics therapeutic practice and also therapeutic organizing forms.* The growing pressure for professionalization and accreditation take coaching even closer to these psychotherapeutic models. Not only are therapeutic practices being imported, but so are the therapeutic organizing forms.

> One of the gifts psychologists can give us as business coaches, perhaps the most valuable is the least obvious. Its not one of the many approaches discussed below … it's the professional

ethos inculcated over years of training, supervised practice and peer expectation. (Scoular, 2011: 89)

Coaching draws on psychotherapeutic practice, and is now being colonized by their organizational forms and protocols which inevitably have a powerful impact on coaching practice. This is a form of organizational isomorphism (where one organization or profession mimics another). DiMaggio and Powell (1983) identify predictors of isomorphism, whereby a profession that is 'dependent on another organization will become the more alike it' and whereby a profession without many models or theories will enable isomorphism to happen more quickly. Coaching is in this position in relation to psychotherapy. Professional codes of practice, accreditation procedures and supervision models are being imported directly from the therapeutic-psychology world, and the process of isomorphism between the two is shaping how coaches think about the practice and profession of coaching.

The macro-social influences and the micro-practices of coaching are inextricably linked. Coaching therefore needs a meta-theory that addresses both the macro and the micro.

I have divided this chapter into the macro and the micro, acknowledging that in practice they are not separated into two distinct areas but ebb and flow in an intricate 'network of activity' that makes up coaching. John Law (1992), one of the Actor Network proponents, explains:

If we want to understand the mechanics of power and organisation it is important not to start out assuming whatever we wish to explain. For instance, it is a good idea not to take it for granted that there is a macro-social system on the one hand, and bits and pieces of derivative micro-social detail on the other. (Law, 1992)

Law's critique – that often we start out by assuming what we want to explain – fits with coaching well. Coaching theory to date acts largely on the assumption that coaching works through similar mechanisms as psychotherapy (Hart et al., 2001; Peltier, 2001). Therefore, coaching theorists focus their gaze on psychotherapy and coaching micro-practices rather than be open to the unfolding and hybrid development taking place in coaching. Coaching is (and can develop to be) much more than therapeutic or psychological techniques, adapted for the workplace through coaching. This problem is demonstrated in a recent and serious empirical attempt at validating coaching theory by Segers and colleagues (2011) who make the wrong assumption from the outset – that coaching is like psychotherapy, therefore it can be researched using the same method. This error undoes their empirical coaching study:

Given the fact that coaching and psychotherapy are based upon similar theoretical constructs (Hart, Blattner, & Leipsic, 2001); have

> functional similarities (Mckenna & Davis, 2009); and draw heavily
> upon the principles and processes of psychotherapy (Judge & Cowell,
> 1997); we are using the Emotionality-Rationality-Activity-Awareness-
> Context (ERAAwC) model from L'Abate (1981) and L'Abate, Frey, and
> Wagner (1982) to structure the field. (Segers et al., 2011: 210)

Yes, coaching draws on psychotherapy constructs but it cannot be reduced
to them. Segers et al. acknowledge the differences between coaching and
therapy but do not explain the differences, or pay attention to how coaching
becomes enmeshed within the therapeutic discourse through this approach:

> Obviously coaching differs from therapy, but we strongly believe that
> a model able to classify the many different therapeutic schools is
> currently the best candidate available to structure the different coach-
> ing schools. (Segers et al., 2011)

Coaching is thus reduced to a therapeutic technique, and what follows from
this line of theorizing is the increasing calls that coaches should be more
psychologically informed. What also follows is that coaching practice is
shaped and formed by the therapeutic language. The discourse of coaching
becomes restricted to the Psy Expert Discourse only, obliterating the other
discourses in which coaches work successfully. The Psy Expert Discourse
accounts for the psychotherapeutic and psychological theoretical aspects,
and I fully agree that psychotherapy has much to offer coaching and that
psychologically informed coaches *can* enhance this discourse of coaching;
yet this is not always the case, and there is also much more to coaching.

Actor Network scholars counsel us not to assume that, in the social, the
macro and micro are separate. Bruno Latour (2005) suggests that to understand the social world the best approach is 'following the actors' (Latour,
2005: 12). This means to ethnographically observe the actors in any network
without forming premature views about how power works, or how things
are organized. In the current coaching network, the premature assumption
is that coaching is like psychotherapy, and the only actors under the gaze are
the coach and coachee; yet many other actors and actants[1] exist in this
network. For example, in the workplace the actants are the managers, the
structures, the systems and processes, the organization, the corporation, the
regulators, the banks and finance systems, old and new technologies, etc.
There are also wider external social influences on coaching, such as those
from popular culture. Take Oprah Winfrey and the many self-help magazines
and 'reality' TV shows that utilize 'Life-coaching' and shape the coaching
discourse in everyday life. New technologies also change the way coaches

---

[1]'Actants' is a term used in Actor Network theory to mean actors in a network that have
agency, but as these can be both human and non-human, they are called actants rather
than actors.

work – the computer, mobile phone and online video capabilities make coaching a much more mobile and virtual practice than psychotherapy for example. Finally, there are the influential institutional actors, the coaching body politic, such as the university, coaching accrediting and training bodies and the big consultancies offering coaching.

It follows that, to develop a coherent body of theoretical knowledge and to develop broad coaching methodologies and frameworks, coaching must look at both the macro and micro, and try to understand how the multiple actants in the 'networks of coaching' evolve and shape coaching practice. For clarity in this chapter, I will order coaching into macro and micro 'fields' as it helps reveal how they interact with each other.

The coaching meta-theory utilizes the four coaching discourses that underpin coaching micro-practices, and shows three areas where the macro-social impacts on coaching. This chapter will now theoretically map coaching micro-practices before addressing the macro-social.

Coaching Micro-practices

The four discourses provide a wider theoretical base than the dominant therapeutic theories that currently dominate coaching theory. The Psy Expert Discourse relates to the theories and practice of psychology and psychotherapy as adapted and applied to coaching, and the other discourses draw on different theoretical resources. Together the discourses provide a robust and broad basis for the micro-practices of coaching to be researched and theorized. As we explore and develop the theories that inform micro-practices of coaching there are three key areas of theoretical development which need to be embraced simultaneously.

1 *Developing existing theories* taken from therapy, psychology, soft management theory, adult learning and development, and other allied human development fields. The task is to adapt them where relevant for application within coaching.

2 *Developing unique coaching theory* that delivers knowledge to explain and inform current coaching practice. These will draw on new coaching research and diverse and hybrid theories and practices. In a reciprocal feedback loop, coaching theory will also have an impact on other 'helping techniques' such as counselling or managerial techniques. This is an exciting area and as yet is under-developed. Coaching brings a particularly active and social lens to dyadic helping relationships that is expanding to team coaching and other interventions. New synergies found between theories and discourses will help to produce an emergent coaching theory and innovative coaching developments.

3 *Developing coaching in innovative, new directions*; encouraging research and theorizing that draws on imagination and experimentation to develop coaching in innovative directions. Developing 'cyber-coaching' for example is an obvious area where coaching is forging ahead

yet is under-researched. Resources and research are required to develop the ontology of coaching and explanatory theories, thereby taking coaching beyond evidence-based practice into a more generative and imaginative understanding of both what coaching accomplishes and supports its future developments. Currently research and theories are focused too narrowly and try to replicate psychological and HR attempts to measure outputs and behaviours.

This chapter will now examine coaching micro-practices, utilizing the four coaching discourses as part of the narrative that informs the coaching meta-theory.

Theoretical mapping of coaching micro-practice

Figure 12.2 shows how the micro-practices of coaching can be mapped – offering practitioners a framework to develop their practice, and academics a framework to develop theory and research studies.

For each discourse:
- *The Coaching Stance*
- The Focus of Work

Soul Guide
'Mirror to the Soul'
Inner-self and Experience

Network Coach
'Emergent Strategist'
Networked-self and Connectivity

Coaching

Psy Expert
'Technician of the Psyche'
Outward-self and Performance

Managerial
'Role Coach'
Role-self and Productivity

Figure 12.2   **Theoretical mapping of coaching micro-practice**

1   *The coaching gaze*

The coaching gaze is important, and like a rabbit in the headlights, some coaches get caught in one gaze, hypnotized by one way of seeing. This pertains to their personal background, training and experience. Some coaches have the capacity to have a dual gaze, others can take up the Network Coaching position and their gaze becomes more about the connected system and can include other discourses.

Soul Guide Discourse   The coaching gaze is focused on *experience*, the coachee's experience in the here and now – their subjective and bodily experience – and the coach will use their own experience to coach (transference and counter-transference in psychoanalytic terms). Together the coaching relationship offers a 'here and now' living experience to work with, and a skilled coach will utilize this.

Psy Expert Discourse   The coaching gaze is towards *performance* – the coachee's personal performance at work, or their performance in living more generally. The aim is to explore this, identify goals and help the coachee change their behaviour and thinking to improve their performance.

Managerial Discourse   The gaze is towards *productivity*: how to support the coachee take up their role and influence their team, to make the enterprise they are working on more productive.

Network Coach Discourse   The gaze is directed at *connectivity*, helping the coachee locate themselves in a network of activity, of where to influence change, the nodal points in a network, and where to make connections themselves and where to help others to connect (this includes connecting them to the right resources and technologies). Also, the coach takes an ethical viewpoint, to help the coachee make connections between their values and the company's values, and between their work and the social and environmental world.

2   *The coaching stance*

This refers to the coach's stance, i.e. what the coach does, their 'activity' in coaching and how they take up their roles.

Soul Guide Discourse   The coach's stance is to be a *mirror to the soul*. This activity is paradoxical as it is contemplative and reflective. However to take this stance is often a lot harder than jumping to external activity and the 'busyness' of other discourses. To be a *mirror to the soul* enables the coachee to reveal their innermost selves.

Psy Expert Discourse   The coach's stance is to be a *technician of the psyche*. The coach uses coaching tools, techniques and methods to work on cognition and behaviour. The coach presents with an expertise drawn from the Psy professions to help the coachee improve their performance and achieve their personal/work goals.

Managerial Discourse   The coach's stance is to be a *role coach*, helping the coachee analyse his/her various roles, e.g. how they take up a leadership role, how their roles are understood by others, and the tensions between their multiple roles; also how their role impacts on output and efficiency.

Network Coach Discourse   The coach's stance is to be an *emergent strategist*. The coach works with a strategic mindset, not getting drawn into operational minutia or small goals, but keeping the coachee in a generative mindset. The coach helps the coachee to identify patterns that lead to emergent strategies to implement new business models, and seeing new opportunities and new directions.

3   The object of the work

This indicates the aspect of the self the coachee is working on, i.e. the object of their work.

Soul Guide Discourse   The coachee works on their *inner self*: how they feel; what their anxieties, inner secrets and concerns are; what desire they have; and how they can find meaning, identity, well-being.

Psy Expert Discourse   The coachee works on their *outward self*, on their personal performance, how they act and behave, and how they relate and are perceived by others.

Managerial Discourse   The coachee works on their *role self*. The coachee reflects on their roles both in work and in life (the roles of mother, lover, daughter, sibling, scapegoat, hero, etc. may be explored). They explore whether they are in the right roles: have they got trapped in certain roles, are they prioritizing the roles well, how does it feel in the role, what are the role challenges and what needs to change?

Network Coach Discourse   The coachee works on their *networked self*. The coach helps the coachee locate themselves in their network. What patterns do they see across different networks they are currently in, or have been in the past? Are they central and well connected or marginal and disconnected in their networks? How do they and others perceive them – with agency, with lots of connections, a lone figure or perhaps marginal with power, or marginal and disempowered? The networked self also implies others; human and non-human 'actors'. The object of the work for the 'network' coachee are the connections and influences in their network.

Note on team coaching

On the discourse map, team coaching can be situated in the same way as individual coaching. The coach can work on the team's internal dynamic, how others see them and their external behaviour and performance, their role and output, or their connections in the wider network.

Summary

Theoretically showing coaching micro-practice in this way offers a broad base from which to further research and develop coaching practice. These discourses draw upon different theory and practice to inform each of them; in coaching they are not discrete, and depending on the coaching or mentoring approach, will operate in parallel, in an integrated fashion, or in tension with each other (see Chapter 10). Some coaches focus on a particular micro-practice that is situated within a specific discourse – a psychologist-coach may stay within the realms of the Psy discourse for example, or they may expand their coaching repertoire and draw upon the other discourses depending on their coaching capability and the context. The context and the coachee also define the discourse to be used, and the contracting process should help determine in which areas the coach/es will work. However, any experienced coach knows that within coaching you can be working on strategy (Network

Coaching) but find yourself in the Soul Guide Discourse in the same session if some powerful personal material is triggered.

Coaches can use the discourses in their practice to:

a   Become aware of the discourses that inform their approach, reflecting on their strengths and limitations, when to use them, and how their personal practice is informed or limited by them.

b   Identify how to develop their coaching practice in some of the discourses they are less skilled, knowledgeable or practised in.

c   Recognize the importance of the Network Coaching Discourse, as it oversees the coaching intervention, helps the coach decide which approach they should be taking at any given time.

Mentoring and the Micro-practices and Discourses

As already stated the skill-sets and dynamics of mentoring cannot be easily separated from the multiple approaches of coaching, as their skill-sets overlap, and depending on the context of coaching or mentoring, and the approach of the mentor or coach, different discourses and different combinations and dimensions will come into play. Each coaching and mentoring contract, session and relationship has to adapt to its local and specific circumstances.

The Coaching Macro-social

Taking a macro-social perspective means to study coaching beyond the dyad of coach and coachee. It takes a broad social science approach to study the macro-social perspectives that influence coaching. There are three areas in the macro-social that are important additions to the current coaching theory:

- Coaching body politic

- Collective coaching influences (informal)

- External social influences

The coaching body politic

The first macro-social position that requires theorizing is coaching as a 'Body Politic'. This examines coaching from an 'institutional' perspective, and how coaching operates within the economic, resource and political-social field. There is a vitally important relationship between coaching organizations, providers, accrediting and training institutions and how coaching is shaped and practised, yet there is little theorizing done to make these links (de Haan, 2008).

The coaching body politic requires research drawing on critical theory to explore how coaching is being formed, controlled and influenced through institutional forms, and how diverse interests impact on coaching practice. Drawing on theoretical resources such as Actor Network theory, organizational theory and post-structural theory, coaching theorists can explore what effects these institutional and organizational actors have.

The question of interests needs exploring, for example, how does power and financial gain sit in relation to accreditation bodies? The call for standards and professionalization of practice involve institutions that regulate, control and charge to administer accreditation. Similarly the calls for the 'psychologization' of coaching involve training bodies and professions who gain from this. Psychologists and others fighting for this agenda are no doubt convinced by their own expertise and how it might help coaching; however there are clearly other interests that need accounting for.

Seligman critiques the current state of affairs, referring to accrediting bodies in a less than positive manner:

> Some [coaches] are 'accredited' by the self-appointed International Coach Federation and by other rump bodies, but most are not ... (Seligman, 2007: 2)

There is a deficit of organizational and institutional theory, and critical theory that is being applied to the study of coaching, which is at a crucial developmental stage with turf wars going on as to who governs and controls coaching practice.

Quality control, regulation and the loss of innocence

Struggles are taking place around the seemingly neutral debates around quality control and improving regulation. However, make no mistake – accreditation and regulation means control, power and the formation of political power elites. This area requires the application of critical theory to reveal how resources, control and power are handled, and to make connections between how different paths strengthen certain forms of practice and weaken others. The point is not only to argue whether regulation is good or bad *per se*, but also to take a macro-social position, and ask who is benefiting and who is losing out from this process.

Coaching is a multimillion dollar business and it is no wonder that the familiar players in the management field are staking out their credentials. University business schools, the large consultancies, psychologists and psychotherapist bodies are all seeing the potential in coaching, with their organizations growing extension bodies to accommodate coaching (coaching psychologists' UKCC coaching, BAC coaching, universities). At the same time, coaching bodies are emerging – the ICF AFC, the EMCC, the WBC – and there are questions as to who appointed them, who they are accountable to and what their agendas are. Taking a critical theoretical position is not to take a Machiavellian or paranoid position, but to analyse and account for power and for the multiple and complex agendas, some of which are explicit and others that are not (even to those enacting them). There are legitimate and healthy debates to be had in regards to monitoring quality and whether there is a need to regulate practice (Sherman and Freas, 2004).

It is important not to continue these debates about micro-technology practices without the macro-social analysis to ask the bigger picture, political-economic questions. The pretence of professional or scientific neutrality in these matters simply creates a veneer that is not convincing. The main concern is to enable coaching to develop as an enterprising, transparent and high-quality practice that is not unduly limited and constrained by special interest groups protecting their own interests.

Collective coaching influences

Coaches work in large numbers in organizations, and have a collective impact as well as an individual and local impact. This is not an organized or formal collective impact (as the body politic) but a collective informal influence that often goes unnoticed and is not theorized. However, it effects how coaching is perceived and how it develops, and coaching's informal and collective influence on managers and organizations requires investigation and theorizing.

Taking a sociological, network and ethnographic perspective is to theorize coaching by looking at its wider social impact outside of formal organizations and institutional bodies. New social movement theory (Melucci, 1989; Della Porta, 1999) helps us to think about how coaching operates in this field. New social movements are not organized like traditional social movements, as organized bodies such as trade unions who laid claim to structural and class power. New social movements are more informal and self-organizing, working less hierarchically, without defined leaders, and focusing more on identity than economic power. Melucci (1989) describes how resistant communities form and attempt to reclaim identity outside of organizational life.

There is an application of this theory to coaching; many coaches are organizational 'outsiders' either by choice or by default, working outside the confines of an institution, and carrying a certain 'liberation' culture with them. This emanates from their 'faith and belief' in coaching, i.e. coaching can be a force for micro-emancipation, individuals freeing themselves from their own tyrannies (anxieties, fears, etc). Coaches can also appear liberated from the 'corporate chains', often working for themselves and from outside an institution by working from home. Whether this is real or rhetoric is worthy of further research. Imagining coaching to be a new social movement is not a great leap of faith; there is something evangelical about many coaches who believe in the power of transformation through their new talking cure. This is particularly true of the Life-coaching fraternity, and it fits with wider social influences of individuality and personal growth.

Coaching works individually and confidentially yet it also has a collective impact, coaching as an 'ICT' is one example.

Coaching as an information communications technology (ICT)

I am guided by Bruno Latour's somewhat playful proposal for how to study material objects. He writes:

> Specific tricks have to be invented to make them talk, that is, to offer descriptions of themselves, to produce scripts of what they are making others – humans or non-humans – do. (Latour, 2005: 79)

To take up Latour's suggestion, one of the 'specific tricks' that might make 'coaching talk' would be to use the metaphor that coaching on a macro scale might be described as an ICT (information communication technology). According to the World Bank:

> [A]n ICT consists of the hardware, software, networks, and media for the collection, storage, processing, transmission and presentation of information (voice, data, text, images), as well as related services. (Cited in Feigenbaum, 2010)

Taking this description we can conceptualize coaching as an ICT, becoming more than the sum of its parts. Coaches and 'coaching' accumulate, disperse and shape data and language, texts, information and emotions. They process and transmit these to others, reproducing and transforming individual and collective actors as they do their transmission and communication work. Coaching creates new networks, within and across organizations, and between coach practitioners themselves.

Coaching as an in-house ICT   Coaching can be used internally in a company as a collective information communication technology. This can be a planned intervention by management and HR, for example if a number of coaches are engaged to change a company culture, to develop a new leadership cadre. The aim here is to achieve both individual and organizational development through an investment in coaching across a certain population. Whilst these initiatives are happening, something else is happening tacitly – the coaches are acting collectively as an information communications technology, spreading news, ideas, carrying and shaping company culture, from individual to individual, department to department.

This ICT function is rarely utilized to its full capacity; it is a two way process, coaching communicating to employees, and coaches picking up data and information that are communicated to them. There are ways to harvest and use this information, yet rarely do HR departments realize the potential of utilizing this aspect of coaching.

Coaching ICTs, acting as a super-organism   Coaching has another collective impact as an ICT that happens in an unplanned way. Let us draw on Weick's (1989) imagination process to develop theory and imagine coaching as a flock of birds or a swarm of bees, with a self-organizing capacity. There are thousands of coaches, flying or buzzing around organizations across the globe, and these coaches communicate with each other in local and global networks. Coaching now becomes a 'super-organism', individual coaches who make up a collective, yet without conventional organizational structures.

> Superorganisms are important in cybernetics, particularly biocybernetics. They exhibit a form of 'distributed intelligence', a system in which many individual agents with limited intelligence and information are able to pool resources to accomplish a goal beyond the capabilities of the individuals. Existence of such behavior in organisms has many implications for military and management applications, and is being actively researched. (Kelly, 1994: 251)

James Lovelock, when developing Gaia theory, drew on the analogy of a super-organism to describe the self-regulating biosphere (Lovelock, 1982).

Coaching acts as a super-organism within society, and within the workplace as an information communication technology. Coaches not only communicate within the sessions they work, they act as 'memes'[2] communicating

---

[2]While genes transmit biological information, memes are said to transmit ideas and belief information.

information between different coaching sessions, picking up language, new ideas, new rhetoric, discourse, knowledge, insights, nuances, management culture, etc. As well as communicating between individual employees, they also communicate to their clients, perhaps a manager or HR department, again picking up and dropping information, and collecting and passing on knowledge and discourse.

Coaches then communicate between themselves, coaches with coaches, through coaching literature, written texts, websites, academic and popular papers, in face-to-face meetings, supervision, teaching sessions and courses, and large conferences. They also communicate with the general public and their families and friends, picking up and dropping insights from and for their work.

Coaching as an ICT acts as a social lubricant in the workplace. Like individual bees moving from flower to flower, coaches move from person to person and company to company, cross-pollinating ideas. Then, like bees, every so often they swarm; and a collective of coaches form a new home, perhaps a new organization, a new training body, a new theoretical group, a new company.

The other analogy is a flock of birds. Birds pick up seeds in the berries they consume, fly away, and in their droppings the seeds are fertilized in a new place where the seedling grows. In this way seeds are dispersed and the eco-system survives. Coaches, like birds, pick up seeds of ideas, seeds of knowledge, fertilize them with their own knowledge and drop them far away in a different setting. Ideas are dispersed and the eco-system of organizational life flourishes. In the eighteenth century, the coffee shop was an important ICT, and became known as the Penny University – it was a place of knowledge dissemination, a technology of communication. Ideas, knowledge, emotions and culture get transmitted in these informal networks. Places like Silicon Valley become clusters of IT specialists, and through socializing and work, a distributed intelligence contributes to the success of Silicon Valley.

Coaches have particular access to private conversations; they pick up nuances, the emotions of work, the subjective goings on, how work feels, as well as the new ideas about business and strategic change. A new way of working attracts flocking behaviour in coaches and there are shifts in movements towards solution-focused coaching or 'mindful coaching' for example.

Collectively coaches become an informal ICT picking up language and ideas and spreading them. At best they are carriers of new ideas, sharing best practice and knowledge; they also carry and reproduce normative cultures that restrict change. They are culture carriers in two directions: from coaching to business, and from business to coaching. Open training courses for managers also have this function, i.e. managers from different companies share learning and stories. Coaches do the same, but with the 'soft material'. They pass on culture and emotional nuance, and they carry news like peddlers of old, interacting face to face, with Skype, email and telephone; they pass on the news, culture, rhetoric, discourse and knowledge. Coaches are carriers of culture, practices, knowledge, narratives and discourses – theirs is a linguistic and practice-based interaction that acts as transmitter and receiver.

External social influences

To explain the rise of coaching and its emergent development, theories are required that account for the external social influences on coaching. For scholars and researchers to further investigate coaching from this macro-social perspective, new theoretical resources are required, drawing on the social sciences. This book has been written with these 'External social influences' in mind. The geneology of coaching looks at historical social influences and the discourse mapping of contemporary external social influences.

External social influences may be natural, technological or political-social, and each of these impacts on the workplace and on coaching. Some say coaching emerged because the external social world became more alienating – people simply need more professionals to help, to talk to. Changing workplace dynamics through globalization, social change and advanced technologies open up a space for coaching in the workplace to tailored, one-to-one support for executives.

Other social issues such as the rise of the confessional society, the subjective turn, and the expansion of therapy culture also pave the way for coaching to emerge. A macro-social theoretical position observes the continued influences and interactions between coaching and the social world.

Yates (1989) claims that certain technologies are adopted when they are perceived to be the solution to a challenge, rather than because they are necessarily superior technologically. Coaching can be very effective but it is by no means proven as the best social technology. By most accounts it is *ad hoc* and diverse in its substance and quality.

If we theorize that the rise of coaching is in response to a challenge, what problem was the technology of coaching a solution to?

Loneliness and alienation

Professor Jonathan Gosling believes an important problem that coaching addresses is that of loneliness, a lack of listeners in society. Previous managers had support structures that no longer exist. For example, 'Organization Man' in the 1950s and 1960s (Whyte, 1956) had a domestic non-working wife in suburbia to come home to and off-load their work woes and successes. Gender roles meant a division of labour; and domestic labour included the role of 'listener' (Butler, 1990). The workplace was also more stable, people often had jobs for life, they belonged to institutions that provided emotional containment and stability, and this meant more sustainable and supportive relationships at work, colleagues you took lunch breaks with and who listened to you. The environment was less competitive, less fast changing, people's jobs were more secure. In the more nomadic work environment of the post-industrial workplace, longevity in role is now seen as failure to advance, and portfolio work is commonplace. The impact is one of increased competitiveness, less stability, less emotional and institutional containment; and when both women and men are working, the domestic realm rarely provides the space for listening to each other in the same way (Putnam, 2000). Scoular, drawing on Rogers' non-directive, listening approach, adds that coaching needs to be a listening profession owing to the 'personal cacophony of emails, Blackberries, Twitter, Blogs, texts, SMS' etc. that we personally inhabit (Scoular, 2011: 75).

Dealing with employee emotions and giving feedback

Reka Czegledi-Brown, a colleague working in talent and HR, believes that coaching solves the management problem of dealing with emotions and giving feedback, coaching becomes the outsourcing of a managerial role, and because of this the manager loses some important contact and feedback from their employees.

Working with the self requires the self to be worked with

Another problem coaching may address is that increasingly employees are asked to bring their emotional and subjective selves to work. The knowledge economy demands the cognitive, creative and subjective self be active ingredients of labour. Coaching steps in to solve the problems of the executive managing their own emotions and selves in the workplace to fit the company demands.

Brand identity and employee engagement: 'we work in organizations and organizations work in us'

The established demarcations of home and work blur, our identities are tied to our work roles, and at parties we are asked 'what do you do?' as this is the clearest signifier of who we are. Employees are expected to engage with the company and brand; no longer is work something you go to and leave – it stays in you, through emails, Blackberries, in our minds and our identities. Coaching becomes a tool of alignment – personal identity to company identity – and this is measured through employee engagement processes.

Wounded self at work

Finally, there is the problem of damaged employees, '*the wounded self*', and the coach has the task of fixing them with their coaching toolkit. There is plenty of evidence of workplaces damaging individuals, through stress, anxiety, depression and conflict. Mental health and well-being issues are increasingly being identified as expensive to workplaces and governments – the cost of an 'ill' workforce or citizenship to society is huge. Coaching can be brought in to help ameliorate these health problems and support employee well-being. In the workplace, where your career depends on your being dynamic, there remains resistance and a stigma to seeing a therapist or counsellor, so coaching has stepped conveniently into this space, offering something akin to therapy, but without the stigma. Whereas the impact of therapy on the social is well documented (Rieff, 1966; Lasch, 1979; Rose, 1990; Giddens, 1991; Furedi, 2003), coaching as a growing influence in society now requires theorizing from this macro-social perspective.

External social influences clearly need to be accounted for in any meta-theory of coaching and new resources are required to achieve this.

Conclusion

This meta-theory aims to set out the table for dinner, not to offer a set menu. To create a coaching meta-theory is to set out the parameters of coaching, identifying its macro-social influences and how coaching operates as a micro-practice. Within these two fields, theories can be developed that enhance our understanding of coaching, and help develop its practice.

This coaching meta-theory is a process, and developing it further will require research, imagination and theorizing, drawing on a wide body of practice experience and theory. Jacques-Alain Miller writes of Freud and psychoanalysis that 'there is nothing extraordinary in posing that, retroactively, the practice one instituted needs to be recast' and this is true also of coaching. This is not a fixed meta-theory but one that requires recasting at some point in relation to practice. Miller (2011) goes on to summarize how theory and practice inform each other (see Figure 12.3), explaining, 'The

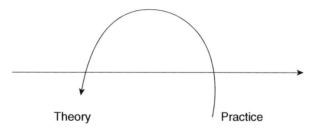

Theory   Practice

Figure 12.3   Theory in relation to practice (Miller, 2011)

theory was necessary in order to institute the practice, and then, retroactively, the practice modified the theory.'

   The essence is here; a meta-theory that is inclusive of the four discourses that underpin coaching – the Soul Guide, the Psy Expert, the Managerial and the Network Coach Discourse. The discourses may be named differently, expanded or contested, but the important thing is that they can now be scrutinized, and can be used to scrutinize existing coaching and mentoring theory and practice.

What makes coaching a distinctive entity?

The meta-theoretical diagram in Figure 12.1 offers a coherent spatial picture of coaching, holding in dynamic relation the four discourses of micro-practice and the macro-social influences. What makes coaching distinctive however, what brings coaching to life, gives it an identity, is by fixing coaching with what Lacan calls a 'point de capiton' – a quilting or an anchoring point.

   The points de capiton are points at which the 'signified and signifier are knotted together' (Lacan, 1993: 268).

> ... a point de capiton (literally an 'upholstery button' though it has also been translated as 'anchoring point'). In the same way that an upholstery button pins down stuffing inside a quilt and stops it from moving about, Zizek argues that a point de capiton is a signifier which stops meaning from sliding about inside the ideological quilt. A point de capiton unifies an ideological field and provides it with an identity. (http://www.lacan.com/zizekchro1.htm)

Lacan recognized that fixing something was also an illusion, yet the point de capiton prevents the endless movement, the endless questions of what coaching is; and the fixing allows the slippage of meanings to be halted, and an identity is formed and fixed in order that it can be acted upon.

   For coaching, the point de capiton fixes the signifiers to the master signifier 'coaching'. These signifiers are the Soul Guide, Psy Expert, Managerial and

Network Coach plus the axes that span between them – wisdom, knowledge, individual and society. It cannot be reduced to the formula that coaching = knowledge + wisdom + individual + society, or that coaching is the integration of the discourses; this is not the case. Coaching is identifiable at the point de capiton, the anchor point at the dissecting point, the intersection of these signifiers, and this makes it possible to theorize and practise from this point. We can then draw on all that is signified, with the endless possibilities for diversity and development. In this way the coaching meta-theory fixes coaching yet does not limit it. Drawing on the meta-theory of coaching we can identify precisely where contemporary coaching can be fixed, at the *point de capiton*.

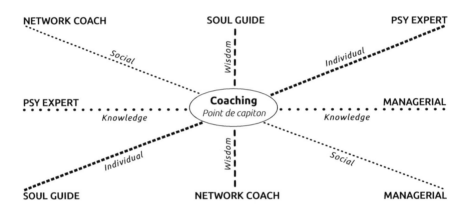

Figure 12.4   **Coaching: born at the 'point de capiton', the dissecting point of the four axes that connect the four discourses**

Macro-social

The other part of the meta-theory is the macro-social and I have attempted to order this into three categories: the body politic, informal coaching collective influences and the wider external social influences. Together the macro-social and the micro-practices form and shape coaching practice and the coaching movement as it progressively travels along its journey.

Future theory development

Each discourse has its own body of theory to be developed, and the macro-social of coaching too can draw on theories from across the social sciences and wide bodies of knowledge from philosophy and other resources. I have deliberately not limited my scope here to name or list theories: they are for each coach–academic to bring to the table.

Further research and theory development are required that will develop a resilience and sustainable body of coaching knowledge that will protect coaching before it gets subsumed solely into the territory of psychotherapy and managerialism, omitting the hybrid and wider potential of coaching and mentoring.

This meta-theory broadens the theoretical base of coaching theory – opening it up to scrutiny and research from multiple perspectives. There are many PhDs and research initiatives waiting to be undertaken in this exciting developmental field. This chapter offers a starting place, giving a meta-theoretical framework to research coaching knowledge and practice, to imagine and develop explanatory theories of what is happening in coaching relationships, and also what happens at macro-social levels, and how the two are connected.

Suggested Reading

Ackroyd, S., Harper, R., Hughes, J.A., Shapiro, D. and Soothill, K. (1992) *New Technology and Practical Police Work*. Buckingham: Open University Press.

Cox, E., Bachkirova, T. and Clutterbuck, D. (eds) (2010) *The Complete Handbook of Coaching*. London: Sage, Section 1: Theoretical Approaches.

Hesketh, A.J. and Fleetwood, S. (2006) 'Beyond measuring the HRM-organizational performance link: applying critical realist meta-theory', *Organization*, 13 (5): 677–699.

Joo, B. (2005) 'Executive coaching: A conceptual framework from an integrative literature review of theory and practice', *Human Resource Development Review*, 4 (4): 462–488.

Melucci, A. (1989) *Nomads of the Present: Social Movements and Individual Needs in Contemporary Society*. London: Hutchinson.

Noon, M. (1992) 'HRM: A map, model or theory?', in P. Blyton and P. Turnbull (eds), *Reassessing Human Resource Management*. London: Sage, pp. 16–32.

13 Coaching Formation
Coach Education and Pedagogies

Introduction

This chapter explores coaching education, and reframes coaching education, training and development as Coaching Formation. Coaching Formation is a term I use, as it puts an emphasis on life-long learning, learning through contexts and practice and from other coaches, and focuses on the coaches forming themselves, rather than becoming coaches through learning skills and techniques. The coach then becomes the essential element in the coaching work, rather than the coaching techniques they employ.

This chapter sets out different education and pedagogical thinking, which are parts of the whole; they each play a part in the coaching formation process.

I will briefly outline the state of play in coaching education, identifying the diversity of offerings and some of the weaknesses whilst acknowledging the new growth in 'quality courses' at masters and PhD levels. The challenges being posed by coaching clients is for coaching to be clearer about

---

[1] I have chosen to use the term 'pedagogy', referring to adult and self-directed learning, rather than andragogy, because andragogy is a less-well-known term, and its meaning is contested and the distinctions disputed. For further reading see Knowles (1980), Hartree (1984) and Davenport and Davenport (1985).

what it offers, what outcomes they can expect, and some reassurance on quality. The coaching fraternity responds with an excessive focus towards accreditation, standardization and professionalization, mimicking psychotherapy and other professional practices. This is at the expense of focusing on developing innovative and creative coaching education and new theories. As the saying goes, 'You can't fatten a pig by weighing it', and in coaching, you can't develop high-quality coaching practice through accreditation control systems. At best you can eliminate the weakest practices, but it is only through excellence in coaching education (throughout a coach's career) and the development of imaginative theory and practice that will raise coaching standards and produce higher-quality practitioners.

   This chapter will begin by outlining where we are now, then focus on how to achieve excellence in coaching education through looking at pedagogies of coaching and providing a psycho-social theoretical process , the 'P–M–P coaching process', which underpins coaching training and coaching practice itself.

Coaching Education: The State of Play

Coaching education is itself in a developmental phase. Some exciting developments are happening as it moves into higher education and becomes a 'respectable' academic subject area. Masters programmes and PhD students are inspiring new research, and refereed journals are beginning to analyse coaching and mentoring with more academic rigour. New books, alongside courses, are manifesting quickly, offering a much more in-depth view of coaching (Kilburg, 1996, 2000; Brunning, 2006; De Haan, 2008; Garvey et al., 2009; Cox et al., 2010; Kets de Vries et al., 2010). There is an emergent questioning of the dominant behaviourist pedagogies that currently dominate coaching, for example Laske (2006) identifies the need to develop capability rather than competencies:

> I have introduced, and surveyed, a novel pedagogical approach to coach education that transcends traditional coach training in the direction of strengthening developmentally nascent capabilities, both cognitive and social-emotional. In so doing, I have focused on the need to understand clients in greater depth than behaviourist paradigms, now pervasive, allow for. (2006: 55)

There are numerous coach educators outside universities, offering coach training that varies in quality, price, length and perspective. Courses vary from \$2,000 to \$30,000 per course, with the top-end university business schools such as INSEAD topping the fees (Scoular, 2011). Some courses are accredited, others are not. At the low end of the market, many courses are atheoretical and very technique focused. To become an NLP coach practitioner takes about seven days and to become a Master Practitioner can be achieved in a 14-day course. In contrast to counselling and psychotherapy training courses that can take years, these lower-end coaching programmes are obviously advantageous in terms of having a much lower entry level into the market place of 'helpers' than therapy training, and with the capacity to charge higher fees. By paying around \$2,000 and having 12 evening teleclasses, some courses claim you can become an ICF 'Accredited Certified Life Coach' (New Horizons, 2011).

Coaching education and accreditation bodies are indisputably interlinked; they share mutual interests. Accreditation bodies cannot exist without courses to accredit, and accredited training courses hope to derive extra legitimization and more business as a result. Accreditation at present is messy, as there are too many bodies, diverse standards, and arguments over whether accreditation actually improves quality (Sherman and Freas, 2004). Accreditation is critiqued by Scoular (2011) who says there are too many accrediting bodies (nine in the UK alone). Her critique is that she would like a single body 'with tough standards and sharp teeth'. Unfortunately, in my opinion, the 'standards' and the 'teeth' would limit creativity from emergent approaches, curtailing creativity and development. Accreditation nearly always becomes over-engineered in the helping/education professions. Counselling for example has developed increasingly long form filling and numbers of hours required in supervision and counselling practice. There is a bureaucratic underpinning that mistakes quantity for quality; the numbers of hours does not offer evidence of good practice. Do these accrediting processes produce quality counsellors? Not in my experience. If you are a poor or mediocre counsellor, but good at filling out forms, and resilient, as long as you haven't done anything outrageous you will be accredited.

Coaching is following these models and if put in the hands of a solo accrediting body, it would, through holding a monopoly, immediately limit the possibilities and approaches. There is something generative about an evolving and emergent coaching 'profession' that would soon be curtailed if it was institutionalized too quickly.

This then is the state of play; coaching training is very variable, it can be expensive or cheap. What is clear is that most courses need to engage more with organizational theory, critical theory and the broader social sciences to offer a fuller curriculum. The meta-theory of coaching, which includes both the macro-social influences and micro-practice (the four discourses), is a good place to start. Putting together an enlivening and creative pedagogy is the next step.

Rather than focus on accreditation and standards (a control approach to delivering outcomes), coaching should follow its more generative and entrepreneurial culture and focus on innovative and creative coaching education, training and development. The rest of this chapter will explore coaching education, and how to underpin good practice. I will begin with the psycho-social dynamics of coaching and suggest a coaching process that frames coach training and coaching practice.

The 'P–M–P' Coaching Process

What underpins any coach training or any coaching session is a psycho-social process, meaning how our inner-landscape (psychodynamics) engages with the outer-landscape (the social). Coaching as a practice creates an emotional and psychological space, in order to engage in our physical and material spaces. The Paternal–Maternal–Paternal (P–M–P) coaching process establishes the theoretical and conceptual structure necessary for coaches to create a developmental environment and a safe space for coaching. This facilitates thinking, before leading to change in the external world.

The P–M–P coaching process is not prescriptive, nor is it a coaching method. It establishes the psycho-social form, the underlying structure and the theoretical stances that underpin a variety of coaching practices. Once the coach understands and internalizes these concepts, their practice becomes freer, and they can then work with individual authenticity *and* creativity, whilst retaining a process that holds and guides the sessions. This P–M–P process initially came from research I undertook when studying at the Tavistock Clinic and later in my doctoral research. It developed from my critique of the Kleinian therapeutic and consultancy methods which focus on maternal containment, without reference to the paternal. Box 13.1 sets out the psychoanalytic theory behind the P–M–P process.[2]

---

[2]The research is found on http://independent.academia.edu/SimonWestern/Papers under the title 'Where's Daddy?' (Western, 1999).

Box 13.1   The Psychoanalytic Theory Behind the P–M–P Process

Explaining the 'Paternal and Maternal' Metaphors[3]

Let me set out the maternal and paternal metaphors in psychoanalytic terms. These are not gender-specific roles; they are symbolic metaphors that either gender can inhabit.

- The maternal metaphor represents the internal world, emotional containment, pairing and dyadic close relations, intimacy, oneness, harmony, play, creativity, thinking, formlessness, emergence.
- The paternal metaphor represents the external world, action and activity, structure, form, triadic and complex relations, difference, the reality principle. It refers to Lacan's *symbolic* father rather than the harsher, all-powerful Freudian father. Using Lacan's term the 'Nom du Père' (Name-of-the-Father) or the 'paternal metaphor', it is the 'father' as signifier and not the real father I am referring to. The 'paternal function' is separate from the presence or absence of the actual father, and can be held by either gender; as Lacan (1958; cited in Dor, 1997) says: 'The Father is not a real object so what is he? ... The Father is a metaphor.'

This P–M–P process is theorized from psychoanalytic experience drawing on Freud (1930/2002; Klein 2001) and a Lacanian perspective, and through applying these theories to my own experience of coaching practice and drawing on my experience of leading masters programmes in Organizational Consultancy at the Tavistock Clinic and directing coaching programmes at Lancaster University Management School.

The P–M–P developed from my critique of the Kleinian therapeutic and consultancy methods that focus on maternal containment – or what Bion (1961) names as maternal reverie – without reference to the paternal metaphor. In my coaching and consulting experience, I found the capacity to utilize maternal containment and to interpret the emotions hugely valuable. However, there were problems too with this method, but firstly I will explain maternal containment and how it applies to coaching.

---

[3]The psychoanalytic use of language such as maternal and paternal can be construed as gender stereotyping, even when it is clearly stated that both genders work in both metaphors; yet this remains unresolved and problematic. However, used in psychoanalytic terms, it acknowledges biological and social constructions of gender and roles that do create real differences.

Maternal Containment and the Container–Contained[4]

Melanie Klein's concept of projective identification (1959) revealed that an infant projects [those] feelings, anxieties and emotions it cannot tolerate into the mother. When the mother takes these projections (introjects them) and emotionally contains them, this is called 'maternal containment'. Maternal containment is to hold the difficult emotions and return them in a manageable form to the infant. Bion (1961) developed this further in two ways, firstly in groups that led to the concept being used beyond individuals in organizations, and secondly in his theory of thinking (1962) whereby he said that the returned emotions were not only managed but can be conceived as 'returned meaning'. Raw emotions are made sense of, and converted into meaning and then thinking through maternal containment. This understanding of maternal containment has been transferred to all helping relationships, from therapy to consultancy and coaching. For maternal containment to be achieved, the mother, therapist or coach must have within them the psychic capacity to be an emotional container.

Container–Contained

In coaching, the coach is the container and the coachee the contained:

> … 'container-contained' coming from the mother-infant relationship, is applicable to a wide range of relationships. In process consultancy the consultant acts as a container for the projected anxieties of the organisation which are then contained. (Halton, 1996: 3)

Bollas describes how he creates a maternal container in his psychoanalytic practice using Bion's term 'reverie':

> There are always levels of thought, levels of engagement, levels of response to a question, levels of thinking about something. I can think off the top of my head. I can provide a certain level of response to what you might be discussing, or to what a patient might be saying to me. But for reverie to take place, I have to be able to drift inside myself … in a more associative way … in a less reactive manner. I also have to be relaxed inside

(Continued)

---

[4]This approach to containment draws upon specific psychoanalytic theory and practice, but is described in different ways and can be found in many ancient contemplative practices. Nancy Kline (1999) for example re-works this contemplative and containing approach for coaching in her 'Time to Think' approach, as do some transpersonal approaches to coaching.

(Continued)

myself for this to take place, creating a containing space for the analysand (client). (Bollas, 1997: 39)

Learning from this stance, the coach creates a space that is not a reactive space, but a reflective, associative space, that enables the coachee to contact their emotions and their unconscious. The coach and coachee can then work together to understand the emotional life of the coachee that impacts on the capability to engage, be confident and be creative.

From 'insight to transformation'

When using this maternal approach of 'container–contained' in consultancy and coaching, my experience found three important deficits:

1 *The lack of a paternal container.* Maternal containment didn't happen without a 'paternal container' which was omitted in the theory and practice of this model. Taken from psychoanalysis, 'the couch', the clear roles of the analyst and patient, and the 50-minute strict time boundary all provide a 'paternal container': i.e. clear structures and physical architecture that enable the maternal containment and emotional work to take place. The clear structures, roles and time boundaries were absent when the theory was translated from the 'analyst's couch' to the coaching space. (Amado, 1995: 351)

2 *The pathologizing tendency.* In contrast to positive psychology coaching that denies the shadow and only works with the positive, Kleinian work privileges the shadow and often denies creativity, drive and jouissance. This means that the unconscious and emotional life is only partially worked with. The lens of maternal containment prefers to find envy and dependency rather than creativity and libido (energy) that are required for generative ideas and entrepreneurship. Both the shadow and the creative unconscious need interpreting and need to be welcomed by an open coach.

3 *A theoretical lack: how to turn 'thinking into action'.* Maternal containment is vital to turn raw emotions into meaning and thinking, yet once achieved, there was no theory or method to translate insight and thinking, achieved through maternal containment, into action that made a difference in the external world, through either personal or organizational change.

My aim was to develop a coaching theoretical framework which utilized the positive aspects of maternal containment, ensured that both shadow and creativity (Eros and Thanatos) were worked with, and which then could lead to action and change in the external world.

To achieve this I introduced the paternal concepts from Jacques Lacan, and combined this to work with the maternal stance from the Kleinian tradition. The resulting process provides the psycho-social structural form for coaching practice. Through testing this in many coaching scenarios and having taught and supervised other coaches using this, the process has proved successful.

In psychoanalytic terms, the father enters the safe pairing world of the mother and infant, who are bonded and in a state of 'oneness'. When the father enters as a third person, the fantasy of oneness is broken, and the infant observes mother and father interacting. The infant also experiences itself being observed by a parental pair. This helps the infant to realize its own individual self – that it is a separate being from the mother and that an external world exists, represented by the father. This is the reality principle – there is a world outside the self, the world is not simply 'me and Mother' (Britton, 1989).

Coaching can often replicate this mother–infant dyad – a collusive relation easily occurs that is safe, warm and supportive; yet changes in the external world are never made, as the coaching couple idealize their own relationship at the expense of facing the reality principle. In this scenario, the paternal metaphor is excluded.

On the other hand, coaches can avoid undertaking maternal containment, owing to their dash to techniques, goals, performance and activity. Holding this maternal containing space can create a lot of anxiety, as the coach has to let go of their 'knowing' and expertise, and invite a space of 'not-knowing' that allows the underlying emotions/unconscious to speak.

This process reveals that maternal containment can't take place before a safe space is created (P), then maternal containment takes place that turns emotions to thinking and meaning (M), and then finally this new thinking finds an outlet in the external world, to create change and transformation (P).

Having explained the basic theory, I will now expand on the P–M–P coaching process.

Together, maternal and paternal containment provide the psycho-social framework for the coaching process itself and the training of coaches.

Application to the coaching process

1   Build a container

First, as Anna Freud says, build the house; first, as Klein says, introject the good breast; first, as Bion says, you have to have an adequate container; first, as Bowlby says, have a secure base.(Alvarez, 1992: 117)

Before a bird lays an egg there is the preparation, finding the safest position and creating the nest. Before a therapist undertakes therapy, a safe physical space and contract are formed.

The first task of a coach is to take up a paternal stance (P) and build a paternal container. This is a structured and safe space, a prerequisite for coaching work to commence. Paternal containment means clear contracting and expectations, financial clarity, time and regularity of sessions agreed, confidentiality, having a solid presence, and finding a safe and protected physical environment to work in (e.g. no phone interruptions). Whilst coaching is not therapy and there can be more flexibility regarding time and working space (a person's office may be used in coaching), the paternal containment work is still vital. The process of building a paternal container is important not only to protect the sessions, but also as a signifier of the coach's intent to take up their role with confidence, maturity and care.

2   *Emotions to thinking: trust, play and creativity*

A maternal stance (M) is then taken up by the coach, who sets up the 'container–contained' relationship. The coach is the container (mirroring the maternal function) and the coachee the contained. Maternal containment is the state of 'reverie' that enables the coach to listen to the unconscious and deep emotions that are often not recognized by the coachee. It is in this safe environment, with a coach trained to hold open a containing space, that something new can be discovered. This close pairing, based on trust, underpins a very strong 'coaching alliance'. In this space, play takes place; and to play with ideas, to be creative, is to lose one's inhibitions and goal-focused drive and enter another space. This is the source of creativity and new learning. The coach uses counter-transference and associative intelligence to offer insights and interpretations, thoughts and meaning. This demonstrates that the coach is thinking deeply about the coachee, is in tune with them, and is 'holding them' in mind. Maternal containment is not passive, and the coach is working very hard to translate the emotional contact with the coachee into language and therefore thoughts and meaning: to transform emotions to thinking. The coachee over a period of time internalizes this way of being and learns to transform their own emotions into thoughts through their own associative work. When the coachee has accomplished this for themselves – and not all succeed – they begin to work with others in this way.

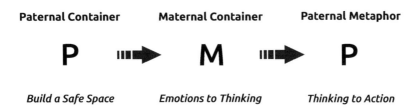

Paternal Container   Maternal Container   Paternal Metaphor

Build a Safe Space   *Emotions to Thinking*   *Thinking to Action*

Figure 13.1 The P–M–P coaching process

3 Thinking to action: the reality principle

Following the maternal containment work and towards the end of a coaching session, and/or after a number of sessions, the coach returns to the paternal stance (P) which prepares the way for the thinking to become action. The safe internal 'maternal space' of processing emotions to thought is interrupted by the entry of the external world (symbolically the oedipal father interrupts the bonded–pairing relationship between mother and infant). Reality has to be faced and negotiated. In coaching terms, this is about application of creative thinking to real workplace or real life challenges, where the coach inserts reality: 'So how are you going to progress these ideas?', 'Where will the challenges be and what resistances will arise?', 'Who do you need to connect with to make this happen?', 'How are you going to overcome your anxiety and retain your capacity to be a confident leader at the next board meeting?'

The coach may introduce a paternal stance, re-inserting boundaries, clarifying contracting around time, or phone calls; or reasserting the reality principle, and ensuring the external world is faced, particularly if the coach and coachee feel like they are in a collusive warm (maternal) bubble that feels great but is not producing results. On the other hand the maternal container is often obliterated in coaching in the dash for goals, results and activity. Coaches can be very fond of doing rather than creating a space for thinking first.

This is not a simple linear process, as the paternal needs reasserting at different times during the maternal containment and vice versa. However, the process itself establishes the psycho-social dynamics of coaching, and gives the coach a framework to work with.

A coaching training programme should mimic this process, clearly contracting and creating a safe learning environment (P), ensuring that the coach trainees experience the trainers as 'maternal containers', allowing deep thinking spaces to occur, and working with the trainees to read and understand the emotional dynamics of the group (M). Finally before the coaches leave the programme, they are supported to face the reality principle: How are they going to practise as coaches? How are they going to get clients? What are they going to do with their learning to make an impact? (P).

If a coaching training course embodies and models this process, working with it repetitively at each module across the whole learning experience, then a parallel-process learning takes place.

1   Coaches on a training course internalize this process and then use it in their coaching practice.

2   Coachees receiving coaching internalize the process and use it in their managerial roles in their work and life.

Coaching Pedagogy

Coach education, training and development in its many diverse forms requires a coaching pedagogy which enables learning to take place in sync with coaching culture and coaching theory.

A coaching pedagogy should draw upon other learning approaches but it is important for coaching to identify what is specific to it – what are the philosophical and practical implications of how coaching is taught and learnt and what are the aims and principles that underpin coach training? The excerpt in Box 13.2 from an unpublished paper of mine sets out some ideas.

Box 13.2   Designing a Creative Coaching Pedagogy

Designing pedagogies for coach training should be a form of art yet it is often reduced to a more mundane and functional activity. Paulo Freire, the famed educationalist, describes the latter approach as 'banking' where the educator 'deposits' knowledge into the educatee (1970: 45). Programme design is often based on this model of 'banking education' where trainers sit down and decide on the theory, knowledge and skills they have to impart, then they plan how to deposit it into the learner. Instead it is a helpful analogy for those designing coach training to step into the shoes of an artist or choreographer. The art of programme design is to embrace experiential learning and move away from the functionalism of breaking down coaching into specific skills, techniques and imparting knowledge as if they are objects to be consumed. This model of consumption, with the trainee as customer, is problematic, as consuming a learning package undermines reciprocal learning.

To design a creative learning process is to think spatially, to imagine aesthetics, to understand the relationship between 'form and function', to envisage patterns and shapes. Observing architecture, film, ballet, opera and theatre is to learn from choreography and film direction. Opera stages, for example, show different constructions that utilize time and space to connect difference; music is merged seamlessly with storytelling, dance and theatre. Together a harmony of experience is created. Behind the scenes there has been a lot of planning, thoughtful preparation, but the experience on the day is a holistic experience and is creatively engaging. Identifying how a training programme works and how learning takes place is a complex matter of putting things together, ordering a process, and seeing where connections and synthesis take place, where theory works alongside experience, where skills and practice fit into the mix. It is seeing where conscious learning makes way for unconscious processing, where disruptions and cuts are necessary to jolt the learning experience, to awaken participants to their own experience. It is to create a stage, to engage an audience and then turn to the audience to become directors of their own learning. To design an effective training programme that embraces experiential and associative approaches is to create an event, something that is memorable. It is to design an experience that engages each person and creates a collective experience, one that teaches but also reveals, and continues to reveal long after the event has finished. It is to create a learning space that can be occupied by learners, who camp out there for a while, play for a while, and experiment with new forms of the self and the whole learning group.

In designing the pedagogy for coach training events, I draw upon religious practices and rituals, learning from centuries of experience that are embodied in worship liturgies. A liturgy is about embodying wisdom through experience, rather than consuming knowledge. To achieve a creative course pedagogy takes an understanding of structure and emotion, thinking and experience, individual and group dynamics, and paternal and maternal containment.

To create a coaching training programme the best preparation is to hang out in architecturally beautiful and interesting places, and to see how space works, then see how connections are made, where the escalators and walkways are, where the light comes into the building; or go to the opera, or a jazz or a classical concert, or a high-church service, and observe people, patterns, shapes, colours, liturgy, space and audience engagement. Then start to plan your course.

Eight principles of a coaching pedagogy

Reflecting on my experience of designing a pedagogy to deliver a new master's-level coaching course at Lancaster University Management School, eight pedagogical principles emerged that can be used as a guide or template for coach training programmes (see Box 13.3).

Box 13.3   Eight Principles of a Coaching Pedagogy

1   Human Experience

Coaching is a people activity and therefore human experience must be central. This may sound obvious but it's often overlooked. Coaching training often displaces the true 'object' of the coaching activity, 'the person', in favour of a substitute object, 'coaching techniques or tools'. If the object of coach training is to learn methods, tools and techniques, it produces coaching practice that mirrors this. When humans' experience is displaced by what the coach does and their expert techniques, rather than the experience between the coach and coachee, then the essence of coaching is lost. Laing (1967) sums up this position most eloquently in his book *The Politics of Experience*:

> ... we need a phenomenology of experience, of person relating to person ... Any theory not founded on the nature of being human is a lie and a betrayal of man ... 'an inhuman theory will inevitably lead to inhuman consequences'. (1967: 45)

In any coach training, human experience needs to be placed at its heart. This means to expect the trainers and learners to be open to their experience on the course, and to ensure any coaching models and techniques that are taught come secondary to the focus on the coachees' experience.

2   Self-knowing

A coach who hasn't done the work on themselves cannot do the work on others. Self-knowing is about personal insight and also relational insight, i.e. how you relate to others and how they relate to you.

A key part of a pedagogy is to create a *'laboratory of experience'* where participants contract to learn in the here-and-now about their personal and group process, whilst also learning theory and skills. Self-awareness is not a solitary exercise as we are inextricably linked to and created by others. Discovering ourselves has to be achieved through others, and a coaching course should be a place to explore these dynamics. Coaches should work from an authentic place and each coach brings something special – coach education should recognize and work to enhance this. There is no place for coaching conformity! Teaching to give feedback is common in coach training – learning how to accept feedback undefensively, are and to learn from it, are very important.

3 Emancipation, Ethics and Critical Thinking

A pedagogy should encourage critical thinking – for example, questioning normative assumptions, structural power relations and diversity issues. Unless we train coaches to think about the power structures of coaching relationships, and how management and organizations can create conformist and controlling cultures, how can coaches resist colluding in such structures of dominance, or find ways to challenge them? Developing ethical approaches works with coaches to clarify their own values, in order to help them to work with coachees to clarify theirs. The emancipation agenda is to train coaches to question systemic violence (Zizek, 2008), that is, the things in society and workplaces that oppress others, for example the sexism, racism and discrimination that often go unspoken but exist in the system. Training coaches to coach with a micro-emancipation agenda is also important: to coach individuals to find their autonomy, their unique individualism, to help them find their voice, their vocation, to release their passion and energy in their lives.

4 Learning from Experience, Observation and Practice

A good pedagogy will create learning opportunities where coaches can learn from experience – from the experience of coaching, of being coached, and of being part of a learning organization. Experiential learning is learning that sticks. Creating experiences to learn from is an essential part of pedagogical design as it involves personal reflection, creating a culture of openness, trust and sharing. To learn this way means to learn how to observe others, how to be observed by peers and trainers, and to observe yourself practising skills (video/audio-recording). An experienced coach finally learns how to observe themselves whilst coaching in the moment, so they can adapt their coaching accordingly.

5 Learning from Each Other

A coaching pedagogy should provide a minimum of 50 per cent of space for lateral learning opportunities. This can occur on the training course itself and outside of the course, taking place through discussions, pairing work, group work, peer-coaching, observation, online chat forums, buddy systems, etc. Learning from each other, sharing stories, knowledge, skills, best practice, tips, emotions and feelings is both formative and inspiring. Learning from each other is also to learn from difference. It helps demonstrate to coaches how coachees can learn from dialogue and observing the coach.

(Continued)

(Continued)

6   Learning from Play

> The significant moment (of play) is that at which the child surprises him or herself. (Winnicott, 1971)

To learn is to be able to play; a child learns through play, and adults learn through playing with ideas. Creating a safe space for people to play is to free 'learners' from having to know, to be knowledgeable, to be right. Learning means to open a space to learn something new, to surprise oneself; and to achieve this they need to step into a space of not-knowing. Humour, play, fun, creativity, art, making films, playing roles, playing games, playing with each other's ideas – to be a great coach means to allow a coachee to be able to play with ideas. Coaches need to learn to do this themselves first, and a training course should ensure there is room for playing.

7 Robust Theory

As identified in Chapter 11, coaching at present is weak on theory and research. Robust theory is really important for coaches to develop practice. Serious theoretical concepts are important, and coaching education needs to review what theory is taught and what is missing. At different levels in coach training, theory will be more or less present. However, at all levels some theory is necessary – even in short courses, reading lists and some concepts should be taught. Coaches sharing a common language, knowing some theoretical principles, can explore their practice in a more informed way. The coaching meta-theory set out here gives a guide for this. In masters- and diploma-level courses, the traditional seminar and reading group is a good pedagogical way to learn theory. Trainers need to 'know their stuff' and teach a wide range of theory. Bringing in guest tutors to give seminars from expertise across a university, from sociology, feminist studies, theology, management studies, etc., is necessary to broaden the syllabus. As Kurt Lewin (1946) teaches us, 'there is nothing so practical as good theory'. Practising skills and ways of 'being' as a coach are then informed by conceptual knowledge, and in turn practice informs theory.

8   Portfolio Assessment

Assessment impacts on learning and practice. A coaching pedagogy requires assessment that covers coaching practice, skills and theory. Assessment can limit learning, creating anxiety and risk-averse behaviour or conformity of thinking. Portfolio assessment presentations giving trainees a wide remit allows for coaches to present to their learning in innovative ways – this is my favourite assessment method as it frees trainees up, develops their creative and communication skills, and allows peers to learn from the experience and give open feedback. Within a portfolio assessment brief can be a written assignment and other required material, peer and self-assessment, and video and recording coaching sessions for example.

Quality control is vital in coaching, and assessment offers one way to let trainee coaches know their deficits as well as let them know their strengths. Done in a helpful and thoughtful way, assessment is a vital part of any learning and should be a carefully planned part of the pedagogy.

Examples of pedagogy used in coaching education

These examples are from training programmes I have worked on, and they have been well received by participants. I share these to stimulate further thinking by coach trainers.

Learning laboratory

In any face-to-face training session an essential part of the learning comes from the peer learning from the participants. This usually takes place through the informal discussions and set exercises. However, one aspect that is omitted from discussion is the group dynamic itself, which provides a wonderfully rich learning environment if it can be accessed.

Coaching, like other forms of interpersonal learning, relies heavily on the interpreting and sense-making of others – their words, behaviours, experiences and emotions. Coaches require a high level of self-awareness and an awareness of interpersonal relationships to achieve this. Face-to-face training offers a unique opportunity to learn from experience to create a 'learning laboratory' where interactions, thoughts, feelings and reflections can be accessed and used as data for learning material. The learning laboratory evolves from Kurt Lewin's (1946) influential work amongst others who developed experiential group learning methods such as the T group. To achieve a 'learning laboratory' environment requires confident trainers who are skilled in reading group dynamics and are prepared to show a real authentic openness about their part in the dynamic. The participants and trainers contract to be open, to examine their own behaviours and thoughts. Trainers who can be open can discuss the power relations in the room, how they are experienced by and experience the group; are they deferential, are they passive, are they combative? What does it mean and who owns what part of this dynamic?

This contracting is about building trust (mirroring building the *'coaching alliance'* with a coachee) and it is a two-way process: not the trainers setting out a contract for the participants, but a dialogue ending in mutual agreement. As can be seen, all of this provides *parallel process learning*. Coach training is not simply about skills and knowledge acquisition, as what is learnt is often tacit and by processing emotions and experiences in the classroom. A pedagogy can be designed to maximize this tacit, parallel process learning.

Like in the learning laboratory, the coach–coachee relationship tells the coach a lot about how the coachee relates to others. In the world of psychoanalysis, this is called 'reading the counter-transference and the projections received from the patient'. How a coachee relates – their body language, defences, their spirit and engagement, when they come alive, when they slump in the chair – are all data for the coach to work with. Honing these skills in the safety of a classroom is a vital part of coach training, and the best way to develop this capability is to create a shared experience where staff and participants can observe their own reactions, inner-theatres, defences and dynamic relations with others in a safe environment.

Developing associative intelligence

Developing 'associative intelligence' means to work with the emotions and thoughts, the conscious and unconscious. Developing associative intelligence is to use the self as a sensor, to develop the capacity of a coach to become insightful. To associate is to make connections between things, between emotions, relations, in the virtual and material world – in coaching it is to encourage a transgression from linear thinking to associative and generative thinking. It fits with Network Coaching and the Soul Guide Discourses – both utilize associative intelligence.

Freud revealed two main ways to the unconscious, the dream and free association. Free association on the couch does more than give access to the unconscious as it also develops our awareness of the 'unconscious', and some claim it develops the unconscious life itself (Bollas, 1997). Lacanian psychoanalysts think of the unconscious as something between people, not just deep within us.

When applied to coach training we try to develop the coach's capacity to access their own unconscious process and to associate this with the coachee's unconscious. In terms of coaching utilizing associative intelligence, we encourage the unconscious in the room to speak.

This coaching approach is working in a completely different ball-park to GROW coaches or the Psy Expert, who use tools and techniques to focus on cognitive and behaviour change. It moves into an area of using the authentic self, to become a receptive container for the other, to make oneself available, to be open to the emotional and the unknown, and to tune into the coaching session so that the unconscious and the emotions speak their own truth. The work is multilevel; it is where Soul Guidance takes place, where personal insights happen. A talented coach working with 'associative intelligence' is able to stop a coaching session mid-track, to pause, to hesitate, and can completely change track, to disrupt the session by speaking what is felt and experienced but often remains unspoken, and perhaps is known at some deep level but not yet consciously thought. In the hesitation, the gap, the subjective truth is revealed.

Psychoanalysis teaches us that in the absence of something (the lack), desire is formed. In contrast to the headlong dash to personal growth, to improving personal performance, associative intelligence creates connections to a deep knowledge of the self, and is able to speak to this. It speaks the unconscious into existence and it connects the unconscious/the soul with the cosmos – the link here is between the coach working in the discourses of Soul Guide and Network Coach. Developing 'associative intelligence' is also to develop our capacity to be associative to the aesthetics, material objects and architectures around us, to nature; it is to be aware of our bodies in space and time. Developing associative intelligence is a task of highly competent coach training, influenced by psychoanalytic approaches. One way to develop associative intelligence is the Free Association Matrix (see Box 13.4). When directing the Lancaster University Coaching Course, each day began with a yoga session to engage the body, individually and collectively, which was then followed by a Free Association Matrix, to engage the unconscious, individually and collectively, and to develop the coach trainees' capacity for associative intelligence.

Box 13.4   Free Association Matrix

'Free Association Matrix' (FAM) is a technique I designed that draws on Gordon Lawrence's Social Dream Matrix (1999). To develop associative capacity, I therefore asked people to 'free associate' (Freud's other road to the unconscious); yet in the FAM the free association is as a collective rather than in the dyad of the psychoanalytic pair (Western, 2008a: 92).

The FAM begins as a 'disruptive intervention'. The chairs are placed in *ad hoc* patterns, as a maze of chairs facing in all directions disrupts normative expectations of group work. We ask participants not to ask questions, not to discuss things, only to speak associatively: to associate to their thoughts, emotions, feelings, bodily experience and to others in the room.

(Continued)

(Continued)

After 40 minutes there are 'sense-making' exercises to try to capture some themes, patterns and learning from the associations shared. We work to encourage the unconscious to speak in the room, to develop the individual and group unconscious, and also to develop participants' capacity to interpret group dynamics at unconscious levels. The effect of the Free Association Matrix is transformative as it changes the training environment from a classroom to a place of unconscious enquiry. Over a period of time, participants shift from being self-conscious in the matrix to completely relaxed in it.

I have used this technique over many years now, and it provides an action–learning experience of both doing unconscious work, then reflecting and learning from this work. This free associative method built on the participants' ability to see how the threads of their own unconscious, and that of the social unconscious, entwine.

When using it with a global OD team in a bank, they were initially confused and threatened by this 'strange process'. After three days of using it, one person spoke at the end, saying, 'If everybody in the bank spent 20 minutes in an FAM, the whole bank would perform better and it would transform the culture.'

Democracy wall

In each training room I set out a democracy wall and invite all in the room, trainers and learners, to use it as they will. At the end of each day we visit the wall which has captured thoughts, questions, comments and reflections from the day, including feedback, insights, preoccupations, suggestions and improvements to the course. This sets out a transparency and openness from the beginning, and it offers a space for people to jot down thoughts during sessions and breaks that can be picked up later without interrupting sessions.

Hot seats: coaching in the moment!

Two seats are set out in a coaching pairing at the front of the training room. Live coaching sessions are used to work through issues that arise in the classroom, giving individuals the opportunity to coach, and to be coached, and also to learn from observing the tutors work as coaches. Different people occupy the hot seats, and we sometimes do *Tag Coaching*, asking different people to take different roles, whilst a coaching dialogue continues. This deals with the live issue in the room, modelling transparency and building trust, whilst learning about coaching at the same time through observing a live coaching dialogue – killing two birds with one stone!

Doubling

This is a technique whereby the trainer (or another participant) places a hand on a coach practising coaching, and speaks as if he/she is the coach. The coachee responds to the coach rather than the trainer who is 'doubling'. This allows a training intervention and a different perspective, without interrupting the flow of a session.

Coaching triads

Working in coaching pairs with an observer creates a coaching triad. The observer timekeeps the session and then gives feedback to the coach on their coaching skills. The triads take turns in each position – coach, coachee, observer. This exercise installs in the mind of the coach the third position (the observer); and the aim is that when the coach is in a session they become their own observer, taking up the third position that enables them to observe themselves in the moment, and adapt their coaching accordingly (this is one of the abilities of an experienced Network Coach).

These are a just a few examples of coaching pedagogical methods.

Coach Education and the Four Discourses

The chapter will now briefly discuss how coach education works across the four coaching discourses.

Psy Expert Discourse

When training coaches in the Psy Expert Discourse the normative approach is to go straight to the tools and techniques of coaching, the NLP tools, the CBT methods. This is putting the cart before the horse as it teaches coaches the 'tricks of the trade' without teaching the trade itself. Figure 13.2 sets out how coaching in the Psy Expert Discourse should be taught. Drawing on the main theories of psychotherapy, we can say that Psy Expert coaching informs coaching on the four levels of skills, interventions, theories and understanding.

At the base of the diagram is the coaching alliance:

1 *Person centred.* Humanistic counselling approaches and the work of Carl Rogers set out the core conditions needed for any helping relationship. Without learning these, coaches will never build the trusting relationship that enables open, trusting and reflective thinking. The coaching alliance is paramount to the work of coaching.

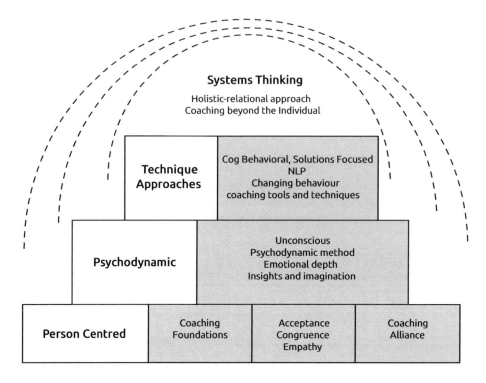

Figure 13.2   Training coaches to utilize the Psy Expert Discourse

2   *Psychodynamic.* The next level of learning should be the psychodynamics of relationships. Coaches should understand the importance of transference, projections and unconscious defences, or they will miss important aspects of the process. I have met a number of coaches in supervision who are blind to the positive transferences they receive (my clients love my coaching) and the huge blind spots they have regarding the client's defences and anxieties that are covered by either aggressive or omnipotent behaviours. Psychodynamics are vitally important and the Psy Expert Discourse is the place to learn the basic psychodynamic processes necessary for coaching.

3   *Technique approaches.* Now we can come to coaching tools, skills and techniques! The coach is now sufficiently grounded in practice; they have the skills to make the coaching alliance, and to actively and empathically listen so that they understand the coachee's challenges. They have the psychodynamics to read some defences and listen to unconscious desire. They can now think about how and when to use techniques to work with their coachee, agreeing what is appropriate, what challenges and behaviours the coachee really wants and needs in order to adapt and modify. The list of tools and techniques is endless, from CBT, NLP, solutions-focused and a myriad of eclectic tools (Zeus and Skiffington, 2002). There is also an array of psycho-metric tests that fit into the technique approach, and many coach programmes select one or two psychometric tests for their personal coaching toolbox.

4 *Systems thinking.* Finally, applying systems thinking from the Psy Expert Discourse draws upon family therapy approaches; this application from the Psy Expert makes the link to the Network Coach Discourse.

Soul Guide Discourse

To train coaches in this discourse is to work with associative intelligence and to draw on ancient contemplative traditions. The Soul Guide draws on humanism, non-directive coaching, philosophy, existentialism, theology, deep ecology, nature, spirituality, art and music, and other influences that inspire and help the coach explore authenticity and meaning. There are many ways to coach in the Soul Guide Discourse and it depends on the experiences and dynamic between the coach and coachee, and the shared understanding they can reach in this domain. There are no rules or techniques: this is not therapy, nor is it spiritual direction.

Training coaches to be Soul Guides is very different to training skills. It is about developing capacity for negative capability (Bion, 1961), to work with the unknown, to hold open a space, and to guide the coachee into the space to allow them to do the 'soul work'. To hold a mirror to the soul means to have done some soul work oneself, and in coach training the focus implies more personal development, free association approaches, holding one's silence, artwork to explore the unconscious, sharing personal journeys, and other practical guidance. Some coach trainees really develop in this discourse and engage, whilst some have very limited capacity to work in it. The danger area is those who like to be in this field yet have not done the work themselves, and cannot separate themselves from ego and narcissism (the New Age movement is full of Life-coaches and 'healers' in this space). The Soul Guide space is open to conversations about values, meaning, belief systems, faith, spirituality, philosophy, existential joys and angst, life, death, love and beauty. It may also include childhood events and patterns that continue to come alive in the present. This is the domain of ontology – of being, what it means to be in the world – and also of the transpersonal – what it means to have a soul.

The coaching potency in this discourse comes from another source, which is counter-intuitive to the Western mind but familiar to all contemplative traditions. The coaching space becomes a sanctuary, a retreat in the world, and at times the coach, like in the Zen tradition, awakens the coachee with an interpretation, a thought, a gift, an act of generosity or perhaps a jolt.

Managerial Expert Discourse

To educate in the Managerial Expert Discourse is to situate the coachee in role, in their team, their department or their organization. The coaching task is role analyst, that is, to help the coachee analyse how they perform in their role, and how they can impact on organizational success. The theory required for coaches draws on team dynamics, organizational theory, change theory and management and leadership theory. The coach is required to understand the world of management, teams and organizations, in order to support the coachee to work on change, efficiency and productivity. Tools such as SWOT analysis are common in this field. Training coaches in organizational role analysis and role biographies gives them methodologies to work with coachees (Long, 2006; Reed and Bazalgette, 2006); and I would advocate at master's level that coaches and trainers read Goffman (1968), Sartre (2001), Butler (1990) and MacIntyre (1985) to explore the different ways of understanding role, identity and performativity, in order to develop a greater understanding of 'social role' and social construction of identity. The coaching task is focused on role and output, and the coach training focuses on becoming a role analyst, enabling the coach to explore the meaning or tensions in the roles, and how to support a manager/leader to take up their roles with confidence to increase productivity and organizational success.

Network Coach Discourse

To teach the Network Coach Discourse is to draw on network and systemic theories, and Actor Network theory, as it offers a contemporary insight into how the social world is organized. Ecological readings and contemporary organizational theories are also useful. Educating Network Coaches is to change the focus from behaviour and performance to spatial awareness. Theory and practice merge in this discourse – how we conceptualize both our organizations and social-network frames informs how we work in them.

Observing organizations

One exercise I use is observing organizations, where trainees are asked to choose a formal or informal organization and observe it (for either an hour or a series of visits). I then ask them to record their observations, what they saw, what they thought and what they felt. Reporting back to the class, so much is learnt about both what is seen, and what is not seen. I have learnt to do the exercise at least twice, with the second time looking for that which was not present the first time. Often this supports the Actor Network scholars, who claim that social scientists see only people, and not other machines, processes, material objects and technology; when these are identified as part of a network of activity the report coming back is often very different, and new connections are made.

Discourse mapping

Another part of training in the Network coaching discourse is to get the coachees (or observers) to map which discourse they are working in during coaching sessions (or training sessions) and to notice change during sessions. This awareness is invaluable because as they become aware, they develop a reflective capacity that enhances their coaching ability; they are no longer entrapped within a discourse, but have the insight and choice to move from one to another as appropriate.

Network mapping

Training coaches in the art of network mapping is a very helpful training exercise to develop Network coaching. I work with a network mapping exercise I have developed from structural family therapy (Minuchin, 1974) that brings insights of how power works in networks, and how an individual locates themselves in relation to others. The trainees begin to see inter-dependencies, their connections and the gaps in where and how they relate. We seek nodal points in the network that can maximize and influence change.

Working seamlessly across the discourses

Working between and across discourses is the real skill of a coach. There are times to focus on the linear space between the Psy Expert and Managerial in order to improve the coachee's personal performance and apply this to role and team outcomes. To know when to work in the Soul Guide Discourse, and then when and how to link this with the Managerial, Psy or Network Coach perspective is an advanced coaching skill that relies on having a Network Coaching perspective. Learning comes from good theory and conceptually understanding the discourses, then from coaching practice, reflection and observing good practice in others: watching role plays, live coaching sessions, working in triads and reflecting on their practice.

Coach training and development drawing on the P–M–P process establishes the safe space that allows experimentation, risk and creativity to emerge. Supervision and dialogue with other coaches then help transfer the learning into coaching practice in the 'real world'.

Coaching Formation: Continuing Coaching Development, Supervision and Communities of Practice

I like to think of coaching as a vocation rather than a profession. The former signifies that coaches are dedicated to their work, that it is more than a professional role, as a successful coach really does have to bring their authentic and emotional selves to their coaching – it is essentially human-relational work.

I spend time in monasteries, and when observing monks, I had a breakthrough understanding of what formation means. Coaching Formation emanates directly from the religious idea of spiritual formation, and I turn to the Christian monastic tradition that has developed over the past 1,700 years since the early Desert Fathers.

When on retreat at the Camaldolese (Benedictine) Hermitage in Big Sur, California, I observed how the monks underwent their spiritual formation and realized that coaches could learn much from the monastic tradition. The idea of spiritual formation challenges our modern idea of learning. The monastic tradition does not place an emphasis on the monks' spiritual life being learnt through teaching, training or personal development. To undergo formation as a monk is not to undergo a series of separate developmental acts, but is a holistic experience which arises from living in the community. It is an ongoing process of formation, and each monk is continually formed by, and also contributes to, the living tradition and formation of the community. A monk doesn't learn monk skills, they undergo a formation experience that lasts a lifetime.

The monastic communities have mastered and tailored the ability to create successful and sustainable contexts in which the lives of their monks are formed. A novitiate monk chooses to join a monastic community having discerned a certain charism (a God-given gift) and takes a vow to follow the Monastic Rule of the particular order they join. The monastic setting, the Rule and the community, overseen by an abbot, provide a Paternal Container, the safe containing space that is a prerequisite for 'developmental or formative' activity to take place. Within this physical and spiritual container, the monk is supported and encouraged to form the 'monk within' alongside others undergoing the same formation process.

The monks' life is *formed* through partaking in daily spiritual practices, for example prayer, work, reading the scriptures and, vitally important, the liturgy (the form of the religious service). It is the whole rather than any of the parts of this process which form both the novitiate monk and the community. The monks call this holistic experience *'the life'*. In addition to this process there is spiritual direction. The spiritual director is a guide, a mentor, a 'loving father' in the monastic tradition. Their role is to be receptive and to support the monk in finding their path, not to teach that path, nor to develop the person, but to observe, reflect and guide the new monk through the formation process. The formation process is a communal process, as well as an individual one.

Coaches are not monks, and the settings are different – however much can be learnt from this formation process. Training and education courses are important for coaches (even monks go to universities and study theology). However if coach education puts an emphasis on coaching formation, it changes the way coaching courses are taught and assessed. The coach educator no longer 'deposits' expert knowledge into the trainee (Freire, 1970: 45), but creates a context of peer and personal learning. It also puts the focus on continued formation, and brings to the fore ongoing coach development, not just through attending continued professional development (CPD) courses but through different practices such as supervision, mentoring or peer coaching, and communities of practice forming around special interests, whereby coaches work together in learning groups that may be online as well as in person. Coaching supervision should not copy clinical therapeutic supervision approaches, but take what is useful and develop specific coaching supervision or reflective practices that enhance coaching rather than mimic therapy. Perhaps coaching supervision should be called 'Individual Coaching Formation' in order to differentiate it, as language is important. Coaching Formation could then reflect on the coach's practice, but the formation process could also support the coach in planning other developmental activities, help them find their own coach to do personal work, identify a community of practice to join, and suggest reading and also learning from non-coaching sources.

Conclusion

Establishing coaching forms for coaching formation to take place is the key to coaching's future success. Coaching courses need to take a coaching formation stance rather than feed coaching with knowledge, expertise and techniques to 'bank'. The whole approach to coaching education needs to be addressed, and rather than attempt to standardize and professionalize it, coaching needs to become more vocational and take coaching formation seriously, to switch the object of learning from the skill and technique to the person.

Coach and mentor education cannot be a prescriptive method, owing to the diversity of approaches; however there are three fundamentals that underpin it.

1 *The 'P–M–P' coaching process* informs the coach trainer of the process that holds and guides
   the coaching trainees, whilst at the same time modelling the process that underpins their
   coaching practice. It is a theoretical and conceptual process with applications that inform how
   a coach takes up their role at any given time in a coaching relationship.

2 *The 'coaching alliance'* is developed through high-quality relationships, learning to listen in
   a different way from everyday conversation, while Rogers' (1961) core conditions are still the
   benchmark for developing the trust and acceptance needed in a 'helping relationship'. In
   addition a 'coaching alliance' is a different contract from a 'therapeutic alliance', and the
   P–M–P process helps define coaching as both an exploration of the person and of the organization and external world.

3 *The Coaching Network.* Coaching education needs to take a Network Coach stance to work
   across the four discourses and draw on the coaching meta-theory, in order to support coach
   formation and address the macro and micro issues that affect coaching.

Coaching education and development should work on these fundamentals
of how a coach conceptualizes a process that frames, 'holds' and informs
their practice. Then it can focus on how a coach builds a coaching alliance
and the basic requirements for coaching and mentoring to work. After this,
each coaching development will work in different discourses at different
levels: *skills, practice* and *theory* are the triangular method that frames most
courses.

This chapter offered some insights into how coach education can be
thought about, through theory, concepts and pedagogy. It is for each coach
trainer and educator to design their courses, events and supervision sessions, bringing their own creativity, knowledge and experience and ensuring
that the learning is always two-way.

Promoting innovative, imaginative coaching education alongside developing robust and diverse theoretical insights are the best guarantees of
coaching quality and future success.

14 Epilogue

Coaching and mentoring
Untidy ending
Free associations
Final words: coaching – a Virtuous Vocation

The themes that arise in this book explore ideas, some of them challenging and provocative, others hopefully bringing clarity or at least insightful glimpses of the underpinning themes of coaching and mentoring.

Coaching and Mentoring

Coaching and mentoring have been merged in this book, as they are under-pinned by the same fundamentals; they emerge from the same journey from 'friendship to coaching/mentoring' as discussed in Part II. Like identical twins they look the same, they are based on similar skill-sets, shaped by the same social contexts; but they have different personalities. Traditionally they offered something more easily differentiated; yet recently their paths con-verged, and they have been merged by language and practice. We read about coaching skills for mentors, and 'coaching managers' might previ-ously have been described as mentors. The blurring has made clearly demar-cating territory nigh impossible. Each term, mentoring or coaching separately, can describe a wide range of activities and practices, and this diversity means that some mentoring approaches are more akin to coaching, and some coaching approaches are more akin to mentoring.

Coaching itself has expanded exponentially in the world of business; it is also becoming socially significant as Life-coaches and Executive coaches are now familiar terms, and popular culture has identified with the term 'coach'. Garvey wonders if a term will be invented to cover both practices but I think it more likely that coaching will continue to expand and colonize more of the mentoring territory. It seems that a stronghold of mentoring is in the 'social-activist' space referring to projects that are linked to producing the 'good society'. The other strong element in mentoring is its focus on mutuality, whereby it benefits both parties, such as older youths mentoring younger youths in colleges. If coaching heads down the path of professionalization and accreditation, this may further demarcate the two. Coaching will be associated with professional expertise and intervention, in individual lives and the workplace. Mentoring will be associated with voluntarism, mutuality and working on social rather than profitable projects.

Untidy Ending

To offer a neat and tidy conclusion is not desirable or possible in a text like this, nor should it be desirable for coaches in their practice.

As any experienced coach knows, it is better to end a coaching session with untidy endings, leaving the coachee with some 'yeast in the dough' that they will work on between sessions, consciously in their waking hours, and hopefully also in their daydreams and their sleeping dreams. The coachee will work on real tasks between sessions, putting their coaching work into practice in their personal lives and their work-roles. Coaching should provoke and inspire this dual work, the task-focused, and the internal-emotional and cognitive work. The coachee may be working between sessions at a deeply personal level (Soul Guide); they may be trying out new behaviours they have been working on in coaching (Psy Expert); they may be working with their team, taking a new leadership role (Managerial); or they may be developing a new strategy, engaging with stakeholders or developing sustainable initiatives (Network Coach). This work is done both consciously and unconsciously, and between sessions the coach can agree 'homework tasks' but just as often the 'in-between work' emerges unplanned as ideas flow, and emotions and learning are triggered by events. The coach works between sessions, holding the coachee in mind, reflecting on their work together.

Coaching acts retroactively as coaching sessions set off a stream of thought and actions in the coachees' life and workplace, and the outcome is only known when reflecting backwards. The outcome may also not be known for a long period – seeds can take a long time to flower – and this is a challenge to the coaching community who often promise and design quick fit solutions.

Very often there is desire from the client and coachee for a 'false security blanket', to believe and obtain 'quick wins' and a feeling of achievement that ideally can be quantified. Frustrating senior executives is not an easy sale, yet it is through working through frustrations and complexity, alongside the capacity for play and creativity, that real learning and sustainable change takes place. Play always has some element of frustration, whether a child struggles on the climbing frame to reach the top, or an adult plays with ideas but frustratingly can't quite get the clarity of vision they want, until finally it appears from an unexpected source. This is a coaching dilemma: how to sell the hard stuff of reality, whilst creating the space to play?

Free Associations

As a coach inspired by psychoanalytic practice, I always ask my coachees to take a breath when we begin a session, and then to free associate, to say what comes to mind, what is preoccupying them, what lingers in their uncon-scious. This starting place (and I revisit this space during sessions) gets us to the place we need to be in the shortest time possible. Counter-intuitively, working without goals, helping the coachee pause from their rush to out-comes, can identify and achieve clarity much more effectively, and at the same time open up strategic and Soul Guidance coaching opportunities that otherwise would have been missed.

The anchor points to this approach are to take a Network Coach stance that connects the associations to the task of living and working, and to leap beyond the individual into the otherness of the world. In a parallel process to coaching, I offer some free associations at the end of this book, undigested thoughts that reveal what they reveal, before finishing with a few final words.

Threads that run through the book

Coaching is underpinned by four identified discourses, and these require theoretical and practice development, especially on the dynamics that occur when working in-between and with multiple discourses. Different approaches are informed by different discourses and the task of the coaching commu-nity is to value them all, and learn how to utilize them, play with them and engage with each and all of them in different contexts.

Professionalization and institutionalization of coaching

Does coaching really want to lose its dynamic, entrepreneurial and creative energy to become like psychotherapeutic and management institutions – mimicking their over-engineered accreditation processes, standardizations and risk-averse training programmes? Whilst coaching is a bit on the 'wild-side' (Sherman and Freas, 2004) this is not necessarily a bad thing as change comes from those at the margins; for example the 'hippy' environmentalists were considered eccentric, but were actually ahead of the mainstream, warning us of global warming and the loss of natural resources. Being tolerant of fringe coaching approaches is not too much to ask in return for retaining dynamism and the early coaching energy that brings innovation with it. I strongly refute the claims that coaching can be a dangerous or damaging practice (Berglas, 2002) as this is simply repeating the mantras of pathologizing therapy that always looks for and finds risk, danger and the wounded self. Talking to somebody about their life and work will rarely do damage, particularly as the coach is not imbued with the symbolic power of the priest or therapist, and in the workplace the manager who works with the coach is often in a more powerful place, and not easily led too far astray by a coach. Coaches may wander into unknown territory, they may work from a narcissistic place, they may not always be very skilled; but many accredited counsellors, too, fail in these areas. Coaching begins from an assumption that the coachee has personal autonomy (even though this is shaped by social culture and context) and coaches should not patronize pathologies or victimize the client group.

Coaching formation and accreditation: raising quality and standards

Trying to raise quality and standards is admirable, yet controlling approaches to try to monitor standards such as accreditation are not the best way to raise quality (see Chapter 13 on education). This is best achieved through sharing best practice, developing good coaching scholarship, broad-based theory and research, and most of all through developing excellent coaching education and continuing development opportunities, including supervision, and forming communities of practice to share learning and develop new ideas, i.e. to create opportunities for Coaching Formation to take place. Clients will choose courses on the basis of reputation, and this will support good practice and limit bad practice. I am not totally against accreditation *per se*, but am concerned at the amount of energy spent in coaching on 'controlling practice' rather than innovating and developing it. For me it seems like a very counter-intuitive and un-coaching way to go about things.

Developing theory

Substituting psychotherapy theory for coaching theory with a few adaptations condemns coaching to become a second-rate form of therapy, and limits coaching practice to the Psy Expert Discourse. Developing the Psy Expert Discourse and utilizing therapy and psychological know-how is important (I utilize my therapeutic background to great effect in my coaching). However, coaching is also more than this, and is the reason why I moved from therapy to coaching. Coaching offers me a more generative space to work, and allows me to combine interests, in working deeply with individuals, and in teams and organizations, on leadership and strategy. There is a wealth of research and theorizing to be done within the coaching meta-theory set out in Chapter 12. Coaching has begun on this path of richer research streams and theorizing, and the future looks promising if coaching can get beyond theorizing about coaching skills and outcomes. Coaching has a unique position, and if it retains its hybridity, and develops theory across the four discourses, and includes the macro-social influences, the future is exciting.

Ethics and emancipatory approaches

Throughout the book, there are references to ethics and emancipatory approaches. These warn against the drift towards the instrumentalization of coaching practice – to evidence-based research and technique-based approaches that put coaching in the same frame as managers who, as MacIntyre claims, operate as if they were scientists, as morally neutral characters whose expertise is in efficiency and effectiveness, without questioning the means to the ends. Coaching is heading in this direction, claiming the universal ability to change behaviour and output, to deliver effectiveness. Yet without looking at the big picture, coaches just become another cog-in-the-machine of ever-increasing productivity, blind to the ethical consequences on the individuals they coach and on the wider impacts. Coaching can and should take strategic, ethical and emancipatory approaches, and I would hope to see ethics and emancipatory approaches that address the macro as well as micro issues much higher on coaching courses and on coach conferencing agendas and in the journals in the future.

Modernism and the instrumentalization of human experience

The techniques and tools of coaching provide easy wins for coach trainers, but restrict coaching to micro-change approaches and reductionism. Soul Guide and Network Coaching are being swamped by cognitive behavioural, NLP and solution-focused coaching, each borrowed from therapy and applied with instrumental mindsets. This book claims that these approaches have their place but, if they dominate, it castrates coaching, and shifts human experience and systemic thinking to the margins. Human experience is relational and holistic – it cannot be broken down to behaviours – and technocratic functionalist coaches should not dominate the coaching space.

Social and organizational dynamics

Developing coaching will hopefully mean that the more advanced courses engage in debates and develop coaching practice and theory that embrace the latest thinking on organizational dynamics and social theory. We are in such a fast-changing social and work environment that advanced executive coaches need to expand their knowledge base. Then they can work in the Network Coach Discourse, and support leaders who work in complex systems and dynamic networks that require new leadership thinking and an understanding of contemporary organizations. A critical stance drawing on post-structural theory, network theory, critical organizational and management theory, and feminist theory is also necessary, to counter coaching theory that is lightweight and dominated by positive psychology and technocratic approaches. Developing coaching theory and interventions that address organizational power dynamics, working with diversity and inclusion agendas, and promoting socially responsible and sustainable business models are much needed in the coaching field.

Coaching networks and macro-interventions

Coaching has a huge, untapped potential beyond the focus on individual change. The data coaches are getting from their coachees is invaluable to organizations and to researchers who want to find out what is going on at multiple levels in organizational life. OD coaching approaches miss out on sharing best practice, identifying cultural trends, stress risks, unseen challenges and missed opportunities for innovation, if the data and knowledge gained by coaches is not harvested.

Final Words: Coaching a Virtuous Vocation

Alasdair MacIntyre finishes his acclaimed text, *After Virtue*, by reflecting how in past epochs of change, new forms of community were established, such as Benedictine monasteries that enabled virtues and civility to survive 'the dark ages' (although they were not fully aware of what they were doing). In contemporary times he suggests that the barbarians are not at our frontiers threatening our civilization, but have been governing us for some time, ' … and it is our lack of consciousness of this that constitutes part of our predicament' (MacIntyre, 1985: 263). MacIntyre claims that the contemporary task is to create new local forms of community that will enable 'moral life' to survive our challenging times, saying that what is needed is a 'new – doubtless very different – St Benedict' (1985: 263).

Reflecting on this, it is my belief that new local 'communities of virtue' that will carry culture forward will be diverse and plural, not institutionalized like the medieval monastery. Probably the most important community site in late modernity is the workplace, as other communal sites and institutions such as the Church (particularly in Europe) or social clubs have long been in demise. In China and Asia, materialism and economic success have surpassed ideological Marxism, and traditional values are under threat as globalization impacts. The new world they are creating will also have to develop new forms of morality and virtuous communal narratives that will bind success with sustainability, and humanity with profit and gain. The economic realm and the workplace is therefore a vitally important and contested site for the future of the planet and for how we as humans live together. The workplace is at the centre of the struggle for our humanity and survival. So what has this to do with coaching?

Creating local communities that enable virtues and humanity to develop in the face of a collective materialistic blindness means creating networked, virtuous communities in the workplace. Coaches have emerged as potential carriers of culture (see Chapter 12 on macro-social influences). Coaches can inspire and support, offering thinking spaces and critical reflection, and become carriers of a virtuous culture, collaborating with others to create moral spaces, ethical leadership and sites of resistance to the hegemony of growth, exploitation and instrumentalism that diminish us all.

To achieve this, coaches and coaching institutions, training bodies and purchasers should reflect on the discourses that are now shaping coaching, and how they might influence coaching in light of this. Coaches need to become radically conscious, awake and engaged in creating a better society rather than repeating the mistakes of the past century. If coaching carries on offering techniques and technologies that instrumentalize happiness and human emotions, turning employees into objects that are coached to undergo behavioural modification in the name of market forces, increased performance and productivity, then coaching is no more than a collusive force on the side of destruction.

Coaching perhaps needs its own St Benedict, or some leadership to form networked coaching communities that resist Fukuyama's *End of History* (1992), where we are presented with no alternative to continued growth, exploitation and ruination of nature and of our mental and emotional environments.

Re-inscribing individuals and communities with ethics, virtue and the ability to become conscious of the connectivity, and the interdependency we have with each other and with the natural environment, is necessary in order to think our way out of the abyss. Coaches can play an important part – after all, their core task is to be thinking partners to the leaders of organizations. If enough coaching practitioners claim an ethical stance, and work with individuals *and* organizations towards a progressive and emancipatory agenda, then coaching will become a virtuous vocation. Coaches can help create the network of leaders, in all walks of life, that will resist destructive and oppressive tendencies, and work towards creating the 'good society'.

Appendix

This appendix gives a brief outline of a coaching approach that offers a practical application informed by the meta-theory and discourses in this book. This approach is being used and developed by the author.

Analytic-Network Coaching© (A-Nc)

Transforming yourself: influencing your network

Analytic-Network Coaching© offers a new coaching process that fits with the twenty-first century 'network society'. It offers coaching depth, connectivity and breadth, bringing ethics together with the capacity to map networks and intervene in them to strategically influence change.

   This coaching process and approach has emerged from the author's coaching and workplace experience, and through research and theoretical development. Drawing on the coaching meta-theory, Analytic-Network Coaching© has been developed to offer a coaching process and methodology that is theoretically robust. It also has the breadth of approach that transcends the limitations of many coaching approaches, as it draws on all four discourses in this text. This approach is accessible for coaching practitioners, and at the same time addresses the challenges of contemporary leaders and organizations.

Why 'Analytic-Network'?

Analytic

The word 'analytic' signifies two approaches within this coaching process:

1   A systematic coaching process. Firstly 'analytic' signifies a *systematic approach* that takes the coach and coachee through five frames to analyse the coachee's experience, their relation to others, their leadership and to their networks, so they can make strategic changes and interventions that produce more dynamic and sustainable change.

2   A psycho-social coaching approach. Secondly, 'analytic' signifies an applied *psychoanalytic approach* to coaching. Psychoanalysis is the longest-established form of psychotherapy, and the aspects brought into A-N Coaching are very different from the dominant coaching brands based on behavioural or goal approaches to change.

Drawing on the psychoanalytic approach, we pay attention to the uncon-scious, the patterns that inhibit us and the dormant creativity that lies within us. More than this, psychoanalysis provides a method to work between the coach and the coachee, where the coachee can learn to interpret their own processes and patterns in relation to the coach. The unconscious is not just a dynamic deep within our minds; it is also a dynamic between pairs, groups, organizations and societies. A-N Coaching is a psycho-social approach to coaching, not focused simply on the internal life of the individual. Key ele-ments of this approach are to develop:

- *The Coach as Container*: offering structural and emotional containment to the coachee (this enables 'emotions to become thinking') and for the coachee to 'think-in-the-face-of-anxiety' rather than just be reactive.

- *Emergent Thinking*: the coach fosters an attitude of open curiosity – the ability to tolerate the unknown – and in doing so creates a space for something new to be thought, and for the coachee to develop the capability for adaptive and emergent thinking.

- *Associative Intelligence*: encouraging new ideas and thoughts to emerge from the unconscious.

This approach gets beyond the coach fixing the coachee with expert tools, and offers the coachee a way of interpreting themselves, others and the social, in order to become dynamic change agents.

Network

The word 'network' is used to signify the network society (Castells, 2000) in which we live and work. The internet provides us with our mirror: vast inter-connected networks of activity, consisting of humans and technology con-nected in virtual and real time. Drawing on Actor Network theory (Law, 1993; Latour, 2005) we utilize the metaphor of the network to think outside the box, and beyond organizations and departments with clearly demarked roles, functions and boundaries. The concept of the Network Society undoes much of leadership and management theory of the past century; linear hierarchies, fixed structures and roles are not 'fit for purpose' in this new environment.

Systems theory provides some insights into this domain but open and closed systems theory is limited by the lack of a contemporary networked understand-ing of how power and knowledge operate within the social field. The recent financial crisis and the Arab Spring are examples of how networks are increas-ingly interdependent and 'un-manageable', because of the speed and complexity of communications, and the unpredictability of social networks that cannot be controlled. In contemporary organizations the task is not to manage but to understand and influence through creating networks of dispersed leaders who find nodal points in the networks. Coaches need to be familiar with the latest change theories in social and organizational thinking in order to help their clients.

The Analytic-Network Coaching© Process

The process has been designed not as a linear, functional approach, but as five frames that are interdependent and connected. The process is transformational for the individual and offers HR and managers a coaching process that provides *results for the organization, beyond improved individual performance.*

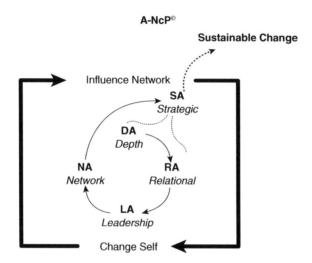

Figure A.1   **The A-NcP© connects five frames: Depth Analysis, Relational Analysis, Leadership Analysis, Network Analysis and Strategic Analysis, to create an inter-dependent whole. Individuals are coached to become authentic leaders who are *catalysts of influence* in their organizational networks.**

1 **Depth Analysis**. *Coaching the Inner self*. Coachees are encouraged to identify their values and to discover and work from their 'true, authentic self' in order to review conscious and unconscious patterns in a way that releases dynamic creativity. In this 'soul work' the coachee also works on their values, their desire and their purpose. Depth analysis allows the coachee to work from a solid base, from the place Jean-Paul Sartre calls 'good faith'.

2 **Relational Analysis**. *Coaching the Relational self* to improve relationships through understanding the dynamics that exist between the coachee and others. Its focus is on small teams/groups, families and friends, and these days on distant and virtual relationships. We analyse relational dynamics and the underpinning emotions and unconscious dynamics that entrap the coachee in certain ways of relating and experiencing relationships. The coach utilizes their own relationship with the coachee (transference and counter-transference) as live data to inform the analysis.

3 **Leadership Analysis**. *Coaching the Leadership self* to develop the coachee's leadership role, help the coachee develop their 'inner-leader' and exercise leadership and followership, and how they take up and react to authority and power and influencing others. The leadership analysis is done in alignment to their personality and context, rather than following a universal leadership competency model. This analysis utilizes the Wild Questionnaire (indicator of leadership, found on www.simonwestern.com) to see what the coachee's preferences are in terms of the leadership discourses, i.e. Controller, Therapist, Messiah or Eco-Leadership. The analysis then goes beyond individual leadership to address how leadership can be distributed, how to enable leadership to flourish within an organization, and what leadership contexts require what kind of leaders.

4 **Network Analysis**. *Coaching the Networked self*. Using a network mapping exercise the coachee situates themselves on the map and builds their network around themselves. The coach analyses this with the coachee, seeing where power and resources lie, where strong and weak connections are, and the coach offers interpretations to the coachee, associating to the holistic picture (map) they face. Externalizing the network map carried in the coachee's mind has the immediate impact of enlightening and offering a spatial model for the coachee to begin a process of identifying connections they need to make, and nodal points they need to influence. Coachees inevitably feel empowered through Network Analysis because it reveals possible changes which previously felt very stuck.

5 **Strategic Analysis**. The final frame reviews the previous four frames and enables the coachee to 'evaluate, consolidate and innovate'. Strategic Analysis focuses on:

a emergent strategy for the coachee

b emergent strategy in their network and workplace

This means analysing and evaluating what's working and then identifying strategies to consolidate what's working, i.e. doing more of the same, developing potential and capacity and building on success. The coachee identifies where to make personal strategic changes that will be sustainable, and to take strategic decisions in the workplace. Innovation helps the coachee to see things from a different place, in a different way. This can lead to new business models, career leaps and to realize which frames need more coaching to develop yet unknown futures.

Each frame is an important piece of coaching on its own, and yet used together, the A-Nc process becomes *'greater than the sum of its parts'*.

The Analytic-Network Coaching© process is *not* a prescriptive coaching formula or a set of tools or techniques, but a process. It provides the conceptual framework which coaches and coachees internalize, so that the process becomes a part of how they think and work.

There are two ways to approach A-N Coaching:

• Consecutive frames

• Adaptive frames

Consecutive frames

Coaching through the five frames consecutively allows clients to pursue a holistic process that coherently moves from the inner self to the relational self, before moving into a person's role and specifically focusing on leadership, then on how to influence their network, before reflecting strategically on the whole process.

Adaptive frames

Once a coach internalizes the five-frame process, they are then freer to work across the boundaries and adapt the coaching to the coachee's context and needs. Clients may come and want to work on a specific area first, perhaps leadership or their team relationships. The coach begins in the appropriate frame but the coach always holds in mind the holistic view and is aware of the other frames, and will turn to them appropriately. The A-Nc process means the coach will be working in a particular frame, and also with the whole process in mind.

In either approach, what is important is that the Analytic-Network Coaching process is holistic in the sense that the frames inform each other, and the sum of the five frames is greater than the individual parts.

Box Appendix 1   Emancipatory Ethics

Our approach is underpinned by a set of ethical values: we believe our coaching approach will help individuals and organizations achieve success because of these ethics, not in spite of them.

1 *Individual values and development*. To help each individual discover their 'charism', their unique gift to the world.
2 *Humanizing organizations*. Striving for more humane organizations, accounting for human experience as well as for financial gain.
3 *Environmental sustainability*. To act responsibly towards our natural environment locally and globally.
4 *Speaking truth to power*. To counter the psycho-social patterns (often hidden) that reproduce power elites and perpetuate social disadvantage to any individual or group.

(Continued)

(Continued)

5 *Emancipation*. Ethics and freedom are symbiotic. Our coaching process aims to help individuals discover their creativity and autonomy, and to identify social patterns that promote conformity and totalizing social structures that entrap us.

6 *Good Faith and the Good Society*. To commit ourselves to working from a place of 'good faith' to help create the 'good society'.

For some coaches these ethics may be underpinned by a personal faith, for others by a deeply held humanism; it matters not what underpins it but how we enact it.

For further information about Analytic-Network Coaching contact Dr Simon Western at simon@analyticnetwork.com or visit www.analyticnetwork.com.

References

Ackroyd, S., Harper, R., Hughes, J.A., Shapiro, D. and Soothill, K. (1992) *New Technology and Practical Police Work*. Buckingham: Open University Press.

Action Coach Business Coaching (2010) *What is Business Coaching?* [Online]. Available at: www.actioncoach.com/what-is-business-coaching (accessed November 2010).

Aelred of Rievaulx (1977) *Spiritual Friendship* (Mary Laker, trans.). Kalamazoo, MI: Cistercian Publications.

Alvarez, A. (1992) *Live Company*. London: Tavistock/Routledge.

Amado, G. (1995) 'Why psychoanalytical knowledge helps us understand organizations: A discussion with Elliot Jaques', *Human Relations*, 48 (4): 351–357.

Anderson, S. and Cavanagh, J. (2000) *Top 200: The Rise of Corporate Global Power*. Washington, DC: Institute for Policy Studies.

AnitaRoddick.com (2006) *About Anita* [Online]. Available at: http://www.anitaroddick.com/aboutanita.php (accessed July 2011).

Armstrong, D. (2005) *Organization in the Mind* (R. French, ed.). London: Karnac.

Arnaud, G. (2003) 'A coach or a couch? A Lacanian perspective on executive coaching and consulting', *Human Relations*, 56: 1131.

Aspey, L. (2011) *Therapist Coach: Coaching for a Changing World*, BACP [Online]. Available at: http://www.bacpcoaching.co.uk/Conf%202011/index.php (accessed 10 May 2011).

Bachkirova, T. (2011) *Developmental Coaching Working with the Self*. New York: Open University Press.

BACP (2011) *What happens in the Silence? The Real Art of Coaching* [Online]. Available at: http://www.bacpcoaching.co.uk/Conf%202011/keynote.php (accessed June 2011).

Barker, C. (2005) *Cultural Studies: Theory and Practice*. London: Sage.

Barley, S. and Kunda, G. (1992) 'Design and devotion: Surges of rational and normative ideologies of control in Managerial Discourse', *Administrative Science Quarterly*, 37: 363–399.

Bass, B. (1990) 'From transactional to transformational leadership: Learning to share the vision', *Organizational Dynamics*, 18: 19–31.

Bass, B. (1998) 'The ethics of transformational leadership', in J. Ciulia (ed.), *Ethics, The Heart of Leadership*. Westport, CT: Praeger.

Bateson, G. (1972) *Steps to an Ecology of Mind: Collected Essays in Anthropology, Psychiatry, Evolution and Epistemology*. Chicago: University of Chicago Press.

Bateson, G. (1979) *Mind and Nature: A Necessary Unity*. New York: Bantam.

Baudrillard, J. (1988) 'Simulacra and simulations', in *Selected Writings* (Mark Poster, ed.). Stanford: Stanford University Press, pp. 166–184.

Bauman, Z. (1989) *Modernity and the Holocaust*. Ithaca, NY: Cornell University Press.

Bauman, Z. (2001) *The Individualized Society*. Cambridge: Polity.

Bauman, Z. (2003) *Liquid Love*. Cambridge: Polity.

BBBS (1995–2011) *Big Impact, Proven Results* [Online]. Available at: http://www.
bbbs.org/site/c.9iILI3NGKhK6F/b.5961035/k.A153/Big_impact8212proven/
results.htm (accessed November 2010).

BBC News (2010) 'Unilever says sustainability key to new business model', BBC
News Business, 15 Nov. [Online]. Available at: http://www.bbc.co.uk/news/
business-11755672.

Beck, A. (1976) *Cognitive Therapy and the Emotional Disorders*. London: Penguin Books.

Beck, D. and Cowan, C. (1996) *Spiral Dynamics: Mastering Values, Leadership, and
Change: Exploring the New Science of Memetics*. Cambridge, MA: Blackwell Publishers.

Beck, M. (2011) Available at: http://marthabeck.com.

Belisle, M. (2002) *The Privilege of Love*. Collegeville, MN: Liturgical Press.

Bell, E. and Taylor, S. (2003) 'The elevation of work: Pastoral power and the New Age
work ethic', *Organization*, 10 (2): 329–349.

Bell, E. and Taylor, S. (2004) 'From outward bound to inward bound: The prophetic
voices and discursive practices of spiritual management development', *Human
Relations*, 57(4): 439–466.

Bellah, R., Madsen, R., Sullivan, W.M., Swidler, A. and Tipton, S.M. (1992) *The Good
Society*. London/New York: Vintage Books.

Bellah, R.N., Madsen, R., Sullivan, W.M., Swidler, A. and Tipton, S.M. (1996) *Habits
of the Heart: Individualism and Commitment in American Life* (2nd edn). Berkeley:
University of California Press.

Beradi, F. (2009) *The Soul at Work: From Alienation to Autonomy*. Los Angeles, CA:
Semiotext(e).

Berglas, S. (2002) 'The very real dangers of executive coaching', *Harvard Business
Review*, 80: 86–92.

Bertalanffy, von L. (1968) *General Systems Theory: Foundations, Development, Application*.
London: Allen Lane.

Bettleheim, B. (1982) *Freud and Man's Soul*. New York: Knopf.

Bettleheim, B. and Janowitz, M. (1950) *Social Change and Prejudice*. New York: Free
Press.

Bhaskar, R. (2010) *The Formation of Critical Realism*. Oxford/New York: Routledge.

Bion, W.R. (1961) *Experiences in Groups*. London: Tavistock Publications.

Bion, W.R. (1962) 'Theory of thinking', in *Second Thoughts: Selected Papers on
Psychoanalysis*. New York: Jason Aronson.

Bion, W.R. (1984) *Attention and Interpretation*. London: Karnac. (1970, Tavistock
Publications.)

Bluckert, P. (2006) 'The foundations of a psychological approach to executive coaching', *Industrial and Commercial Training*, 37 (4): 171–178.

Bollas, C. (1997) *Freely Associated: Encounters with A. Molino*. London: Free Association
Books.

Brautigan, R. (1967) *All Watched Over by Machines of Loving Grace*. San Francisco: The
Communication Company.

Briggs Myers, I. (2000) *An Introduction to Type* (6th edn). Oxford: Oxford Psychologists
Press.

Bright, A. (2009) 'Here, Now', *The Point*, Vol. 1., p.34.

Britton, R. (1989) 'The missing link: Parental sexuality in the Oedipus complex', in
J. Steiner (ed.), *The Oedipus Complex Today: Clinical Implications*. London: Karnac,
pp. 83–101.

Brotman, L.E., Liberi, W.P. and Wasylyshyn, K.M. (1998) 'Executive coaching: The need for standards of competence', *Consulting Psychology Journal: Practice and Research*, 50: 40–46.

Brunning, H. (2006) *Executive Coaching: Systems-Psychodynamic Perspective*. London/ New York: Karnac Books.

Buell, C. (2004) 'Models of mentoring in communication', *Communication Review*, 53 (1): 56–73.

Burns, J. (1978) *Leadership*. New York: Harper & Row.

Burrell, G. (1997) *Pandemonium: Towards A Retro-Organization Theory*. London: Sage.

BusinessCoaching.co.uk (2011) *Outstanding Business Coaching for Outstanding Businesses* [Online]. Available at: http://www.businesscoaching.co.uk/ (accessed June 2011).

Butler, J. (1990) *Gender Trouble: Feminism and the Subversion of Identity*. London: Routledge.

Butler, J. (1999) *Subjects of Desire*. New York: Columbia University Press.

Butler, J. (2004) *Undoing Gender*. New York: Routledge.

Calhoun, C. (1995) *Critical Social Theory*. London: Blackwell.

Callon, M. and Law, J. (1995) 'Agency and the Hybrid Collectif', *South Atlantic Quarterly*, 94 (2): 481–507.

Campbell, D. and Huffington, C. (eds) (2008) *Organizations Connected: A Handbook of Systemic Consultation*. London: Karnac.

Campbell, J. (1959) *The Masks of God. Vol. 1: Primitive Mythology*. New York: Viking Penguin.

Canizeras, K. (2001) *Nike's Social Responsibility Exposed as a Lie*, Organic Consumers Association [Online]. Available at: http://www.organicconsumers.org/corp/ nikesham.cfm (accessed July 2011).

Capra, F. (1996) *The Web of Life*. New York: Doubleday.

Carrette, J. and King, R. (2005) *Selling Spirituality: The Silent Takeover of Religion*. London: Routledge.

Case, P. and Gosling, J. (2010) 'The spiritual organization: Critical reflections on the instrumentality of workplace spirituality', *Journal of Management, Spirituality & Religion*, 7 (4): 257–282.

Casey, C. (1995) *Work Self and Society after Industrialisation*. London: Routledge.

Castells, M. (2000) *The Information Age: Economy, Society and Culture, Vol. I: The Rise of the Network Society*. Cambridge, MA/Oxford, UK: Blackwell.

Chesterton, G.K. (1908/2004) *Orthodoxy*. Whitefish, MT: Kessinger Publishing.

Christopher, J.C. and Hickenbottom, S. (2008) 'Positive psychology, ethnocentrism, and the disguised ideology of individualism', *Theory & Psychology*, 18 (5): 563–589.

Clegg, S.R., Rhodes C., Kornberger, M. and Stillin, R. (2005) 'Business coaching: Challenges for an emerging industry', *Industrial and Commercial Training*, 37 (5): 218 –223.

Clement, C. (1987) *The Weary Sons of Freud*. London: Verso/New Left Books.

Cobb, K. (2005) *The Blackwell Guide to Theology and Popular Culture*. Oxford, UK: Blackwell.

Collins, J. and Porras, J. (2000) *Built to Last*. London: Random House Business Books.

Collinson, D. (2003) 'Identities and insecurities: Selves at work', *Organisation*, 10 (3): 527–547.

Collinson, D. (2009) *Fast Moving Fronts* [Online]. Available at: http://sciencewatch. com/dr/fmf/2009/09novfmf/09novfmfColl/ (accessed September 2011).

Coopey, J. (1995) 'The learning organization: Power, politics and ideology', *Management Learning*, 26 (2): 193–213.

Cornelissen, J. (2006) 'Making sense of theory construction', *Organisation*, 27: 1579–1599.

Costea, B., Crump, N. and Amiridis, K. (2008) 'Managerialism, the therapeutic habitus and the self, in contemporary organizing', *Human Relations*, 61: 661–685.

Covey, S. (1990) *Seven Habits of Highly Effective People*. New York: Free Press.

Cox, E., Bachkirova, T. and Clutterbuck, D. (eds) (2010) *The Complete Handbook of Coaching*. London: Sage .

Craig, P. (2010) *Viewpoint: Looking for Help at Work? Get Mentor, Business Week*, 2 March [Online]. Available at: http://www.businessweek.com/managing/content/mar2010/ca2010031_423652.htm (accessed May 2011).

Cullen, J. (2009) 'How to sell your soul and still get into Heaven: Steven Covey's epiphany-inducing technology of effective selfhood', *Human Relations*, 62: 1231.

Davenport, J. and Davenport, J.A. (1985) 'A chronology and analysis of the andragogy debate', *Adult Educational Quarterly*, 35 (3): 152–159.

Davos (2011) *Unilever's Paul Polman Believes we Need to Think Long Term, The Telegraph* [Online]. Available at: http://www.telegraph.co.uk/finance/financetopics/davos/8261178/Davos-2011-Unilevers-Paul-Polman-believes-we-need-to-think-long-term.htm (accessed April 2011).

de Haan, E. (2008) *Relational Coaching*. Chichester, UK: Wiley and Sons.

De Meuse, K.P., Dai, G. and Lee, R.J. (2009) 'Evaluating the effectiveness of executive coaching: Beyond ROI?', *Coaching: An International Journal of Theory, Research and Practice*, 2 (2): 117–134.

Deal, T. and Kennedy, A. (1982) *Corporate Cultures*. Reading, MA: Addison-Wesley.

Deetz, S. (1995) *Transforming Communication, Transforming Business: Building Responsive and Responsible Workplaces*. Cresskill, NJ: Hampton Press.

Deleuze, G. (1988) *Foucault* (Sean Hand, trans.). Minneapolis: University of Minnesota Press.

Deleuze, G. and Guattari, F. (1972/2004) *Anti-Oedipus: Capitalism and Schizophrenia* (Robert Hurley, Mark Seem and Helen R. Lane, trans.). London and New York: Continuum.

Della Porta, D. (1999) *Social Movements: An Introduction*. London: Blackwell.

Derbyshire, D. (2007) *Most Facebook Friends are False Friends, The Daily Mail* [Online]. Available at: http://www.dailymail.co.uk/sciencetech/article-481050/Most-Facebookfriends-false-friends.html (accessed April 2011).

DiMaggio, P.J. and Powell, W. (1983) '"The iron cage revisited": Institutional isomorphism and collective rationality in organizational fields', *American Sociological Review*, 48: 147–160.

Dor, J. (1997) *Introduction to the Reading of Lacan*. London/New York: Jason Aronson.

DuBois, D.L., Holloway, B.E., Valentine, J.C. and Cooper, H. (2002) 'Effectiveness of mentoring programs: A meta-analytical review', *American Journal of Community Psychology*, 30: 157–197.

Ducharme, M.J. (2004) 'The cognitive-behavioral approach to executive coaching', *Consulting Psychology Journal: Practice and Research*, 56: 214–224.

Ehrenreich, B. (2009) *Bright-Sided: How the Relentless Promotion of Positive Thinking has Undermined America*. New York: Henry Holt and Company.

Emerson, R.W. (1841) *On Self-Reliance*. Essays First Series.

European Mentoring and Coaching Council (EMCC) *Code of Ethics* [Online]. Available at: http://www.emccouncil.org/fileadmin/documents/EMCC_Code_of_Ethics.pdf (accessed July 2011).

Fairclough, N. (1995) *Critical Discourse Analysis: The Critical Study of Language.* London/New York: Longman.

Fairclough, N. (2001) *Language and Power.* London/New York: Longman.

Fanon, F. (1970) *Black Skin, White Masks.* London: Paladin.

Feigenbaum, A. (2010) 'Concrete needs no metaphor: Globalised fences as sites of political struggle', *Ephemera*, 10 (2): 119–133. [Online] Available at: http://www.ephemeraweb.org/journal/10-2/10-2feigenbaum.pdf (accessed January 2011).

Fernández-Ríos, L. and Cornes, J.M. (2009) 'A critical review of the history and current status of positive psychology', *Annuary of Clinical and Health Psychology*, 5: 7–13.

Fitzpatrick, M. (2000) *The Tyranny of Health: Doctors and the Regulation of Lifestyle.* London: Routledge.

Fleetwood, S. and Hesketh, A.J. (2006) 'HRM-Performance research: Under-theorised and lacking explanatory power', *International Journal of Human Resources Management*, 17 (12): 1979–1995.

Flood, R.L. (1999) *Re-thinking the Fifth Discipline.* London: Routledge.

Foley, M. (2010) *The Age of Absurdity: Why Modern Life Makes it Hard to be Happy.* New York: Simon & Schuster.

Foucault, M. (1972) *The Discourse on Language.* New York: Pantheon Books.

Foucault, M. (1977/1991) *Discipline and Punish: The Birth of the Prison.* London: Penguin.

Foucault, M. (1978 [French publication, 1976]) *The History of Sexuality, Vol. I: An Introduction* (Robert Hurley, trans.). New York: Pantheon.

Foucault, M. (1980) *Power/Knowledge: Selected Interviews and Other Writings, 1972–77* (Colin Gordon, ed.). London: Harvester.

Foucault, M. (1990) *Politics, Philosophy, Culture, Interviews and Other Writings, 1977–1984.* London: Routledge.

Four Incorporeal Creatures (2011) *St Ambrose of Milan on Brotherly Love and the Three Holy Hebrew Youths* [Online]. Available at: http://4incorporealcreatures.wordpress.com/?s=st+ambrose (accessed July 2011).

Freire, P. (1970) *Pedagogy of the Oppressed.* New York: Continuum.

Freud, S. (1917) *A Difficulty in the Path of Psycho-Analysis. The Standard Edition of the Complete Psychological Works of Sigmund Freud, Volume XVII (1917–1919): An Infantile Neurosis and Other Works*, pp. 135–144. J. Strachey, 1986 – Hogarth Press.

Freud, S. (1930/2002) *Civilisation and its Discontents.* London: Penguin.

Freud, S. and Breuer, J. (1895/2004) *Studies in Hysteria* (N. Luckhurst, trans.). New York: Penguin Press.

Friedman, M. (1962) *Capitalism and Freedom.* Chicago: University of Chicago Press.

Fukuyama, F. (1992) *The End of History and the Last Man.* London: Penguin.

Furedi, F. (2003) *Therapy Culture.* London: Routledge.

Gable, S. and Haidt, J. (2005) 'What (and why) is positive psychology?', *Review of General Psychology*, 9 (2): 103–110.

Gallwey, W.T. (1974) *The Inner Game of Tennis* (1st edn). New York: Random House.

Gallwey, W.T. (2000) *The Inner Game of Work.* New York: Random House.

GapInc. (2007/8) [Online] Available at: http://www2.gapinc.com/GapIncSubSites/csr/Goals/SupplyChain/SC_Overview.shtml (accessed 17 July 2011).

Garvey, B. (2010) 'Mentoring in a coaching world', in E. Cox, T. Bachkirova and D. Clutterbuck (eds), *The Complete Handbook of Coaching*. London: Sage, Chapter 10.

Garvey, B., Stokes, P. and Megginson, D. (2009) *Coaching and Mentoring: Theory and Practice*. London: Sage.

Gergen, K. (2001) *Social Construction in Context*. London: Sage.

Giddens, A. (1991) *Modernity and Self Identity: Self and Society in the Late Modern Age*. Cambridge: Polity Press.

Giddens, A. and Pierson, C. (1998) *Conversations with Anthony Giddens: Making Sense of Modernity*. Stanford: Stanford University Press.

Glaeser, E. (2011) *Triumph of the City*. New York: Penguin.

Goffman, E. (1968) *Asylums*. Harmondsworth: Penguin.

Gray, D. (2006) Executive Coaching: Towards a dynamic alliance of psychotherapy and transformative learning processes, *Management Learning*, 37(4): 475–497.

Gray, J. (2003) *Al Qaeda and What it Means to be Modern*. London: Faber and Faber.

Gray, J. (2007) *Black Mass: Apocalyptic Religion and the Death of Utopia*. New York: Farrar, Strauss and Giroux.

Griffin, D. (2002) *The Emergence of Leadership*. New York/London: Routledge.

Grint, K. (1997) *Leadership: Classical, Contemporary and Critical Approaches*. Oxford: Oxford University Press.

Grossman, J.B. and Rhodes, J.E. (2002) 'The test of time: Predictors and effects of duration in youth mentoring relationships', *American Journal of Community Psychology*, 30: 199–219.

Gunter, H. (2007) 'Remodelling the school workforce in England: A study in tyranny', *Journal for Critical Education Policy Studies*, 5 (1): 1740–2743.

Habermas, J. (1987) *The Theory of Communicative Action*, Vol. II. Cambridge: Polity Press.

Hackman, J. and Wageman, R. (2005) 'A theory of team coaching', *Academy of Management Review*, 30 (2): 269–287.

Halton, W. (1996) 'Anxiety and the individual', unpublished paper, D10 Course, Tavistock Institute.

Hamel, G. (2011) 'First, let's fire all the managers', *Harvard Business Review*, 89: 48–60.

Hamlin, R., Ellinger, A. and Beattie, R. (2006) 'Coaching at the heart of managerial effectiveness: A cross-cultural study of managerial behaviours', *Human Resources Development International*, 9 (3): 305 –331.

Haraway, D.J. (1991) *Simians, Cyborgs and Women: The Reinvention of Nature*. London: Free Association.

Harper, A. (2008) 'Psychometric tests are now a multi-million-pound business: What lies behind a coach's decision to use them', *International Journal of Evidence Based Coaching and Mentoring*, Special Issue No. 2, pp. 40–51.

Hart, V., Blattner, J. and Leipsic, S. (2001) 'Coaching versus therapy: A perspective', *Consulting Psychology Practice & Research*, 53 (4): 229–237.

Hartree, A. (1984) 'Malcolm Knowles' theory of andragogy: A critique', *International Journal of Lifelong Education*, 3: 203–210.

Hawkins, P. (2011) *Leadership Team Coaching*. London: Kogan Page.

Hay, J. (2007) *Reflective Practice and Supervision for Coaches*. Buckingham: Open University Press.

Heelas, P. (1996) *The New Age Movement: The Celebration of the Self and the Sacralization of Modernity*. Oxford: Blackwell.

Heelas, P. (2008) *Spiritualities of Life: New Age Romanticism and Consumptive Capitalism.* Oxford: Blackwell.

Heelas, P. and Woodhead, L. (2005) *The Spiritual Revolution: Why Religion is Giving Way to Spirituality.* Oxford: Wiley Blackwell.

Hertz, N. (2001) *The Silent Take-Over.* London: William Heinemann.

Hesketh, A.J. and Fleetwood, S. (2006) 'Beyond measuring the HRM-organizational performance link: Applying critical realist meta-theory', *Organization*, 13 (5): 677–699.

Hirschhorn, L. (1988) *The Workplace Within: Psychodynamics of Organisational Life.* Cambridge, MA: MIT Press.

Hirschhorn, L. (1998) *Reworking Authority, Leading and Following in the Post-Modern Organisation.* Cambridge, MA: MIT Press.

Hochschild, A.R. (1983) *The Managed Heart: Commercialization of Human Feeling.* Berkeley, CA: University of California Press.

Hoggett, P. (2000) *Emotional Life and the Politics of Welfare.* Basingstoke: Macmillan.

Holden, R. (1998) *Happiness Now!: Timeless Wisdom for Feeling Good Fast.* London: Hay House Publishers.

Holder, J. (2011) *What is Coaching?* [Online]. Available at: http://www.jackeeholder.com/coaching.html (accessed August 2011).

Hunt, J.M. and Weintraub, J.R. (2007) *The Coaching Organization: A Strategy for Developing Leads.* London: Sage Publications.

Impact Factory (2010) *Coaching and Mentoring* [Online]. Available at: http://www.impactfactory.com/gate/coaching_mentoring_skills_training_development/freegate_1825-1104-1118.html (accessed April 2011).

International Coaching Federation (2008) *What is a Coach?* [Online]. Available at: http://www.coachfederation.org/ICF/For+Coaching+Clients/What+is+a+Coach/FAQs/ (accessed June 2008).

Ives, Y. (2008) 'What is "Coaching"? An exploration of conflicting paradigms', *International Journal of Evidence Based Coaching and Mentoring*, 6 (2): 100–109.

Jackson, N. and Carter, P. (2011) 'In praise of boredom', *Ephemera*, 11 (4): 387–405. Available at: www.ephemeraweb.org.

James, O. (2009) 'Is Cognitive Behavioural Therapy really the answer to Britain's depression "epidemic"?', *Daily Mail* [Online]. Available at: http://www.dailymail.co.uk/health/article-1162512/Is-Cognitive-Behavioural-Therapy-really-answer-Britains-depression-epidemic.html#ixzz1WVCQMfNo (accessed April 2011).

Jodie, S. (2010) *Entrepreneur and Mom*, Meredith Haberfeld Coaching [Online]. Available at: http://www.meredithhaberfeld.com (accessed February 2011).

Johnson, J. (2005) *What is an Ecosystem?* [Online]. Available at: http://www.stolaf.edu/depts/cis/wp/johnsoja/whatisdiscourse/whatisanecosystem.html (accessed August 2011).

Johnson, P. and Duberley, J. (2005) *Understanding Management Research.* London: Sage.

Joo, B. (2005) 'Executive coaching: A conceptual framework from an integrative literature review of theory and practice', *Human Resource Development Review*, 4 (4): 462–488.

Kaushik, A. (2008) *10 Insights from 11 Months Working at Google* [Online]. Available at: http://www.kaushik.net/avinash/2008/02/10-insights-from-11-months-of-working-at-google.html (accessed June 2011).

Keats, J. (1970) *The Letters of John Keats: A Selection* (R. Gittings, ed.). Oxford: Oxford University Press.

Keller, T.E. (2005) 'A systemic model of the youth mentoring intervention', *Journal of Primary Prevention*, 26 (2): 169–188.

Kelly, K. (1994) *Out of Control: The New Biology of Machines, Social Systems and the Economic World*. Boston: Addison-Wesley.

Kets de Vries, M. (2006) *The Leader on the Couch*. San Francisco: Jossey-Bass.

Kets de Vries, M., Guillen, L., Korotov, K. and Florent-Treacy, E. (2010) *The Coaching Kaleidoscope: Insights from the Inside*. Hampshire, UK: Palgrave Macmillan.

Kilburg, R.R. (1996) 'Toward a conceptual understanding and definition of executive coaching', *Consulting Psychology Journal: Practice & Research*, 48 (2): 134–144.

Kilburg, R. (2000) *Executive Coaching*. Washington, DC: American Psychological Association.

Klein, M. (1959) 'Our adult world and its roots in infancy', in A.D. Colman and M.H. Geller (eds), *Group Relation Reader 2*. Washington, DC: A.K. Rice Institute.

Klein, N. (2001) *No Logo*. London: Flamingo.

Kline, N. (1999) *Time to Think: Listening to Ignite the Human Mind*. London: Cassel Orion.

Knowles, M. (1980) *The Modern Practice of Adult Education: From Pedagogy to Andragogy*. Wilton, CT: Association Press.

Konstan, D. (1997) *Friendship in the Classical World*. Cambridge: Cambridge University Press.

Kunda, G. (1992) *Engineering Culture: Control Commitment in a High Tech Corporation*. Philadelphia, PA: Temple University Press.

Lacan, J. (1966) 'Au-delà du Principe de réalité', in Écrits. Paris: Seuil.

Lacan, J. (1970) *D'un discours qui ne serait pas du semblant*. Le séminaire, Livre XVIII. Unpublished.

Lacan, J. (1993) *The Seminar. Book III. The Psychoses, 1955–56* (Russell Grigg, trans.). London: Routledge.

Laing, R.D. (1967) *The Politics of Experience and the Bird of Paradise*. Harmondsworth, UK: Penguin.

Lasch, C. (1979) *The Culture of Narcissism: American Life in the Age of Diminishing Expectations*. New York: Warner Books.

Laske, O.E. (2006) 'From coach training to coach education: Teaching coaching within a comprehensively evidence based framework', *International Journal of Evidence Based Coaching and Mentoring*, 4 (1): 45.

Latour, B. (2005) *Reassembling the Social*. Oxford: Oxford University Press.

Law, J. (1992) *Notes on the Theory of the Actor Network: Ordering, Theory and Heterogeinity*, Centre for Science Studies, Lancaster University [Online]. Available at: http://www.lancs.ac.uk/fass/sociology/papers/law-notes-on-ant.pdf (accessed January 2011).

Law, J. (1993) *Organizing Modernity: Social Ordering and Social Theory*. Oxford: Wiley-Blackwell.

Lawrence, W.G. (1999) 'Won from the void and formless infinite: Experiences in social dreaming', in W.G. Lawrence (ed.), *Social Dreaming @ Work*. London: Karnac Books.

Layard, R. (2011) 'Flourish: A new understanding of happiness and well-being – and how to achieve them, by Martin Seligman – review', *The Guardian* [Online]. Available at: http://www.guardian.co.uk/science/2011/may/15/flourish-science-of-happiness-psychology-review (accessed May 2011).

lead2lead. *Leadership Exchange Programme* [Online]. Available at: www.lead2lead. com (accessed July 2011).

Lewin, K. (1946) 'Action research and minority problems', *Journal of Social Issues*, 2: 34–46.

Lewis-Duarte, M. (2009) 'Executive coaching: A study of coaches' use of influence tactics', thesis for Doctor of Philosophy in Psychology, Claremont Graduate University, California.

Life Coach Directory (2011) *Spirituality* [Online]. Available at: http://www.lifecoach-directory.org.uk/articles/spirituality.html (accessed August 2011).

Linley, P.A. (2006) 'Coaching research: who? what? where? when? why?', *International Journal of Evidence Based Coaching and Mentoring*, 4 (2): 1–7.

Long, S. (2006) 'Drawing from role biography in Organizational Role Analysis', in J. Newton, S. Long and B. Sievers (eds), *Coaching in Depth: The Organizational Role Analysis Approach*. London: Karnac, pp. 127–143.

Lovelock, J. (1982) *Gaia: A New Look at Life on Earth*. Oxford: Oxford University Press.

Lyotard, J.-F. (1984) *The Postmodern Condition*. Manchester: Manchester University Press.

MacIntyre, A. (1985) *After Virtue: A Study in Moral Theory* (2nd edn). London: Duckworth.

Mackenzie, C. and Stoljar, N. (2000) *Relational Autonomy: Feminist Perspectives on Autonomy, Agency and the Social Self*. Oxford: Oxford University Press.

Marks, D. (2002) *Perspectives on Evidence Based Practice*, City University, London [Online]. Available at: http://www.nice.org.uk/niceMedia/pdf/persp_evid_dmarks.pdf (accessed December 2011).

Marshall, G.A. (1999) 'Psy-complex' in *Dictionary of Sociology*, encyclopedia.com [Online]. Available at: http://www.encyclopedia.com/doc/1O88-psycomplex.html (accessed January 2011).

Maslow, A. (1976) *The Farther Reaches of Human Nature*. New York: Penguin Books.

Masson, J. (1990) *Against Therapy*. London: Fontana.

Matus, T. (1996) *The Mystery of Romuald and the Five Brothers: Stories from the Benedictines and Camaldolese*. Naperville, IL: Sourcebooks.

McLeod, J. (1997) *Narrative and Psychotherapy*. London: Sage.

Megginson, D., Clutterbuck, D., Garvey, B., Stokes, P. and Garrett-Harris, R. (2006) *Mentoring in Action* (2nd edn). London: Kogan Page.

Meilaender, G. (1999) *Books in Review: Friendship in the Classical World*, Leadership U [Online]. Available at: http://www.leaderu.com/ftissues/ft9905/reviews/meilaender.html (accessed 23 July 2011).

Melucci, A. (1989) *Nomads of the Present: Social Movements and Individual Needs in Contemporary Society*. London: Hutchinson.

Menzies Lyth, I. (1960) 'A case study in the functioning of social systems as a defence against anxiety', *Human Relations*, 13: 95–121.

Miles, M. (2010) *Reverse Mentoring*, Evan Carmichael (Coaching) [Online]. Available at: http://www.evancarmichael.com/Business-Coach/120/Reverse-Mentoring.html (accessed Nov 2010).

Miller, E. (1993) *From Dependency to Autonomy*. London: Free Association Books.

Miller, J.-A. (2005) 'Response to the anti-Freudians', *Le Point* [Online]. Available at: http://www.lacan.com/antimill.htm (accessed April 2011).

Miller, J.-A. (2011) *Lacan's Later Teaching*, Lacanian Ink 21 [Online]. Available at: http://www.lacan.com/frameXXI2.htm (retrieved 4 September 2011).

Mintzberg, H. (2004) *Managers Not MBAs: A Hard Look at the Soft Practice of Managing and Management Development*. San Francisco: Barrett Kochler.

Minuchin, S. (1974) *Families and Family Therapy*. Harvard: Harvard University Press.

Mitroff, I.I. and Denton, E.A. (1999) *A Spiritual Audit of Corporate America*. San Francisco: Jossey-Bass.

Morgan, G. (ed.) (1986) *Images of Organization*. Beverly Hills: Sage Publications.

Morwood, J. and Taylor, J. (eds) (2002) *The Pocket Oxford Classical Greek Dictionary*. Oxford: Oxford University Press.

Moscowitz, E. (2001) *In Therapy We Trust: America's Obsession with Self-Fulfillment*. Baltimore: John Hopkins University Press.

Naess, A. (1989) *Ecology, Community and Lifestyle*. Cambridge: Cambridge University Press.

Neenan, M. and Dryden, W. (2004) *Cognitive Therapy: 100 Key Points and Techniques*. Hove: Psychology Press.

Nelson, B. (1965) 'Self-images and systems of spiritual direction in the history of European civilization', in S. Klausner (ed.), *The Quest for Self-Control*. New York: Free Press.

New Advent (2009) *Asceticism* [Online]. Available at: http://www.newadvent.org/cathen/01767c.htm (accessed July 2011).

New Horizons (2011) *Become a Certified Life Coach Program* [Online]. Available at: http://www.startcoachingnow.com/coach_training.html (accessed July 2011).

New York Times (2011) 'Berlusconi Steps Down and Italy Pulses with Change' [Online]. Available at: http://www.nytimes.com/2011/11/13/world/europe/silvio-berlusconi-resign-italy-austerity-measures.html?r=1.

Newton, J., Long, S. and Seivers, B. (2006) *Coaching in Depth: The Organisational Role Analysis Approach*. London: Karnac.

Noon, M. (1992) 'HRM: a map, model or theory?' in P. Blyton and P. Turnbull (eds), *Reassessing Human Resource Management*. London: Sage, pp. 16–32.

Northouse, P.G. (2004) *Leadership, Theory and Practice* (3rd edn). Thousand Oaks, CA: Sage.

Obholzer, A. and Roberts, V.Z. (eds) (1994) *The Unconscious At Work*. London: Routledge.

O'Connell, B. (2006) 'Solution-focused therapy', in *Sage Handbook of Counselling and Psychotherapy* (2nd edn). London: Sage, pp. 338–342.

Oprah Winfrey Online (2011) *Best Life Week, Falling off the Wagon* [Online]. Available at: http://www.oprah.com/oprahshow/Best-Life-Week-Falling-Off-the-Wagon (accessed August 2011).

Ouchi, W. and Price, R. (1978) 'Hierarchies, clans and Theory Z: a new perspective on organization development', *Organizational Dynamics*, 7(2): 24.

Parker, M. (1992) 'Post-modern organization or postmodern theory?', *Organization Studies*, 13: 1–17.

Parker M. (2002) *Against Management: Organization in the Age of Managerialism*. Cambridge: Polity Press.

Passmore, J. (2006) *Excellence in Coaching: The Industry Guide*. London: Kogan Page.

Peltier, B. (2001) *The Psychology of Executive Coaching: Theory and Application*. New York: Brunner Routledge.

Peters, T. and Waterman, R. (1982) *In Search of Excellence: Lessons from America's Best Run Companies*. New York: Harper Collins.

Peterson, K. (2002) 'Life Coaches all the rage', *USA Today* [Online]. Available at: http://www.usatoday.com/news/health/2002-08-04-lifecoach_x.htm (accessed May 2011).

Popper, K. (1963) *Conjectures and Refutations: The Growth of Scientific Knowledge*. London: Routledge and Keagan Paul.

Power, M. (1997) *The Audit Society: Rituals of Verification*. Oxford: Oxford University Press.

Putnam, R. (2000) *Bowling Alone: The Collapse and Revival of American Community*. New York: Simon & Schuster.

Quantcast (2010) *Audience Profile, Facebook.com* [Online]. Available at: http://www.quantcast.com/facebook.com (accessed November 2010).

Redekop, B. (2010) *Leadership for Environmental Sustainability*. New York, NY/ Milton Park, UK: Routledge.

Reed, B. and Bazalgette, J. (2006) 'Organizational role analysis at the Grubb Institute of Behavioral Studies: Origins and development', in J. Newton, S. Long and B. Sievers (eds), *Coaching in Depth: The Organizational Role Analysis Approach*. London: Karnac, pp. 43–62.

Rhodes, J.E. and Lowe, S. (2008) 'Youth mentoring and resilience: Implications for practice', *Child Care in Practice*, 14 (1): 9–17.

Rieff, P. (1966) *The Triumph of the Therapeutic: Uses of Faith after Freud*. London: Chatto and Windus.

Roby, D. (1977) 'Introduction', in Aelred of Rievaulx (1977) *Spiritual Friendship* (Mary Laker, trans.). Kalamazoo, MI: Cistercian Publications.

Rogers, C. (1951) *Client-centered Therapy: Its Current Practice, Implications and Theory*. London: Constable.

Rogers, C. (1961) *On Becoming a Person*. London: Constable.

Rogers, J. (2004) *Coaching Skills: A Handbook*. Buckingham: Open University Press.

Rose, N. (1985) *The Psychological Complex: Psychology, Politics and Society in England 1869–1939*. London: Routledge.

Rose, N. (1990) *Governing the Soul: The Shaping of the Private Self*. London: Routledge.

Rose, N. (1996) *Inventing Our Selves: Psychology, Power and Personhood*. New York: Cambridge University Press.

Rose, N. (1999) *Powers of Freedom: Reframing Political Thought*. Cambridge: Cambridge University Press.

Rose, N. (2004) 'Power and psychological techniques', in R. House and Y. Bates (eds), *Ethically Challenged Professions: Enabling Innovation and Diversity in Psychotherapy and Counselling*. Ross-on-Wye, UK: PCCS Books, pp. 27–45.

Rose, N. (2005) *Power in Therapy: Techne and Ethos* [Online]. Available at: http://www.academyanalyticarts.org/rose2.htm (accessed August 2011).

Rose, N. (2011) *Power in Therapy: Techne and Ethos* [Online]. Available at: http://www.academyanalyticarts.org/rose2.htm (accessed 28 July 2011).

Roseneil, S. (2006) 'The ambivalences of Angel's "arrangement": A psychosocial lens on the contemporary condition of personal life', *The Sociological Review*, 54: 4.

Rostron, S. (2009) *Business Coaching International: Transforming Individuals and Organizations*. London: Karnac.

Rowan, J. (2010) 'The positive psychology approach to coaching', in E. Cox, T. Bachkirova and D. Clutterbuck (eds), *The Complete Handbook of Coaching*. London: Sage.

Sachdev, P. (2011) 'Positive psychology, psychotherapy and the pursuit of happiness', a dissertation for MA Integrative Counselling, Dept of Psychology, London Metropolitan University.

Sartre, J.-P. (2001) *Being and Nothingness: An Essay in Phenomenological Ontology*. New York: Citadel Press.

Scoular, A. (2011) *The Financial Times Guide to Business Coaching*. London: FT/Prentice Hall.

Segers, J., Vloeberghs, D. and Henderick, E. (2011) 'Structuring and understanding the coaching industry: The coaching cube', *Academy of Management Learning & Education*, 10 (2): 204–221.

Seiler, A. (2005) *Coaching to the Human Soul: Ontological Coaching and Deep Change, Vol. 1.* Melbourne/Brisbane: Newfield Institute.

Seligman, M.E.P. (2002) *Authentic Happiness: Using the New Positive Psychology to Realize Your Potential for Lasting Fulfillment*. New York: Free Press.

Seligman, M. (2007) 'Coaching and positive psychology', *Australian Psychologist*, 42 (4): 266–267.

Seligman, M.E.P. (2011) *Flourish: A Visionary New Understanding of Happiness and Wellbeing*. New York: Free Press.

Seligman, M. and Csikszentmihalyi, M. (2000) 'Positive psychology: An introduction', *American Psychologist*, 55 (1): 5–14.

Senge, P. (1994) *The Fifth Discipline*. London: Century Business.

Senge, P., Scharmer, C.O., Jaworski, J. and Flowers, E.S. (2004) *Presence: Exploring Profound Change in People, Organisations and Society*. London: Nicholas Brealey.

Sherman, S. and Freas, A. (2004) 'The Wild West of executive coaching', *Harvard Business Review*, 82 (11): 82, 84–90.

Skelton, D. (2011) 'Government of the technocrats, by the technocrats, for the technocrats', *New Statesman*, 16 November [Online]. Available at: http://www.newstatesman.com/blogs/the-staggers/2011/11/european-greece-technocrats.

Snyder, G. (1990) *The Practice of the Wild*. San Francisco: North Point Press.

Social Media Today (2010) *41.6% of the US population has a Facebook Account* [Online]. Available at: http://socialmediatoday.com/index.php?q=roywells1/158020/416-uspopulation-has-facebook-account (accessed January 2011).

Sparrow, S. (2007) 'The benefits of transpersonal coaching', *Personnel Today* [Online]. Available at: http://www.personneltoday.com/articles/2007/09/18/42277/the-benefits-of-transpersonal-coaching.html (accessed August 2011).

Stead, V. (2005) 'Mentoring: A model for leadership development?', *International Journal of Training and Development*, 9 (3): 170–184.

Stein, M. (2011) Personal communication.

Stern, L. (2004) 'Executive coaching: A working definition', *Consulting Psychology Journal: Practice and Research Journal*, 56 (3): 154–162.

Suarez-Villa, L. (2009) *Technocapitalism: A Critical Perspective on Technological Innovation and Corporatism*. Philadelphia: Temple University Press.

Sullivan, N. (2003) *A Critical Introduction to Queer Theory*. New York: New York University Press.

Sutton, R. and Straw, B. (1995) 'What theory is not', *Administrative Science Quarterly*, 40 (3): 371–385.

Swan, E. (2006) *Executive Coaching: Psychobabble or Spaces for Doubt?*, Working Paper Series CEL. Lancaster: Centre for Excellence in Leadership.

Taris, T.W. and Schreurs, P.G. (2009) 'Well-being and organizational performance: An organizational-level test of the happy-productive worker hypothesis', *Work & Stress*, 23 (2): 120–136.

Taylor, F.W. (1947) *The Principles of Scientific Management*. New York: Harper and Brothers Publishers.

TeacherNet [Online]. Available at: www.teachernet.gov.uk/teachingandlearning/socialandpastoral/mentoring/ (accessed November 2010).

The Independent (2010) 'Cameron defends wellbeing measure', 25 November [Online]. Available at: http://www.independent.co.uk/news/uk/politics/cameron-defends-wellbeing-measure-2143595.html (accessed September 2011).

Tolle, E. (1999) *The Power of Now: A Guide to Spiritual Enlightenment*. Novato, CA: New World Library.

Tolle, E. (2005) *A New Earth: Awakening to your Life's Purpose*. New York: Penguin.

Torbert, W.R. (1993) *The Power of Balance: Transforming Self, Society and Scientific Inquiry*. Newbury Park, CA: Sage.

Tourish, D. and Pinnington, A. (2002) 'Transformational leadership, corporate cultism and the spirituality paradigm: An unholy trinity in the workplace?', *Human Relations*, 55 (2): 147–172.

Tourish, D. and Tourish, N. (2010) 'Spirituality at work, and its implications for leadership and followership: A post-structuralist perspective', *Leadership*, 6 (2): 207–224.

Turkle, S. (2011) *Alone Together: Why We Expect More From Technology and Less From Each Other*. New York: Basic Books.

Turner, P. (2010) 'Aligning organisational coaching with leadership behaviour', PhD thesis submitted to Birmingham City University, October.

TVU (2002) *Mentoring is Not New!* [Online]. Available at: http://hermes.tvu.ac.uk/Elearning_Showcase/Mentoring_v6_Site/unit1/tvu1page2.htm (accessed November 2010).

US Senate (2011) *Wall Street and the Financial Crisis: Anatomy of a Financial Collapse* [Online]. Available at: http://hsgac.senate.gov/public/_files/Financial_Crisis/FinancialCrisisReport.pdf (accessed August 2011).

Van Deurzen, E. (2008) *Psychotherapy and the Quest for Happiness*. London: Sage Publications.

Vernon, M. (2007) *The Meaning of Friendship*. New York: Palgrave Macmillan.

Wallis, P. (2007) *Apprenticeship and Training in Premodern England* [Online]. Available at: http://eprints.lse.ac.uk/22515/1/2207Wallis.pdf (accessed June 2011).

Walvin, J. (1997) *The Quakers: Money and Morals*. London: John Murray.

Wanberg, C.R., Welsh, L. and Hezlett, S. (2003) 'Mentoring: A review and directions for future research', in J. Martocchio and J. Ferris (eds), *Research in Personnel and Human Resources Management*. Amsterdam/London: JAI Press.

Weakland, J., Fisch, R., Watzlawick, P. and Bodin, M.A. (1974) 'Brief therapy: Focused problem resolution', *Family Process*, 13: 141–168.

Weick, K.E. (1989) 'Theory construction as disciplined imagination', *Academy of Management Review*, 14: 516–531.

Weick, K.E. (1995) *Sensemaking in Organizations* (Foundations for Organizational Science Series). London: Sage Publications.

Weick, K.E. (2004) Rethinking Organizational Design. In R. Boland and F. Collopy (Eds.) *Managing as Designing*. Stanford, CA: Stanford University Press, pp. 3–18.

Weissberg, R.P., Caplan, M. and Sivo, P.J. (1989) 'A new conceptual framework for establishing school-based social competence promotion programs', in L.A. Bond and B.E. Compas (eds), *Primary Prevention and Promotion in the Schools*. Newbury Park, CA: Sage, pp. 255–296.

West, L. and Milan, M. (2001) *The Reflecting Glass*. New York: Palgrave.

Westen, D., Novotny, C.M. and Thompson-Brenner, H. (2004) 'The empirical status of empirically supported psychotherapies: Assumptions, findings and reporting in controlled clinical trials', *Psychological Bulletin*, 130 (4): 631–633.

Western, S. (1999) 'Where's Daddy? Integrating the paternal metaphor within the maternal, Tavistock tradition of organizational thinking', Conference ISPSO Paper (see http://www.ispso.org/Symposia/Toronto/1999western.htm).

Western, S. (2006) 'Look who's talking', *Coaching at Work*, 1 (2): 31–34.

Western, S. (2008a) *Leadership: A Critical Text*. London: Sage.

Western, S. (2008b) 'Democratising strategy', in D. Campbell and D. Huffington (eds), *Organizations Connected: A Handbook of Systemic Consultation*. London: Karnac, pp. 173–196.

Western, S. (2010) 'Book Review: "With God on all sides: leadership in a devout and diverse America"', *Journal of Management, Spirituality & Religion*, 7 (4): 351–356.

Western, S. and Findlater, C. (2008) 'Telecoaching', unpublished pilot research paper.

Western, S. and Gosling, J. (2002) 'Pairing for leadership', unpublished conference paper.

Western, S. and Sedgmore, L. (2008) 'A privileged conversation', *Journal of Management Spirituality & Religion*, 5 (3): 321–346.

Wexler, P. (1996) *Holy Sparks: Social Theory, Education and Religion*. New York: St Martin's Press.

Wheatley, J. (2006) *Leadership and the New Science*. San Francisco: Berret Koehler.

Whetten, D. (1989) 'What constitutes a theoretical contribution?', *Academy of Management Review*, 14 (4): 486–489.

Whitmore, J.K. (2002) *Coaching for Performance: Growing People, Performance and Purpose*. London: Nicholas Brealey Publishing/Wiley-Blackwell.

Whitworth, L., Kimsey-House, H., Kimsey-House, K. and Sandahl, P. (2007) *Co-active Coaching: New Skills for Coaching People Toward Success in Work and Life*. Mountain View, CA: Davies-Black Publishing.

Whyte, W.H. (1956) *The Organization Man*. New York: Simon & Schuster.

Wilber, K. (2000) *A Theory of Everything*. Boston: Shambala Publications.

Winnicott, D.W. (ed.) (1971) *Playing and Reality*. London: Tavistock Publications.

Woodhead, L. (2004) *An Introduction to Christianity*. Cambridge: Cambridge University Press.

Woolgar, S. (1991) 'Configuring the user: The case of usability trials', in J. Law (ed.), *A Sociology of Monsters: Essays on Power, Technology and Domination*. London: Routledge, pp. 58–99.

Yalom, I.D. and Yalom, B. (1998) *The Yalom Reader: Selections from the Work of a Master Therapist and Storyteller*. New York: Basic Books.

Yates, J.A. (1989) *Control Through Communication: The Rise of System in American Management*. Baltimore: John Hopkins Press.

Zeus, P. and Skiffington, S. (2002) *The Coaching at Work Toolkit*. Roseville, NSW: McGraw Hill.

Zizek, S. (1992) *Looking Awry: An Introduction to Jacques Lacan through Popular Culture*. London: Verso.

Zizek, S. (2001) *Enjoy your Symptom! Jacques Lacan in Hollywood and Out.* London: Routledge.

Zizek, S. (2003) *The Puppet and the Dwarf: The Perverse Core of Christianity.* Cambridge, MA: MIT Press.

Zizek, S. (2008) *Violence.* London: Profile Books Ltd.

Zofia Life Coach [Online]. *Relationship Coaching. Dating Coaching. Life-coaching.* Available at: www.zofialifecoach.co.uk (accessed November 2010).

Zohar, D. and Marshall, I. (2011) *Spiritual Intelligence: The Ultimate Intelligence.* London: Bloomsbury.

Index

Page references to Figures or Tables will be in *italics*

A VERY SHORT, FAIRLY INTERESTING AND REASONABLY CHEAP BOOK ABOUT COACHING AND MENTORING

Bob Garvey *York St John University*
Written to challenge, stimulate and inform, this book takes a critical look at the rapidly-growing field of coaching and mentoring. Focusing on all types of organization - public, private, large, small and not-for-profit - Robert Garvey inspires and provokes readers by asking questions such as 'Are coaching and mentoring the same?' 'Are we obsessed with skills?' and 'What is performance?' He also delves into contemporary debates such as concerns about standards, competencies and codes of ethics, interspersed with views on power, control and politics. This book will prove an engaging, thought-provoking and, above all, entertaining read for undergraduate, postgraduate and MBA students looking for different ways of thinking about coaching and mentoring.

CONTENTS
Introduction: Why Developing a Critical Perspective on Coaching and Mentoring Matters? \ What Is Mentoring and What Is Coaching? \ Are Coaching and Mentoring the Same? The Definition Debate \ What Are the Discourses and What Are We Not Hearing in Coaching and Mentoring? \ Are We Obsessed with Skills and Competences in Coaching and Mentoring? \ What Is Performance in Coaching and Mentoring? \ The Psychological Influences on Coaching and Mentoring \ Conclusions and Further Questions

READERSHIP
Undergraduate, postgraduate and MBA students interested on embarking on a coaching or mentoring course

VERY SHORT, FAIRLY INTERESTING & CHEAP BOOKS

 2011 • 128 pages
Cloth (978-1-84920-782-9) • £55.00
Paper (978-1-84920-783-6) • £13.99

ALSO FROM SAGE

COACHING AND MENTORING

Theory and Practice

Bob Garvey *York St John University*, **Paul Stokes** and **David Megginson** *both at Sheffield Hallam University*

Coaching and mentoring are fast becoming essential aspects of modern managerial practice. With this growth comes an increasing number of students embarking on mentoring and coaching courses.

The authors (well respected and trusted scholars in the field) provide an authoritative text with a comprehensive overview and critical grounding in the key concepts, models and research studies in coaching and mentoring and answer important questions such as `What does coaching and mentoring involve?', `What is its value?' and `How can the added value of mentoring and coaching be demonstrated?'

Examples are drawn from a variety of sectors, including private businesses, public and voluntary organizations and schools. Contemporary debates are explained and chapters include features such as case studies, research questions and helpful tips to support the reader. To gain a wider perspective, there is a chapter which provides critical comment on the state of the art in the US, while the final chapter offers the first attempt at developing a unified theory of coaching and mentoring by drawing on their respective antecedents.

CONTENTS

READERSHIP

Students on CIPD courses and postgraduate students taking a mentoring and coaching programme; also students taking courses on educational leadership and some social work and nursing students

2008 • 272 pages
Cloth (978-1-4129-1216-7) • £78.00
Paper (978-1-4129-1217-4) • £25.99

ALSO FROM SAGE

20100475R00190

Printed in Great Britain
by Amazon